Critical theory and dystopia

Manchester University Press

Critical theory and contemporary society

Series editors:

David M. Berry, Professor of Digital Humanities, University of Sussex

Darrow Schecter, Professor of Critical Theory and Modern European History, University of Sussex

The *Critical Theory and Contemporary Society* series aims to demonstrate the ongoing relevance of multi-disciplinary research in explaining the causes of pressing social problems today and in indicating the possible paths towards a libertarian transformation of twenty-first century society. It builds upon some of the main ideas of first generation critical theorists, including Horkheimer, Adorno, Benjamin, Marcuse and Fromm, but it does not aim to provide systematic guides to the work of those thinkers. Rather, each volume focuses on ways of thinking about the political dimensions of a particular topic, which include political economy, law, popular culture, globalization, feminism, theology and terrorism. Authors are encouraged to build on the legacy of first generation Frankfurt School theorists and their influences (Kant, Hegel, Kierkegaard, Marx, Nietzsche, Weber and Freud) in a manner that is distinct from, though not necessarily hostile to, the broad lines of second-generation critical theory. The series sets ambitious theoretical standards, aiming to engage and challenge an interdisciplinary readership of students and scholars across political theory, philosophy, sociology, history, media studies and literary studies.

Previously published by Bloomsbury

Critical theory in the twenty-first century
Darrow Schecter

Critical theory and the critique of political economy   Werner Bonefeld

Critical theory and contemporary Europe
William Outhwaite

Critical theory of legal revolutions   Hauke Brunkhorst

Critical theory of libertarian socialism   Charles Masquelier

Critical theory and film   Fabio Vighi

Critical theory and the digital   David Berry

Critical theory and disability   Teodor Mladenov

Critical theory and the crisis of contemporary capitalism   Heiko Feldner and Fabio Vighi

Previously published by Manchester University Press

Critical theory and demagogic populism   Paul K. Jones

Critical theory and epistemology   Anastasia Marinopoulou

Critical theory and human rights   David McGrogan

Critical theory and feeling   Simon Mussell

Critical theory and legal autopoiesis   Gunther Teubner

Critical theory and sociological theory   Darrow Schecter

Critical theory and dystopia

Patricia McManus

MANCHESTER UNIVERSITY PRESS

Published by Manchester University Press
Oxford Road, Manchester M13 9PL

www.manchesteruniversitypress.co.uk

British Library Cataloguing-in-Publication Data
A catalogue record for this book is available from the
British Library

ISBN 978 1 5261 3973 3 hardback
ISBN 978 1 5261 3975 7 paperback

First published 2022

Typeset
by Cheshire Typesetting Ltd, Cuddington, Cheshire

Contents

Acknowledgements

I would like to thank Darrow Schecter for suggesting I do this book; and Theodore Koulouris for stopping me from stopping. University Senior Management Teams are good at getting in the way of things getting done: they played a blinder over the last few years. I would also like to apologise to those in University of Brighton Falmer Branch of University and College Union and to those on Co-Com, for not being around as much during the time it took me to finish this.

To Caroline Wintersgill and to Thomas Dark, your patience is much appreciated and I am sorry I gave it so much exercise. To the librarians at the University of Brighton Falmer library, thank you.

Thank you to the Brightonians – Eugene, Shad, Naomi, Cathy, John, Theo and Karen. Thank you to Kevin for making all moments better.

Nothing would happen without the McManus family. I send my thanks to my Father, Paddy, and to my Mother, Maria, the kindest and wisest person I know. To my sisters, Catherine, Niamh, Philly, Gráinne, Róisín; to my brother Pauraic; and to the new generation: Naoise, Donnacha, Theo, Amin, Siobhan, Kate and Killian. I would be nowhere without you all.

This book is for my brother Maurice because we miss him.

Introduction

Dystopia

This is a book about a subgenre[1] of fiction which has come to be known as dystopian fiction. This is a type of fiction differentiated from others not so much because it is about oppression or about suffering but because it is about the organisation of oppression and suffering, the planned or designed production of suffering, or, in those instances where suffering is dramatised as absent, the planned production of subjects incapable of suffering.[2] The dystopia imagines a future inhabited by people who are to the text's readers spectres of a world which is narrated as legible, as a possibility germinating in the present, and which therefore takes on the guise if not of a warning then of a rebuke of some kind to the reader's present.

Before reading a selection of twentieth- and twenty-first-century dystopias, it is necessary to say a word or two about the vocabulary used to approach such fiction. So dense is the imbrication of utopia and dystopia in their historical relationship (and in the politics embedded in perceptions and fears about that relationship) that it is necessary to insist that we cannot see them simply as antonyms. Likewise, so pervasive is the understanding of dystopia today as a stand-alone 'bad place' or 'bad time' that it is necessary to recall to thought the density of *utopia* in the formation of dystopia – as a concept and as a genre of fiction. This is all the more important as in the following pages we will be using the work of Theodor Adorno to help us think the historical alignments and shudders involved in the genre of dystopia. In our own day, 'utopia' may be a buried or residual energy in those alignments but it is nevertheless a formative one for the genre of dystopia itself. For Adorno, 'sedimented content' was a way of thinking about the layers of life which, compressed over time and praxis, constitute literary form. In *Aesthetic Theory*, Adorno insists repeatedly that '[h]istory is the content of artworks. To analyse artworks means no less than to become conscious of the history immanently sedimented in them.'[3] In thinking of the form of dystopia – a core concern of this book – we can position utopia as its sedimented content. The desired defeat of utopia, and the fear of utopia, are mobilising moments in the founding and shape of the genre itself, and are arguably still active in its forms even as contemporary dystopias themselves seem to have forgotten they ever had any relationship with utopia.

The dystopia is a creature of utopia, impossible to imagine without the formal invention of the concept and narrative form of that tradition of fiction which we can date with some precision to Thomas More's *Utopia* (1516), that 'truly golden handbook, no less instructive than delightful' in which More depicted a 'Utopian commonwealth'.[4] The six-line stanza which precedes the letters which open *Utopia* makes clear More's conception of his own text's continuity with the older tradition of state-visioning, and his departure from that tradition:

> Remote, in distant times I was 'No-place',
> But now I claim to rival Plato's state,
> Perhaps outshine it: he portrayed with words
> What I uniquely demonstrate with men,
> Resources, and the very best of laws.
> So, 'Happy-place' I rightly should be called.

Where Plato relied on 'words' to create his *Republic*, More utilises narrative, the relations between 'men,' resources and laws rendered dramatically in such a way as to 'demonstrate' the transmutation of *ou*-topia into *eu*-topia. The drama of utopia as a narrative form is a drama of space, the ground of which is the voyage and the voyager. Louis Marin points out how the utopian journey acts as the organising figure of the narrative itself:

> With that figure, a narrative begins, with a before and an after, a point of departure and a point of arrival, a happy coming-back or a final permanent exile. The locus has become space: directions, speeds, travel-timing give motion to the map with the tracings of various routes.[5]

As the figure is a moving one and a connecting one, the space wandered across should also be a temporal one, connecting the 'before and after' not just of the traveller's own voyage but of the sites they voyage to and from. Utopia is itself no 'new world' but predates and outshines the present from which our traveller, Raphael Hythloday, journeys, for example. Indeed, in its encounters with the Roman Empire and the Egyptians, it demonstrates a capacity to absorb and learn which puts More's contemporary Europeans to shame. When Peter Giles expresses his expectation that 'our governments … are more ancient, so that long practice has introduced many things that enhance life', Hythloday is quick to correct him:

As to the relative antiquity of governments … you'd be in a better position to judge if you had read the histories of their world: if these are to be trusted, they had cities there before there were inhabitants here.[6]

More ancient than 'us Ultra-equatorials (for that's what they call us)',[7] and quicker to learn from novelty, to absorb and transmute the new to their advantage, Utopia and the Utopians constitute a civilisation which enables an evaluation of More's Europe as falling short in forms of government, distribution of resources and manners.

The utopian fiction's use of space involves a peculiar use of time. Physically and militarily, Utopia is a sport as much as an ideal, a corner of the world which is not of the world and which heeds not the latter's modes of development. Utopos is the formative figure of time for Utopia, he who took Abraxa to its current ideal state: it is he who 'raised' the 'brutish and uncultivated' inhabitants of the former to 'such a level of civilisation and humanity that they now outshine virtually all other nations'.[8] Utopos is a figure of conquest: he conquered the place which hitherto would be called Utopia, he conquered its inhabitants and he conquered space when he organised the physical or geographical secession of the place of Utopia from the landmass of which it was once a part. As an island, Utopia stands alone: the 'Utopian Quatrain' which prefaces More's text gives Utopia its own voice:

The leader Utopos turned me from a non-island into an island. Out of all lands I alone, without abstract philosophy, have pictured for mortals the philosophical city. I share my own things freely; not unwillingly I accept things that are better.

The founding of Utopia with More is thus one part of the 'constitutive secessionism' of utopia traced by Fredric Jameson, a 'withdrawal or "delinking" from the empirical and historical world'.[9] That delinking is most formal and most constitutive when it comes to the treatment of time. As a narrative device, the islanding of Utopia – its human-made distinctiveness – cuts it off from the temporal patterns organising the image of Europe in the text. The teleology of 'progress' is given to Utopia and is quarantined there. It is not frozen as Utopia 'accept[s] things that are better' but it is hard to see how those things can be encountered on other than Utopia's hard terms. A better society has been reached and it now rests within itself, cut off from what would become the developmental or historical time of modernity.

Some two hundred years later, in 1747, an anonymous poem was printed by George Faulkner in Dublin, which re-temporalised utopia, casting it as the successor to the wretchedness it solves or negates. This poem uses the term 'dystopia' to describe that wretchedness, and puts that time in the past, a time of factions, of the absence of wealth, of bad air and insects. Here dystopia precedes utopia, is the foundation for the latter and is that

which utopia cancels. The poem, *Utopia: Or, Apollo's Golden Days*, hymns
the brief reign of Philip Stanhope, fourth Earl of Chesterfield, as the Lord
Lieutenant of Ireland from December 1744 to November 1746. Though he
had spent only a matter of months in Ireland and had his mind much in the
sway of matters at the English court, Stanhope is praised by the poem in
the figure of Apollo, commanded by Jove to take human form and to visit
Ireland:

> But Heav'n, of late, was all distraction,
> And, more than ever, rent in faction;
> Caus'd only by a wretched isle,
> On which we thought no God would smile
> …
> Unhappy isle! Scarce known to Fame
> Dustopia was its slighted name
> …
> Jove saw and sent Apollo.
> Again a God forsake the skies
> To make a sinking nation rise
> … To mortals, Stanhope he appears
> Come to dry dustopia's tears.[10]

This early use of the term which would become 'dystopia' is mentioned
here as a way of underlining the concept's proximity to the concept of utopia
and to the latter's complex historical embeddedness in notions of 'civilisation', and 'governance' and colonisation's articulation of these as twins.

Dystopia did not become the name for a type of fictional narrative of
the future until the middle of the twentieth century. When it did adhere
to the fictions – many of which predate it – it was at a time when utopia
itself had faltered. At the turn of the nineteenth century, two of the most
popular fictions in the Anglo-American world were utopian fictions. The
sales figures for Edward Bellamy's *Looking Backward, 2000–1887* (1888)
and those for the fictional answer to it written by William Morris, *News
from Nowhere* (1890), were only the most commercially successful tip of
the popular interest in utopian fictions. Nor was fiction the horizon of that
interest. As Matthew Beaumont notes in some detail, the *fin-de-siècle* interest in utopia stretched from politics to fiction and back again:

> In the face of a widespread perception that capitalist society had arrived at
> some sort of historical turning point, the end of the last century was perme-
> ated with anticipatory or utopian consciousness.[11]

Utopia, which had itself become a recognisable and popular literary genre
by the middle of the nineteenth century, was already caught up with antici-
pating and rebutting reproaches of itself as 'utopian'. This slippage of the

term 'utopian' to become a term of reproach – utopian dreamer, spinner of illusions – was part of the dominant or homogenising layer of the history of 'utopia's' adventures as a concept in the later eighteenth and nineteenth centuries. By the 1880s and the 1890s, however, decades pierced by knowledge of the Paris Commune, not the implausibility of utopian dreaming but the seeming convergence of the latter with the logic of the world was at stake. This is a moment which has been traced by Lucian Hölscher in his essay 'Utopia':

> From the end of the nineteenth century the utopia critique was also increasingly based on the understanding of a possible convergence between utopia and history ... [I]n comparison to the anthropological foundation of the utopia critique in the eighteenth and nineteenth centuries the theoretical standpoint had greatly changed: it was no longer based on the certainty of impossibility but, entirely to the contrary, on the understanding of the possible realization of Utopian social constitutions.[12]

By the late nineteenth century, that is, utopia seemed both possible and utterly undesirable to its critics. The first usage of 'dystopia' to name a form of fictional narrative about the future was in scholarship on the classic dystopias.[13] The name caught on. It was useful for scholars as it neatened the sprawl of categories which had been generated by the form's clear but complex relations with utopia,[14] and it was useful for publishers. Prior to the term 'dystopia' being applied to the fictional form, the names used to understand such fictions were varied but had in common a negative relationship with utopia. In Adorno's essay on Huxley's *Brave New World*, for example, the term 'negative utopia' is used to indicate the novel's acceptance of the notion of progress simultaneously with a castigation of that same progress.[15] Likewise, in another early exploration of the 'anti-utopias', George Woodcock called his essay 'Utopias in Negative' (1956).[16]

We need to note that dystopia is no inheritor of the utopian narrative form, nor is it a simple antagonist. Dystopias are not immanently anti-utopian, even in their classical moment, as utopia cannot be confined by its negation: in a world where universal leisure and the satisfaction of all bodily needs are so easily practically possible, what a state or other totalising force does cannot cancel out utopian possibilities though the text may pass over them in silence. This does not mean, however, that dystopias are anti-anti-utopian.

Fredric Jameson's aside in the opening paragraph of *An American Utopia* (2016) that there has been an 'overwhelming increase in all manner of conceivable dystopias, most of which look monotonously alike' can – at least provisionally – act here as the historical question to be explored. Why the increase and what is it that this plethora of dystopias share to make them appear so monotonous?[17] In an essay also spurred by Jameson's aside, Mark Bould suggests that one reason for the 'monotony' may be the totalisation of the present or the present's success at presenting itself as such a totality, closed and pragmatic and inevitable. Classic dystopias, in this argument a subgenre of science fiction, depend for their political purchase on creating and maintaining a textual distance from their contemporaneous moment, a way of throwing that present and its dangers, its violence, into relief. It is that distance – more so than even the content of the fictional world, the world that is dystopian – which once provided a sharp way of critiquing the present: the dystopian text here becomes less a warning about the future than a revelation about the present. Given decades of neoliberalism and the force with which its slogan – 'there is no alternative' – has been hammered home repeatedly, it is possible, suggests Bould, that

> we already inhabit the worst of all possible worlds – the one that actually exists – so perhaps there is no critique left that dystopias can effect ... dystopia can no longer gain sufficient distance from our own world to generate the cognitive estrangement upon which SF's political potential hinges.[18]

This is an argument which I will explore in some more detail a little later. For now though, we should note that, at one level, descriptive but fundamental all the same, the argument does not work. For whilst such an explanation may flatter the exceptionalism which marks some writing on the present, if our present is already dystopian, then why so much writing about futures which are worse? Relatedly, what is there in our present which prevents imaginative distance from it that did not exist in the 1930s or the 1940s, or the 1990s? Our present is indeed woeful but it has been for a long time now. And whilst dystopias are markedly shy of tracing the past within the present, the layers of imperialism, of slavery, of enclosures and of expropriation and exploitation which brought 'the West' into the twentieth century, they are now themselves more than a century old.

I will argue here that Jameson's aside – that there is a proliferation of dystopian fictions and that they are monotonous – makes sense only in the light of the point his aside illustrates: that there 'has been a marked diminution in the production of new utopias over the last decades'. There is a relationship that is between utopia and dystopias. That relationship is not one necessarily of antagonism but the period of dystopia's formal innovation, the period of the dark imaginations of writers from E.M. Forster through Aldous Huxley and Katharine Burdekin to George Orwell and Anthony Burgess, was a period of anti-utopian dystopias. The classical dystopia, in other words, fed from both the utopian fictions and the mass political movements of socialism and of fascism, not from the *possibility* of large-scale political change but from the *certainty* of it even as the direction of that change was itself not given.

That our own moment is different is clear but the nature of the difference remains to be explored. In particular, why do we still have so many dystopian fictions? It is not sufficient to say because we live in a world which is terrifying and which may become more so. That is well known. Why write and why read a dystopian fiction now? How are such things possible in the absence of any extant utopian traditions to draw on whether negatively or not? Is there something at stake in all this or is the popularity of dystopian fiction part of a free-floating world of cultural production, geared towards commercial legibility, either indifferent to politics or committed to the reactionary fantasy that 'things could always be worse'?[19]

There is more to be said about what constitutes dystopian fiction, about how a text is to be identified as dystopian, about what distinguishes those texts from other subgenres of fiction with which they may seem to overlap, or with which they may seem to be intimately engaged in an antagonism so deep they may appear as siblings, utopian fiction. For the moment, however, it is important to touch on this study's approach, on why and how critical theory will be used here, as that approach governs all. This book uses the work of Theodor Adorno to understand the coming into existence and the contemporary success of this form of fiction, future fictions of organised brutality. The aim is to arrive at an understanding of the odd shapes of dystopia historically, and from this to build an understanding of the pervasiveness of dystopian fictions in our own moment, in the first decades of dystopia's second century. This is a book about form, not just about the forms dystopia may take – the various shapes of tyranny, coercion, subjugation and suffering – but also about the forms of the things lost to tyranny, things which are frequently not even named by the dystopian texts themselves but the absence of which motivates the misery of what is there: autonomy, freedom, equality, difference, hope. It reads these properly social forms through the literary scholarship of Theodor Adorno as materials rather than as content, in a way of seeing or reading literature which pays most attention to its shape and to how that shape is achieved, how a novel's and a subgenre's own 'formal law' is realised.

It builds on the work of previous scholars of dystopia, in particular the argument that any dystopian fiction is involved in a peculiar relationship with its own present, a relationship of complex antagonisms and loyalties, both of which escape any simplistic notion of 'theme' or of 'message' including those of the oft-invoked warning or prophecy kind. As it is concerned with the look and feel, the logic and self-image, the history and the experience of modernity's myriad forms of domination, it may seem as if the scholarship of the first generation of Frankfurt School writers would work well with such a study. And in some ways it does but the object of enquiry here is not primarily a political or a social but a cultural one. Throughout this study, though we will engage with the history of the term 'dystopian' as an adjective to castigate some actual phenomena in the realm of politics or of social formations, or to castigate the entirety of the present itself, a term not as much used as 'utopian' but still significantly if uselessly mobilised to evaluate bogeymen of the left and of the right, such considerations will serve only to situate the fictional interventions: it is these latter which will be the focus of and provide the substance for the critical analysis which follows.

To think of dystopian fiction in the terms left to us by Theodor Adorno is difficult, and may even seem self-defeating. Much of what is thought of as dystopian fiction, if not the subgenre or the idea of the genre itself – throughout the hundred-plus years which I will argue constitute its history – would surely fall into the category of the 'culture industry'. Though Adorno and Horkheimer, Benjamin, Brecht and Bloch may have given us a rich conceptual apparatus with which to understand the workings of power, its sources, purposes and effects, dystopian fictions cannot be simply read through that apparatus. They do not belong to it in any unmediated way no matter how tempting it may be to see this or that fictional innovation confirming or illustrating some thesis about instrumentally-driven science or thought, or about reification or what happens to a body or to the seeing of bodies under the sway of reification's regime.

Indeed one of the purposes of this volume is to lift dystopian fictions out of the interpretative framework which casts them as soothsayers, as warnings which retrospectively corroborate what we knew or should have known at each point along the violence and pain of the twentieth century: that we knew, that we should have known – as if knowing was itself a form of prevention. It is our job here to make this very strange form of fiction strange again: why should human beings write so much, with such imagination, about the production of pain and the pleasures of that production?

In his essay 'Trying to Understand *Endgame*', Adorno notes that, for the *dramatis personae* of Beckett's play, the 'end of the world is discounted, as though it could be taken for granted'.[20] Clov knows things have finished: 'if [the seeds] were going to sprout they would have sprouted. (Violently) They'll never sprout!'[21] Dystopian fiction spurns any dealing with Clov's 'euphemisms' however: if the 'violence of the unspeakable is mirrored in the fear of mentioning it' for Beckett, then dystopian fiction does something to that violence by rendering it speakable, not only mentionable but narratable and hence readable. For Adorno, any alleged drama of the atomic age would be a mockery of itself, solely because its plot would comfortingly falsify the historical horror of anonymity by displacing it onto human characters and actions and by gaping at the 'important people' who are in charge of whether or not the button gets pushed.[22]

This 'historical horror of anonymity' is not what the bomb does to bodies but what the system of which the bomb is both an insane sign and its negation does to bodies, rendering them as so much disposable matter if necessary, their suffering if it occurs incalculable and yet not unthinkable as it is built into the threat of nuclear annihilation, a designed suffering which does not need names as it knows only numbers. Any narrative of this situation would not truly be a narrative of this situation if it gave names, if it paused over lives and their value as a way to index or to 'humanise' the situation which is one of a historical horror premised on the blotting out of names in incalculable number.

The early dystopias, those which constitute the basis of the model referred to in the scholarship as 'classical dystopias', hover over this antinomy: there is rarely a 'button' to be pushed but neither the regime itself, typically 'totalitarian' in these early decades, nor those it rules receive as much narrative attention as the senior bureaucrats of rule. The 'historical horror of anonymity' is there – as it must be if a totalitarian state is to show itself totalitarian – in Zamyatin's numbered hordes, in Huxley's Gammas, Epsilons and Deltas, and in Orwell's 'proles' – but, almost incidentally, cast into being context or backdrop for the drama of the bureaucrat's dual role: to explain the regime's function, subsuming the anonymous to their allocated parts, and to confirm the efficiency of that function by crushing the individualised rebels or misfits. Using the terms Adorno used to castigate Sartre's error in setting *The Die Is Cast* and *Dirty Hands* among the 'political leaders and not in obscurity among the victims', dystopian fictions use 'political leaders' and their structurally necessary opponents, to give shape to their horrors, and use the obscure, the anonymous, to act as substance, not shape, for those horrors.[23]

Language imposes limits

I want to use Adorno's essay 'Commitment' to help bring his understanding of how language must be used by literature to the question of dystopia. Before doing so, however, it is necessary to put some more specificity on what can usefully be meant by dystopia as a subgenre, and on the historicity of its conventions as they first emerged in their codified or repeatable form. To do this, I wish to use Darko Suvin's notion of a novum as being the formal signature of science fiction, the field of study Suvin's own work was central to codifying, and that to which the dystopia belongs, alongside – even though frequently in opposition to – utopian fiction.

Why Suvin? To think in terms of genre is to attempt to ensure that formal questions do not shrink into a matter of textuality but remain historical questions. Adorno's own work on literature and on art more generally is a consistent prompt in this direction but that work cannot be applied immediately to the subgenre of the dystopia; some mediating categories are needed and one such is the novum. To work with genre is to work with form-in-history, form moving historically. Suvin's account of the novum was a key step in the study of science fiction as a genre as it insisted on taking formal procedures as inseparable from the ideas which then constituted a large part of science fiction's appeal. Suvin's work on utopia as first and foremost a literary construct – the 'first point and most fundamental element of a literary definition of utopia is that any utopia is a *verbal construction*' – was key to his parallel insistence on treating individual utopian texts as belonging, however contingently, in a subgenre we call utopia.[24] Suvin argued in *Metamorphoses* that defining the context of the work of art means inserting that work into the 'tradition and system of its genre'. The description of genre Suvin works with here is useful enough to reproduce:

> a socioaesthetic entity with a specific inner life, yet in a constant osmosis with other literary genres, science, philosophy, everyday socioeconomic life … Understanding particular utopias really presupposes a definition and delimitation of their literary genre (or, as we shall see, subgenre), its inner process, logic and *telos* … its *differentia generica*.[25]

In the short history of its formal study, there was once a tendency to treat individual dystopian texts as without genre, as utterances without either language or the histories language-use embeds or entangles fictional utterances with. This in part can be understood as the weight of an older tradition of literary criticism which posits that to read a novel at all, one has to read it as singular. This was a tradition at its most powerfully normative in Anglo-American scholarship in the 1950s and 1960s. As such it marked the early moments of the scholarship on dystopia – Chad Walsh's *From Utopia to Nightmare* (1962), for example, treats dystopias as the penetrating insights of 'advanced minds and sensibilities' set to work to critique utopian plans.[26] The literary critic's job is then to assess the value of the dystopian novel's critique in terms of its acuity and fidelity to human nature.

In some recent scholarship, there has been a principled return to this position, one which this book wishes to argue against. Gregory Claeys's monumental *Dystopia: A Natural History* (2017) can be read as a summation, defence and elongation of this tradition. Though he notes that dystopias 'are not reducible to the history of ideas', it is in terms of 'ideas' that Claeys produces his 'natural' history: it is dystopias' contribution to such a history of ideas which forms his focus 'rather than an analysis of their literary forms.'[27] As this history squeezes out historicity itself from such ideas, turning away from their form of presentation, their participation in modes of perception and action which themselves have agency in the conflicts which constitute social life, agency and conflicts sometimes subterranean, sometimes open and proud, the dystopia becomes a site not of ideas as such but rather of truths about collectivity or collective life, its dangers and temptations. Positioning 'the crowd' as 'one ancestor of the collectivist political dystopia',[28] and using both the classic theories of crowd psychology and historical examples of modern political crowds at work, *Dystopia: A Natural History* dehistoricises as dystopia's premise that rigorous separation between social life and individual life a troubled liberalism experienced as one symptom of its troubles in the late nineteenth and early twentieth centuries.

In other words, the literary history which treats dystopia in terms of ideas is in danger of mistaking as normative what the fictions worry over. It is indeed the case that the classic dystopias of the early twentieth century are fascinated by – or 'transfixed' by – the unravelling of the liberal conception of selfhood but that self-same conception cannot be accepted by their reader as her premise too without erasing the historicity of the form in which those anxieties become embedded in a desire to protect individuality from the dangers of 'mass society'. In his essay on *Brave New World*, Adorno noted that Huxley's 'negative utopia' treats subject and object too rigidly, polarises them in a crude alternative which fetishes the individual as an organic form for humanity and can hence see social life only in terms of the degradation of that individuality. Accordingly

> exteriority and interiority move into a primitive antithesis: men are the mere objects of all evil, from artificial insemination to galloping senility, while the category of the individual stands forth with unquestioned dignity. Unreflective individualism asserts itself as though the horror which transfixes the novel were not itself the monstrous offspring of individualist society. The spontaneity of the individual human being is eliminated from the historical process while the concept of the individual is detached from history and incorporated into the *philosophia perennis*. Individuation, which is essentially social, reverts to the immutability of nature.[29]

Contra Claeys then, the dystopia has to be approached as a form if it is not to become documentary evidence for either its author's or its reader's 'ideas' about the age they inhabited. The genre of dystopia is a difficult one to parse, however, and is so in particular at two moments in its history: its consolidation in the first decades of the twentieth century, and its apparent success in the first decades of the twenty-first century.[30] To identify these knots in the moments of the sub-genre's history, and to tease apart their conditions, will require some testing of particular texts. In the chapter which follows this one, I have placed readings which will bring us from Forster's 'The Machine Stops' (1909) up to our own day with Leni Zumas's *Red Clocks* (2018) via Frederik Pohl and C.M. Kornbluth's *The Space Merchants* (1952). That chapter will provide a practical elaboration and test of the argument made more abstractly here. That argument uses Adorno's understanding of the situation of language, and culture more generally, in the late nineteenth and twentieth centuries to rework Suvin's concept of the novum. The reworked novum can then be put to use to read the subgenre of dystopia as formally defined by a commitment to the present which cannot be figured, a negative commitment.

To begin, I want to follow Adorno's remarks in 'The Position of the Narrator in the Contemporary Novel'. That essay, as almost all Adorno's work on fiction, takes as its own examples 'the extremes' or the modernist works from which 'we can learn more about the contemporary novel' than from any '"typical" case'. The essay's object, however, is the situation of the novel more widely, its problematic as the conditions of realism were destabilised on all fronts.[31] In this 1954 essay (originally a radio broadcast), Adorno sketched out the dilemma for the twentieth-century novel in terms which, whilst they take modernist novels as their analytic exemplars, can be made to work with a wider set of co-ordinates. The aim is to situate dystopia in relation to Suvin's novum: that 'imaginary framework alternative to the author's empirical environment', the 'main formal device' of those fictions.[32] The task of so situating dystopia should allow us to see dystopia's use of a future encountered by the reader in *medias res* as a technique, and in being so as a solution to a historical and formal problem rather than a free-floating formal innovation. That problem turns on familiarity and the cancellation of shock it involves. Dystopias are fictions which grapple with the problem of how to render the shock of something which habit has deprived of its shock, of how to render the horror of habit.

Shock, surprise, fear are not productive reading habituses, however. The dystopia is a fictional form which must negotiate the tension between the production of meaning which can estrange its reader, and can yet form the basis of how the text can simultaneously reach out and hold on to that same reader. For the classic dystopias, it is not the terrible which most pointedly estranges but its familiarity, its translation in the future world into the ordinary and everyday.

Plunging the reader into a world which has for centuries or decades been 'dystopian', and having no character – time-traveller, sleeper, adventurer – 'guide' the reader through the shift from present to future, totalises that future. It is all there is: whatever temporal borders it has are lost to the mists of myth (Zamyatin, Burdekin), engineered forgetting (Huxley, Orwell) or to sheer absence (Forster). The reader has thus no textual present when she reads: she is addressed by the dystopian text as someone who is *in* this new world as it is experienced rather than experiencing it from the reports of fictional witnesses to whom it also might have come as a novel or shocking place. Habit or the familiarisation which habit breeds is thus always there in dystopian openings. What must be terrible and dreadful is inaugurated as the daily routine for a social world whose inhabitants cannot see or feel that routine as anything other than what has to be, a 'natural' or a 'good' world.

The explanatory framework set up by *utopia's* temporal layerings, in contrast, builds consensus as the new is inaugurated, peered over, understood. The dystopia takes a much more narratively dangerous route; it does not build or make a consensus in an intradiegetic manner but relies on an internal conflict to generate a diegetic one. Plot rather than pedagogy serves as the narrative backbone. Dystopia's peculiar break with speculative fiction's earlier tropes of the visitor to a strange land or time, the time-traveller or voyager, is a strong index of the subgenre's historicity. It could not assume an interpretative position for its reader but had to make one. Take, for example, the opening lines of three of the classic dystopias:

> Forster: 'Imagine, if you can, a small room, hexagonal in shape like the cell of a bee.'
> Huxley: 'A squat grey building of only thirty-four storeys.'
> Burdekin: 'The Knight turned towards the Holy Hitler chapel which in the orientation of this church lay in the western arm of the Swastika, and with the customary loud impressive chords on the organ and a long roll on the sacred drums, the Creed began.'

Each of these sentences introduces the strange or the new or unprecedented shorn of any shock or with the shock quietened by the mode of address. Forster's injunction to 'imagine' itself notes the difficulty of doing so; Huxley's 'squat' building is silently three times the height of any residential building in London in the 1930s;[33] and Burdekin's juxtaposition of a Knight, a chapel, Hitler and a Swastika is relayed as if it is just a setting for an early morning mass. This quiet is narratively necessary as it is an inhabitant of the dystopia itself who must realise the terrible nature of the regime she lives within, opening up space for marvel and awe, for fear and fury, within the text. But the quiet does a strange thing to the reader's position: they are left relatively alone, subject to an estrangement which is immediate but which is unremarked. As the dystopian inhabitant undergoes their own later estrangement, the reader finds a textual space and vocabulary for resistance to the dystopian regime – for the defamiliarisation of that regime from within – but there is never a textual space opened for the evaluation of the regime from the perspective of the present. That is left to the reader and the narrative language which addresses that reader as one who is expected to be estranged and is yet reconciled by that language at the same time.

In this reliance on the reader, the model of the classic dystopia is a conservative model yet is one which registers the stresses and strains of its own conservatism as it strives to maintain an aesthetic distance which can no longer be 'organic' or part of the story – as with the temporal distance used by the utopia or by the earlier anti-utopian fictions.

For Adorno, 'realism' had been 'inherent' in the novel but had become disturbed by a 'paradox' afflicting the position of the narrator: today 'that position is marked by a paradox: it is no longer possible to tell a story, but the form of the novel requires narration'.[34] Realism *had been* inherent in the novel,

> even those that are novels of fantasy as far as their subject matter is concerned attempt to present their content in such a way that the suggestion of reality emanates from them. Through a development that extends back into the nineteenth century and has become accelerated in the extreme today, this mode of proceeding has become questionable.[35]

It would be wrong here, however, to say that realism was a position no longer possible. Adorno's characterisation of Joyce's work as involving 'the novel's rebellion against realism' suggests that realism lives on in modes vigorous enough to have to be rebelled against. The novel is not free, either, to just turn its back on realism. It may have 'lost' many of its traditional tasks to 'reportage and the media of the culture industry, especially film' but this does not mean it can veer off on its own to pursue 'what reportage will not handle'.[36] Unlike painting, whose tasks have also been in part appropriated by new technologies,

> language imposes limits on the novel's emancipation from the object and forces the novel to present the semblance of a report: consistently, Joyce linked the novel's rebellion against realism with a rebellion against discursive language.[37]

Realism is not here a discreet *style* of fiction but was the epochal job of the novel, that literary form which 'was … specific to the bourgeois age'. At its origins 'stands the experience of the disenchanted world in *Don Quixote*, and the artistic treatment of mere existence has remained the novel's sphere'.[38] Neither 'mere existence' nor the techniques of its treatment have been left untouched by the technologies of the mass media or by the centralisation and consolidation of capital in an era of monopoly or state capitalism. The novel's realism is undermined at all the levels of its conditions of possibility. In a process which originated in the last decades of the nineteenth century, and which Adorno describes as having become 'accelerated in the extreme' by the 1950s, the novel can no longer assume a world that is meaningful. To avoid the false promise of meaning, its narrative apparatus must remake itself, the narrative distance it could once posit and enjoy is no longer there.

The novel at the time of Henry Fielding's *Tom Jones* (1749) was capable of sensing alienation as a process, and of negotiating the delicate dialectic between an awkwardly singular individuality and the external world which is experienced at first in terms of its 'rigidified conditions' before the latter loosen so as to accommodate a subject who has 'grown into' his or her individuality by accommodating it to an external world now no longer so utterly alien or 'enigmatic'.[39]

The reader had her role here. So long as the narrator was capable of spinning into objective harmony the subject's coming into possession of their place in the world, the reader was invited to see everything, to be there. For such proximity or intimacy to occur, the narrator had to maintain an aesthetic distance of a peculiar sort. It is this aesthetic distance which is now, in the early twentieth-century novel, unbalanced. Adorno compares the traditional novel – 'whose idea is perhaps most authentically embodied in Flaubert' – to the three-walled stage of bourgeois theatre. The

> technique was one of illusion. The narrator raises a curtain: the reader is to take part in what occurs as though he were physically present. The narrator's subjectivity proves itself in the power to produce this illusion … There is a heavy taboo on reflection: it becomes the cardinal sin against objective purity.[40]

The 'reader's contemplative security in the face of what he reads' is sustained and required by the aesthetic distance the narrator maintains between the totality of the story and the narrator, and between the narrator and the reader. The reflection which is 'taboo' is not the 'moral' commentary the pre-Flaubertian narrator is prone to. '[T]aking a stand for or against characters' can be tolerated by narrative distance, may even be considered as constitutive of its peculiar mode of confidential address, the formal or impersonal intimacy of the 'dear reader' mode, so long as commentary does not reach out and comment on itself. In the novels of Proust or Kafka, Thomas Mann or James Joyce, that aesthetic distance disappears. In Mann or Musil, 'reflection breaks through the pure immanence of form'. In Proust, 'commentary is so thoroughly interwoven with action that the distinction between the two disappears'; Kafka more directly 'abolish[es] the distance', using 'shocks' to destroy the reader's contemplative security in what she reads.[41]

For Adorno, these were the novels of importance, the 'contemporary novels that count' because they did not dodge or deny their new situation but confronted it and worked it to register not just the loss of a world which might have been made meaningful but the loss of the self who might have inhabited that world, and the loss of a language in which their art might have spoken of them without erasing the difficulties of that inhabitation. These are novels in which subjectivity is 'unleashed' and in its headlong momentum 'turns into its own opposite'. They are 'negative epics',

> testimonials to a state of affairs in which the individual liquidates himself ... These epics, along with all contemporary art, are ambiguous: it is not up to them to determine whether the goal of the historical tendency they register is a regression to barbarism or the realisation of humanity, and many are all too comfortable with the barbaric. There is no modern work of art worth anything that does not delight in dissonance and release. But by uncompromisingly embodying the horror and putting all the pleasure of contemplation into the purity of this expression, such works of art serve freedom – something the average production betrays, simply because it does not bear witness to what has befallen the individual in the age of liberalism.[42]

Now dystopian fictions of the classic type, though they belong to the period Adorno writes about, do not either liquidate individuality or unleash subjectivity. What they do is figure a world in which these things have happened socially or politically rather than aesthetically. They throw into the future, and make full and meaningful there, the horror they otherwise do not embody. The catastrophe warned of does not affect the warning except as it needs that warning to exist at all. Dystopias in this sense do not bear witness to 'what has befallen the individual in the age of liberalism' but rather project those anxieties into a future when it is the collapse or overthrow of the 'age of liberalism' which is the catastrophe which has befallen the individual.

Even in their first or formative phase, the phase of the classic dystopia, the styles used by these fictions vary markedly. The ironic distance utilised by Aldous Huxley or Yevgeny Zamyatin does much more, paradoxically, to maintain the contemplative security of the reader than does the detailed density of the realist style used to create Katharine Burdekin's or George's Orwell's much more concrete-heavy images of foreboding realised. In this way, the case Adorno makes about the destabilising of the traditional distance between narrator and reader may be thought to be embedded in the subgenre too, a destabilising which means that the aesthetic distance of a narrator now 'varies' 'like the angle of the camera in film: sometimes the reader is left outside, and sometimes he is led by the commentary onto the stage, into the prop room'.[43] Nevertheless, dystopias, no matter how genial their parody or how cold their satire, wish *to say something*. In Adorno's terms, they 'sing the praise of binding ties' even if that song is one sung in a negative key. To do this, they must use language in its discursive register, that register where its capacity to mean is left untouched or untroubled by history. The estrangement opened for the reader in the first sentence of the three fictions mentioned above is a partial estrangement only: it has as a thread holding it stable the deeper stability of the narrator. That narrative position is one for which language and with language interpretation still works.

These fictions do not operate language as if they themselves were only reports. No novel could but they do create the semblance of a report, a report from the future, in ways which mean the tensions between the language use they worry about – the future realm of a full and centralised instrumentalisation of language so central to the dystopian-ness of each of the dystopian regimes – is never allowed to breach its bounds and trouble the form's own reliance on language. These are not texts in which language is worked so as to turn on itself. A modernist novel 'rattles the cage of meaning and through its distance from meaning rebels from the outset against a positive assumption of meaning'.[44] A dystopian novel frets about what will happen to meaning in a future unlike the present but not about its own present capacity to hold and to objectify meaning.

In 'The Position of the Narrator in the Contemporary Novel', Adorno makes the case for what we can learn about the contemporary novel from the shapes taken by those novels we now think of as modernist, arguing that it is there that we can access the tendency to the abolition of aesthetic distance as one 'inherent in form'. A novel which follows its own imma nent law of form follows its own inner logic, not the logic of a genre or subgenre. To follow its inner logic, the contemporary novel must recoil from the world which would deny the inner logic of anything not identical to what is acceptable. His account of the pressures bearing down on narrative form have a more general and historicising use to us, particularly when we come to specify the situation of the subgenre of dystopia in relation to Suvin's synchronic account of the novum. The novum as theorised by Suvin is constituted by, or needs or makes, aesthetic distance: regardless of the particular forms it might take or how successfully they may be realised, the need for such a distance is the *raison d'être* of the novum. Such a distance is made – it cannot be assumed. Whatever work the novum does depends on it being able to initiate and sustain a narrative which 'deviates' from the known but can yet be known. For Suvin, a 'novum or cognitive innovation is a totalising phenomenon or relationship deviating from the author's and implied reader's norm of reality'.[45] That 'deviation' is for Suvin the central formalising work constitutive of the subgenre: its

momentum and oscillating rhythms the work of the production of the
novum. This embedding of a shared space – one subjected to all the textual
activity necessary to defamiliarise space and time but nevertheless *there* for
that defamiliarising activity to take place and be constantly rebuilt *as* that
defamiliarisation takes place – usefully brings into the heart of dystopia the
question of readership not as a sociological one but as a formal one, as a
question of the public at a time when the classical model of the public was
being transformed.

The tension between private and public as a thematic of dystopian fiction
has long been recognised. This is a fiction which senses a threat to the private
sphere of bodily autonomy, contemplation, familial relations, thought and
culture from a newly socialised and newly statified public realm or from the
creep of a field of leisure colonised by the commodity work of the culture
industry. This is a thematic we will return to in the next chapter but, for
now, it is its translation into a formal problematic in Suvin's work which is
of use here. The novum is 'totalising' and, for its totality to work, it must
bring its reader with it:

> the essential tension of SF is one between the readers, representing a certain
> number of types of people of our times, and the encompassing and at least
> equipollent Unknown or Other introduced by the novum. This tension in turn
> estranges the empirical norm of the implied reader.[46]

The tension or the estrangement necessary for the novum to work, to be
new yet legible, was elaborated by Suvin as the interrelationship between
cognition and estrangement. Suvin's work and the scholarship it has generated over the last forty years has centred most productively on building a
historical understanding of science fiction as the conjuncture where utopia
found a home. I want to shift the focus to dystopia and to do so by nar-
rowing the Suvinian dialectic of estrangement and cognition to bring it to
bear on dystopian fictions as constituted by a political logic, a pattern of
familiarisation and defamiliarisation which has as its material the forms
and relations of power rather than more broadly social or even anthropo-
logical modes of life.[47]

When thus narrowed, however, the moments of the dialectic become
volatilised a little, the familiarity which estrangement must assume to do its
work becomes more visible, and estrangement itself, or its effects, become
more desperate, less self-assured. It is rarely the science or technology which
estranges in a dystopia but rather the uses to which they are put, and more
specifically the familiarity or conventionality of that use. For the reader,
what should estrange *is* that familiarity, that what is shocking is not shocking, what is cruel and unusual is experienced as normative, as capable of
even irritating in its banality or predictability.

To take one small but influential example, the moment in Huxley's *Brave New World* (1932) where 'Neo-Pavlovian conditioning' is practised successfully on infants. The 'science' is not put into question at all, its efficacy is secure. It is the subjection of babies to the violence of the method, and the consequences of that violence – an aversion to 'nature' and to books – which estranges.

Bowls of roses and brightly coloured books are laid on the floor of a nursery, in front of a group of eight-month-old infants. The

> swiftest crawlers were already at their goal. Small hands reached out uncertainly, touched, grasped, unpetalling the transfigured roses, crumpling the illuminated pages of the books. The Director waited until all were happily busy. Then, 'Watch carefully,' he said. And, lifting his hand, he gave the signal.
>
> The Head Nurse, who was standing by a switchboard at the other end of the room, pressed down a little lever.
>
> There was a violent explosion. Shriller and even shriller, a siren shrieked. Alarm bells maddeningly sounded.
>
> The children started, screamed; their faces were distorted with terror.
>
> 'And now,' the Director shouted (for the noise was deafening), 'now we proceed to rub in the lesson with a mild electric shock.'
>
> He waved his hand again, and the Head Nurse pressed a second lever. The screaming of the babies suddenly changed its tone. There was something desperate, almost insane, about the sharp spasmodic yelps to which they now gave utterance.[48]

That adults would sanction and organise the infliction of pain on infants is the site of the shock here. The conditioning itself 'works'. When next presented with books and roses, the children shrink away in horror: 'Books and loud noises, flowers and electric shocks – already in the infant mind these couples were compromisingly linked' (*BNW*, p. 29). What is being estranged is not delivered only in the application of pain but via the professionalism with which it is done. The pride of the Director, the efficiency of the nurses, the convention and routine of it all. What is estranging is precisely the familiarity of the scene: that in this social order, human beings are – within limits – malleable and are subject to a state apparatus whose bureaucracies daily shape that malleability to the state's needs.

For Huxley's World State, the application of science to every area of human genesis and development – with the aim of perfecting a closed and stable cycle of production and consumption – is successful. For the reader this success is laid out as possible but not as palatable, an evacuation of 'nature' from 'human nature' – 'What man has joined, nature is powerless to put asunder' (*BNW*, p. 29) – which is the last moment in the conquest of history by science.

The work of this dystopia creates not a critical distance alone but a consensus. The narrative work estranges and reconciles, building the latter on the silent assumptions which enable the former. The reader is thrown forward into a time and a space where cruelty to children is shockingly routine, mechanised and posited as necessary for the reproduction of the social order of which it is a dynamic part. The shock is not one that spreads: Neo-Pavlovian conditioning, eugenics and the hierarchical division of labour, these are immune to it. They work. It is the ends to which they are put, the conventionalisation of those ends, which estrange.

The reader addressed is one capable of being amused by this scene from the world of A.F. 632. The irony of the style is cold and incisive enough to be distancing, but locally detailed enough to identify and puncture professional pomposity and vanity. The consequent distant intimacy between narrator or mode of address and reader is one peculiar to Huxley's style but its formal movement is one constituted by that oscillation between estrangement and cognition that Suvin identifies. The circuits of both are reciprocally limited, and for dystopia it is the political organisation of the novum which is estranged and which estranges most completely but it is therefore equally a political cognition which is required most thoroughly for these texts to make sense. The legibility of that political cognition is nowhere positively figured in the text as reconciliation – any challenge mounted to the dystopian order will be defeated in the classic model of dystopia, as in *Brave New World* – but it is the core of the narrative form, an absent core or a negative commitment.

For the estrangement to work, the text must posit what Suvin terms the 'empirical environment', a sphere I am going to move out of his 'cognitive logic' and into the narrower realm of 'political logic'. Once we make that move, we will see with Adorno how difficult it is for dystopias to so posit the familiarity – that shared environment – they must rely on. Not politics per se gets in the way but language itself or rather what happens to language in the era of dystopia's early consolidation in the first decades of the twentieth century. Huxley's satire may be read as a warning about the political uses to which contemporary applied science – 'Procrustes in modern dress'[49] – may be put but it is historically more interesting to read it as a novel. As a novel, the text is an entity which cannot have things fully its own way. From the early 1930s, the text tells us of its suspicion not only of the clichés and slogans of speech in the World State but also of a suspicion of the language it uses itself. The generalisation of mass-produced habit or the habitualisation of perception, itself critiqued by Huxley in the essays and fiction he wrote in the 1920s, cannot leave narrative language, aesthetics or literature outside its maw.[50] The novel puts writing and writers to work in the College of Emotional Engineering, there to produce slogans, hypnopaedic rhymes and 'feely scenarios' (*BNW*, p. 61). These are the debased activities involved in the instrumentalisation of words for immediate affect on bodies which have been designed to be receptive only to such affect.

Emotional engineering requires words to jolt or to excite their interlocutors, to stand out, to draw attention so as to drive meaning home:

> 'I'm pretty good at inventing phrases – you know, the sort of words that suddenly make you jump, almost as though you'd sat on a pin, they seem so new and exciting even though they're about something hypnopaedically obvious.' (*BNW*, p. 63)

Helmholtz Watson, the Emotional engineer good at inventing such phrases, can see these things only as 'phrases', terms without referent or too busy signifying in a way which will excite a response to liaise with a referent. Phrases are language as empty, phrases are interchangeable, units of meaning without integrity, designed to provoke or to stimulate some desire. In this, however, this quality of not having to *mean*, the phrases of emotional engineering are like aesthetic work.

The central character John Savage's encounters with Shakespeare are mocked by the novel as naive or quasi-literate because he reads literally, he attempts to organise his experience and behaviour around the 'values' of a language he mistakes as meaningful not in itself but for him. For the novel, this is to treat language as magical, as capable not of speaking to you but of being you. Following one of his disastrous attempts to communicate with Lenina Crowne, John Savage is repelled by her advances and throws her out. He can do no other as he inhabits a language in which the advances of a woman are ungodly or plain bestial:

> Outside … the Savage was striding up and down, marching, marching to the drums and music of magical words. 'The wren goes to't, and the small gilded fly does lecher in my sight.' Maddeningly they rumbled in his ears. 'The fitchew nor the soiled horse goes to't with a more riotous appetite. Down from the waist they are all Centaurs, though women all above. But to the girdle do the Gods inherit. Beneath is all the fiends.' (*BNW*, p. 154)

A language which is too empty to mean, on the one hand, the merely formal unity of 'phrases', and a language too full of meaning, on the other, too saturated with the needy subjectivity of its user to limit the flow of meaning at all. That these are two sides of the same coin – the dual aspect of language as it becomes codified into the practices of what Adorno and Horkheimer termed the culture industry in *Dialectic of Enlightenment* (1944) – may become clear if we mention briefly the conjuncture recreated by Franco Moretti in his 1980 essay 'From The Waste Land to the Artificial Paradise.'

Tracing what he describes as the 'formidable aestheticizing of culture' which took place in the first half of the twentieth century, Moretti builds out from an analysis of T.S. Eliot's review of *Ulysses* (1922) a historicised account of the liquidation of the aesthetic use of language, not its destruction but its appropriation and exuberant spread by the culture industry. The creation of an aesthetic use of language or the establishment of a linguistic domain where there is no compulsion to refer directly, to be subordinate to the universe of 'external' things, involved a very

> particular semantic situation ... a relatively modern way of judging literary and artistic manifestations. It appears in the *Critique of Judgement*, and was probably motivated by the necessity of 'justifying' aesthetic activity on the basis of principles no longer strictly cognitive.[51]

Those 'principles no longer strictly cognitive' will shortly be the place where we can bring Adorno and Suvin together but, for now, Moretti's essay provides a usefully brief way to historicise the seeming inability of *Brave New World* to find a form for the value of art, for the special type of cognition required by an aesthetic use of language, all the while performing that ability in its own mode of address. For having identified the language of 'emotional engineering' as a language which has sense but no referent – 'empty phrases', the 'sort of words that suddenly make you jump' (*BNW*, p. 63) – the novel tracks an anxiety that all language is now fully cultural, fully public and aesthetic at the same time, subjected to a sundering from the things of this world and a consequent ballooning of the elasticity of sense, of the playful or creative use of language.

The World State controls and relies on the apparatus, practices and products of 'emotional engineering', and it and they are offered up to the reader as already judged, to be understood as an illegitimate and infantalising usurper of the autonomy of subjects who could be individuals, and the theft of that privacy which could be the medium of individuality. Nevertheless, the novel can find no positive way to figure a cognitive use of language which is outside science, is significant yet fictional, playful or aesthetic, except itself, its own practice.

The novel's worry about the unmooring of an aesthetic use of language from art, its seeping into every nook and cranny of cognition left over after 'science' has had its way with language, pushes it to provide a formal opponent to 'engineered' culture in the presence of Shakespeare but this opposition of 'high' and 'mass' culture remains formal: once Shakespeare is read, cognition goes awry.

For Gregory Claeys, John Savage manages to figure 'the less secure but more "natural," romantic, and freer old world ways by contrast to the supposed superiority but obvious puerility of the new'.[52] There can be no nature to secure value in this novel, however, the irony is too absolutising. Nothing is without its social mediation. John Savage is a different social creature from Lenina Crowne but not a more 'natural' one. The novel manages to valorise the individual as private but cannot manage to naturalise that same individuality or the privacy which should be its organic form. That there should be a subject capable of aesthetic cognition or appreciation, that the readers of the novel are addressed as such, is clear but there is no place in the novel where such clarity can find positive form. It is only figured internally as a maxim, moralising because missing any potential agents or mode of realisation. For Claeys, in

> perhaps the novel's definitive line, we are told that the alternative to the system involves recognising 'that the purpose of life was not the maintenance of well-being, but some intensification and refining of consciousness, some enlargement of knowledge.'[53]

Such a recognition is not an alternative to 'the system', however; it is not even the beginning of one: it is more a note to what has been lost – even as the novel's mode of address keeps alive the fiction of its continuing presence. It is only in reading the novel that the business of art or literature can be realised. Adorno was right when he noted the rigidity of the novel's polarisation of subjective and objective. They are reconciled only in the reader, the novel can no longer do it.

Conclusion: negative commitment

At this point, I have given a concrete instance of what I am terming a negative commitment, the type of commitment which I will argue is constitutive of dystopia when conceptualised as a subgenre of fiction. Negative commitment will allow me to use Adorno to translate the critical vocabulary of the novum into a hermeneutic sensitive specifically to the political work of the subgenre, and to the historical conditions and limits of that political work. To complete this Introduction, I want to pause a moment over the term 'commitment'. It is not an easy term to use though it is an easy one to misuse. The first thing to be done, to help avoid that misuse, is to distinguish 'commitment' in its Adornian sense from any notion of a paraphrasable content or 'message'. A committed work of art is not to be known by its 'position' on something, or its campaigning aesthetic. Rather, in

> aesthetic theory, 'commitment' should be distinguished from 'tendency.' Committed art in the proper sense is not intended to generate ameliorative measures, legislative acts or practical institutions – like earlier propagandist

plays against syphilis, duels, abortion laws or borstals – but to work at the level of fundamental attitudes.[54]

How this is to be done, how those 'fundamental attitudes' are to be prepared for, elicited, made a part of art's own integrity rather than added to art, is the question. For the literary critic or historian, this then becomes how those strategies in the work are to be deciphered not so much in the texts as in the reading positions those texts desire. There is much in Adorno's 1962 essay on 'commitment' to help us here. In particular, Adorno's alignment of the 'sphere of consumption, which includes the psychologically motivated actions of individuals' with the 'surface of social life', that busy arena of perception, action, affect, of cause and consequence which is social life when mediated by the vagaries and contingencies of a privatised form of being, against which the social itself – except in the form of what is chosen – must appear as a threat to authenticity. Adorno begins his essay as a response to Jean-Paul Sartre's understanding of commitment (*engagement*) in *What Is Literature?* (1948). Noting that it is now a 'half-forgotten controversy about committed and autonomous art', Adorno nevertheless opens a historical scale on which that controversy contains an important cluster of questions, ones worth poring over if art is not itself to sink into being an arena of choice with something for everyone its slogan:

> the controversy over commitment remains urgent, so far as anything that merely concerns the life of the mind can be today, as opposed to sheer human survival. Sartre was moved to issue his manifesto because he saw – and he was definitely not the first to do so – works of art displayed side by side in a pantheon of optional edification, decaying into cultural commodities.[55]

Sartre's own argument in *What Is Literature?*, and in different ways his own aesthetic practice, fail to live up to the possibilities or to realise the limits of committed art. In his theory, Sartre relies too heavily on subjectivity, not so much the writer's but the human who is the writer, the humanity the writer shares with others in her present moment. This deprivatised subjectivity has yet no objectivity, no form which compels it to share the deeply collective objectivity which is the aesthetic itself. The result is a general stress on *expression*, on what, ultimately or inevitably, the writer wants to say:

> Sartre's question, 'Why write?' and his derivation of writing from a 'deeper choice' are unconvincing because the author's motivations are irrelevant to the written work, the literary product … When using Durkheimian terminology, Sartre calls the work a '*fait social*,' a social fact, he is involuntarily citing the idea of a deeply collective objectivity that cannot be penetrated by the mere subjective intentions of the author. This is why he wants to link commitment not to the writer's intention but to the fact that the writer is a human being.

But this definition is so general that any distinction between commitment and human works or behaviour of any kind is lost. It is a question of the writer engaging himself in the present, *dans le présent*; but since the writer cannot escape the present in any case, no program can be inferred from this.[56]

That 'weakness' in Sartre's 'conception of commitment' is a weakness in his conception of art: it is this which 'strikes at the cause to which Sartre is committed'.[57] Grasping art as contingent on what its maker means to do with it means grasping art as akin to a vehicle, shorn of its objective entanglements and objective needs:

[for] Sartre, the work of art becomes an appeal to the subject because the work is nothing but the subject's decision or non-decision. He will not grant that even in its initial steps every work of art confronts the writer, however free he may be, with objective requirements regarding its construction. Confronted with these demands, the writer's intention becomes only a moment in the process.[58]

It is this greater process, one in which the writer's wishes are but one moment, which Adorno then brings to the practice of Brecht – which practice he likewise finds falls short of the demands of commitment, and of art. Brecht, who wanted to 'educate spectators to a detached, thoughtful, experimental attitude, the opposite of the illusionary stance of empathy and identification', used abstraction as an aesthetic strategy and formal principle. His 'didactic *poésie*' manages to see off aesthetic individuation, the 'traditional concept' of character, and to posit characters as instead the shrivelled-up 'agents of social processes and functions that they are, indirectly and without realising it, in empirical reality'.[59] Brecht's work then escapes the probing for truth in the surface of life, that busy, conflictual, rambunctious arena in which the principle of exchange takes on multiple meanings, each subject to its own reification but each alluring in its own way. Instead, there is a radical distillation, a dramatic abstraction which renders both the 'sovereignty of the subject' and the realm that the sovereign subject is at home in empty of meaning or touched only with the taunt of a meaning which might be promised but cannot be realised. In this, Brecht is for Adorno the greater artist:

he wants to turn the gruesomeness of society into a theatrical phenomenon by dragging it out into the open … Brecht wanted to capture the inherent nature of capitalism in an image; to this extent his intention was in fact what he disguised it from the Stalinist terror as being, realistic.[60]

The theory, and some of the aesthetic work, was crippled, however, by the same stress on abstraction which lent it the power to overcome the lure

of a subjectified social world. Brecht may have escaped the sentimental-
ity of identification or the over-reliance on a work's affect which afflicted
Sartre but the adherence to a radical form of abstraction gives the lie to
particular understandings or the cognition of particular truths when it
insists on denying the complexities of mediation: 'The process of aesthetic
reduction he undertakes for the sake of political truth works against
political truth. That truth requires countless mediations, which Brecht
disdains.'[61] Committed to theoretical accuracy *and to* political truth,
Brecht struggles to capture those truths in images which do not belittle or
caricature them. As much as his dialectical theatre spurned what became
known in SF as 'info dumping', the plays were still frequently unable to
summon up images which could do justice to the 'information' they were
preoccupied with:

> criticism of Brecht cannot overlook the fact that he did not ... fulfil the norm
> he set himself as if it were a means to salvation. *Saint Joan* was the central
> work of his dialectical theatre ... The play is set in a Chicago half-way
> between the Wild West fables of *Mahagonny* and economic facts. But the
> more preoccupied Brecht becomes with information and the less he looks
> for images, the more he misses the essence of capitalism which the parable
> is supposed to present. Mere episodes in the sphere of circulation, in which
> competitors maul each other, are recounted instead of the appropriation of
> surplus-value in the sphere of production, compared with which the brawls
> of cattle dealers over their shares of the booty are epiphenomena incapable of
> provoking any great crisis.[62]

We will come back in a moment to the impossibility of any art practice
managing to image the 'appropriation of surplus-value in the sphere of
production', or the impossibility of figuring the 'essence of capitalism' but
for now it is important to note the political force of Adorno's reading, a
force which is most tangible in the following account of the pitfalls of rep-
resenting fascism according to the agitational strategy of diminishing your
adversary. In *The Resistible Rise of Arturo Ui* (1941), the 'subjective nullity
and pretence of a fascist leader' are exposed in a 'harsh and accurate light'
but the explanatory matrix embedded in the play's use of the 'cauliflower
racket' as an allegorical means of reconstructing the nexus of the fascist
leadership, and also of cutting that leadership down to size, does not work:

> Instead of a conspiracy of the wealthy and powerful, we are given a trivial
> gangster organisation, the cabbage trust. The true horror of fascism is con-
> jured away; it is no longer a slow end-product of the concentration of social
> power, but mere hazard, like an accident or a crime ... Against every dialectic,
> the ridicule to which Ui is consigned renders innocuous the fascism that was
> accurately predicted by Jack London decades before.[63]

·

Even if Brecht had created in Ui a figurehead of a far more potently powerful organisation, there is a deeper problem with his method, one which deserves some attention here as it can serve as a bridge to bring us back to the dystopian novum. Adorno uses the terms 'reduction' and 'simplification' in the passage below to indicate what is more commonly understood as Brecht's commitment to a theatre which used *Verfremdungseffekt* to tell its new or epic stories.[64] Nevertheless, the description Adorno gives provides terms – and relations for them – which we can usefully migrate back to the types of commitment that dystopian fictions spurn and those they practise. For Adorno, the

> primacy of lesson over pure form, which Brecht intended to achieve, became a formal device itself. The suspension of form turns back against its own character as appearance … The substance of Brecht's artistic work was the didactic play as an artistic principle. His method, to make immediately apparent events into phenomena alien to the spectator, was also a medium of formal construction rather than a contribution to practical efficacy … Yet the artistic principle of simplification not only purged politics of the illusory distinctions projected by subjective reflection into social objectivity, as Brecht intended, but it also falsified the very objectivity which didactic drama laboured to distil.[65]

The interaction of estrangement and cognition which makes up the self-momentum or internal dynamic of the novum – that movement which creates 'spatial and historical configurations as partly but irreconcilably different from the novum dominant in the author's age'[66] – can be lined up with two moments in Adorno's understanding of the situation of literature in the twentieth century. Firstly, Adorno's understanding of the autonomy of modern art as a last-ditch attempt to save art rather than a positive assumption of autonomy as something just held by the work. And secondly, his theory of the culture industry as indicating a historical shift, the end of the situation of culture in the 'short intermezzo of liberalism'[67] rather than naming a hierarchy of cultures.

In *Metamorphoses*, Suvin describes a 'feedback oscillation' as the relationship through which the novum works by positing a reader who follows or co-executes that oscillating rhythm, moving

> now from the author's and implied reader's norm of reality to the narratively actualised novum in order to understand the plot-events, and now back from these novelties to the author's reality, in order to see it afresh from the new perspective gained.[68]

This pulling of the addressee into the structure of the work, this dependence on a lop-sided reciprocity between reader and the business of the work, is not at all a democratic one or a relationship of equals. On the contrary, it requires a desubjectification of the reader's own experience beyond and before the work. If she is to follow the pattern of swerves between novelty and cognitive validity, she will be a historical reader but not a personal one. The rhetorical sway of the novum works to position subjects both situated and not situated in time: inside the civilisation which they must recognise as self-threatened, and yet outside it sufficiently to imagine that threat. For the novum to exist at all as not the present, not the world which constitutes the present, it must constantly reach out and touch that present, differentiating itself from it with the reader as the sensitive differentiating instrument, the point of 'interaction between the text and the history in which it is being written and is being read, so that the contradictions and mediations of a history-as-process are [not] passed over in silence'.[69]

Adorno's understanding of the situation of language in the twentieth century does not forbid the novum from behaving in this way but does make its job more difficult as it is precisely the capacity of language to estrange *and* its capacity to cognitively persuade which were torn apart as functions by the dialectic of enlightenment, and which in their separate spheres as aesthetic and scientific modes of language are threatened with a further undoing as liberal capitalism gives way to monopoly capitalism and to the vast language machine of the culture industry.

There is no one place in Adorno's work that is better than another to begin recreating or pointing to his understanding of language. It is, with history, his pervasive object and it is the medium with which he pursues and retreats from that object. In *Negative Dialectics* (1966), he wrote of dialectics in its literal meaning as being 'language as the *organon* of thought', a point which allows then the methodological apparatus of *Negative Dialectics* to be understood, at one level, as the attempt at a 'critical rescue of the rhetorical element'.[70] As our object is a subgenre of the novel, however, the dystopia understood for now as involving the formal work of the novum, we can use the understanding of language in literature that Adorno unfolded in 'Presuppositions' (1961) to describe the elements of a constellation which may allow us to reach and encompass the Suvian novum.

In a discussion of the experiments of Expressionism with language, Adorno stresses how inescapable is the conceptual moment in language. Failing to recognise or to respect that moment allowed Expressionists to envision 'using words as pure expressive values, the way colours or tone relationships are used in painting or in music'.[71] The word itself, any word, resists such an attempted divorce from its significative or communicative being however: the Expressionists had tried to use language to jump over 'the shadow of language' and had inevitably failed. But why would any literary effort struggle so to disentangle the expressive and the communicative values of language? That question pinpoints the historicity of the problem but Adorno's understanding of that historicity posits it as something we must see as internal to the literary work rather than just a registering of an external or social moment or pressure. As frequently happens when Adorno probes in his essays the contemporary configuration of language, history and literature, he reaches for the figure of Karl Kraus. The appearance of Kraus in the passage below should enable us to follow Adorno's understanding to a more precise focus on the situation of the novel as a literary artefact, a creature of language. Calling the appearance of unintelligibility in 'legitimate contemporary art' the emergence in that art of the moment of the absurd 'which is a constituent of all art but has hitherto been largely hidden by the conventional moment' (which moment is the demand for an intelligibility which is now only the sign of a 'non understanding that [does] not recognise itself as such'), Adorno notes that

> Art has come to this point, to be sure, not so much through its polemic against something external to it, its fate in society, as through internal necessity. In literature the arena of this necessity is the double nature of language, as a means of discursive signification – of communication first and foremost – on the one hand and as expression on the other. To this extent the immanent necessity of radical linguistic arrangements does in fact converge with the social criticism to which language tends to cede the work of art. With utter integrity, Karl Kraus, who was hostile to Expressionism and hence to the unqualified primacy of expression over sign in language, in no way relaxed the distinction between literary and communicative language. His oeuvre persists in trying to produce an artistic autonomy for language without doing violence to its other aspect, the communicative which is inseparable from transmission. The Expressionists, on the other hand, tried to jump over their own shadows.[72]

The internal necessity is not the double nature of language but art's autonomy, something which the work can no longer assume. To now achieve or realise autonomy – something which has to be worked out in language as the arena of this necessity – the literary work must mount a defence against being subsumed 'under preformed schemata', and must compel 'a kind of follow-through on the part of the recipient that renounces understanding'.[73] Every work must begin anew this process so as to realise its own autonomy: tradition is no use to it any more as a positive resource but must be used negatively, as material to be dismantled as the new work produces itself. Neither the novel nor poetry can rest easy on the sensuous particularity or expressive nature of language as that nature is dual and each item of language brings dripping with it its layer of discursive or conceptual meaning and all the allegiances and associations struck up or sparked by that layer. Even a 'stammered sound, if it is a word and not a mere tone, retains its conceptual range', whilst the organising work of any linguistic form could never 'dispense with the conceptual element'.[74]

Such antithetical figures as Stefan George and Kraus both 'repudiated the novel, out of an aversion to the non-aesthetic quality of an excess materiality in literature',[75] an aversion, that is, to the linguistic density of terms which may have as many facets of meaning, or as few, as they do places in the world. Concepts here do not link to the specialised vocabularies of science or even of philosophy but to what the latter share with the social world, the spread of an instrumentalising rationality in everyday cognition and in communication itself.

Before even any questions about the associations or implications of narrative form – the consequences for meaning of this formal choice or that – the writer has to reckon with how much or how little (and how) of a captured or subsumed social world is already there in the language she has at her disposal. Prior to

> questions of narration about the world, concepts as such have something hostile to art about them; they represent the unity as sign of what they subsume, which belongs to empirical reality and is not subject to the spell of the work.[76]

Not subject to the spell of the work but already subject (in the concept) to a governing rationality which freezes the moment of meaning, trapping a layer of it which is then presented positivistically as the concept's entire being, a definition which exhausts everything. So concepts do not circulate freely in the social world, they are not part of a discursive realm – of signification or communication – which is dialogic or packed with explosive shocks or reciprocally enriching antagonisms, things which might provide language itself with the immanent materials to burst out of its own concept. That task is one that only literature can take on. What concepts bring in language is a social world already stretched out as a chain of equivalences, each term more or less triumphant in its capacity to enclose and finish meaning, to identify the all with itself.

Nevertheless, the novel has not merely survived on its constant negotiation of the non-aesthetic quality of its materials, it has at times thrived. Because the conceptual or significatory element of language cannot be dispensed with, the literary work of art must treat with it, prevent itself from being absorbed by it but simultaneously respect it. From the point of view of the indispensability or unavoidability of the conceptual element in language,

> even the most authentic works take on in retrospect a pre-artistic, somewhat informational quality. Literature gropes its way toward making peace with the conceptual moment without expressionistic quixoticness but also without surrendering to that moment. Retrospectively one should grant that this is what great literature has always done; in fact it owes its greatness precisely to its tension with what is heterogeneous to it. It becomes a work of art through

the friction between it and the extra-artistic; it transcends that, and itself, by respecting it.[77]

The conceptual moment treated in such a manner by a literary work in its own production may not only be respected but in being respected is woken out of its positivist freeze and starts to move in a field of associations again. Rather than clasping a closed meaning to itself and repelling all others, it sheds its stasis – 'the result of a reification, a forgetting' – and reawakens to something of its life in language. The

> rudiments of that life ... are the associations that can never be fully accommodated within conceptual meanings and yet attach themselves to the words with a gentle necessity. If literature succeeds in awakening associations in its concepts and correcting for the significative moment through those associations, then the concepts begin, so to speak, to move. Their movement is to become the immanent movement of the work of art.[78]

Such possibilities for the literary work of art belong to the past for Adorno. In 'Presuppositions', he warns that 'the tension' experienced by the literary work, its friction with what is heterogeneous to it, that 'extra-artistic' material which yet must find its way inside of it, is disappearing:

> this tension, and the task of enduring it, becomes thematic through the relentless reflection of history. Given the current status of language, anyone who still relied blindly on the double character of language as sign and expression as though it were something god-given would himself become a victim of pure communication.[79]

Modern art is one register of the undoing of the 'double character' of language as certain works sought to defend if not art then at least themselves from an existence in which artistic autonomy shrank to the abstract equivalences of the commodity form. The presentation of this moment for art, the moment of the crisis of language or of meaning, is one of the burdens of *Aesthetic Theory*, a text which in its very first sentence temporalises its own object in terms of the loss of its legibility: '[i]t is self-evident that nothing concerning art is self-evident anymore, not its inner life, not its relation to the world, not even its right to exist'.[80] In relation to the study of the dystopia as a subgenre, we cannot paraphrase ourselves into Adorno's position: what we can do is follow the two moments in Adorno's thinking which cleave closest to our own pursuit of language and the novel form in dystopian fiction, and indicate where the reader can return to those two moments' own place in Adorno's wider project to understand the 'crisis and agony of aesthetic appearance' in the twentieth century.

Though it is too simplistic or static an image to survive long, we can take a step into the relationship between the culture industry and the novel by suggesting that the dystopia has too much of an interest in the things of the world outside it and that this interest exacts the price of its autonomy. As a form, dystopias desire to intervene in the world, to direct their readers' attention, finally, not to themselves but to the world. This does not mean, however, that they yield to unvarnished communication, to a purely instrumentalised language-use. The intervention they make is one made in the name of culture and the type of social order which would secure culture's autonomy. As these are precisely the things forbidden in and by the dystopia which is the imagined future yet must be drawn upon to measure just how fallen that future is, the dystopia must provoke its reader into providing their normative existence as she reads.

Dystopias, in short, begin their life as critical texts, a status which in no way contradicts their conservative ethos. The classic dystopia, the formal model which consolidated itself in the first half of the twentieth century, takes society as its subject and attempts to lay bare the forces within that society which would compel it to create out of itself a dark and miserable future. This is far from the work of modernist texts, those novels which sacrifice the world to secure an autonomy which can only then facilitate the whisper of a future world or the barest echo of a past one. Art can no longer look directly at society as it has not got the materials with which to look. For the novel, this pushes realism to the point of impossibility. That point is not one where realism disappears, however, but is one where it must make a choice about how to express the world it finds itself in: to surrender to the world of communication or to surrender the world so as to avoid being communication.

Notes

1 I use the term 'sub-genre' in this chapter to indicate that dystopian fiction belongs to the much wider genre of science fiction. For simplicity's sake, however, I've shortened this to genre in the remainder of the volume.

2 From the childlike and feminised leisure class of Eloi in H.G. Wells's *The Time Machine* (1895) through Yevgeny Zamyatin's use of happiness as the engineering out of 'imagination' in *We* (1924), and up to contemporary dystopias – whether in the shape of the happy workers in Dave Eggers's *The Circle* (2013) to the competitive happiness of Charlie Brooker's digital subjects in *Black Mirror* (2011–2019) – dystopian fiction has many shapes for power. The crushing of desire is one such shape, its elimination by satisfaction is another.

3 For historicism, the history of the artwork 'accords simply with its position in real history' but, for Adorno's dialectical understanding of literary form, the relationship between history and the artwork which can't escape it is more

complex. Adorno, *Aesthetic Theory* (1970), trans. Robert Hullot-Kentor (London: Bloomsbury, 2013), p. 118. On Adorno's conceptualisation of form, see Josh Robinson, *Adorno's Poetics of Form* (New York: SUNY Press, 2018).

4 Thomas More, Frontispiece to *Utopia* (1516), trans. Dominic Baker-Smith (London: Penguin, 2012), p. 3.

5 Louis Marin, 'The Frontiers of Utopia', in Krishan Kumar and Stephen Bann (eds), *Utopias and the Millennium* (London: Reaktion Books, 1993), p. 13.

6 More, *Utopia*, p. 54.

7 Ibid., p. 54.

8 Ibid., p. 58. Abraxa is the name More gives to the land which was overcome and remade by Utopos as Utopia. For a discussion of the derivation of the term 'Abraxa', see Blandine Perona, 'Between Erasmus and More, Abraxa(s), an Anamorphic Name', *Erasmus Studies*, 39:1 (13 March 2019), 93–6.

9 Fredric Jameson, 'Morus: The Generic Window', in Jameson, *Archaeologies of the Future: the Desire Called Utopia and Other Science Fictions* (London; New York: Verso, 2005), p. 23.

10 On the identification of this poem as one of the earliest printed texts to use the idea of 'dystopia', see Lyman Tower Sargent, 'In Defense of Utopia', in *Diogenes*, 53:1 (2006), 11–17. On the standardisation of the spelling of 'dustopia' to 'dystopia' in excerpts from the poem published in *The Gentleman's Magazine* in 1748, see V.M. Budakov, 'Dystopia: An Earlier Eighteenth-Century Use', *Notes and Queries*, 57:1 (Mar. 2010), 86–8. For the poem itself, see Lewis Henry Younge, *Utopia: Or, Apollo's Golden Days* (Dublin: George Faulkner, 1747).

11 Matthew Beaumont, *Utopia LTD.: Ideologies of Social Dreaming in England, 1870–1900* (Leiden; Boston: Brill, 2005), p. 3.

12 Hölscher's essay was first published in *Geschichtliche Grundbegriffe*. It was republished in translation in *Utopian Studies*, 7:2 (1996), pp. 1–65, trans. Kirsten Petrak. In his essay, Hölscher cites Berdyaev, the same piece of text given by Huxley (from 'Nicolas Berdiaeff') as the epilogue to *Brave New World*: '[t]o use the words of Nicolai Berdyaev's: "*Les utopies apparaissent comme bien plus réalisables qu'on ne le croyait autrefois: Comment éviter leur réalisation définitive? .... Les utopies sont réalisables. La vie marche vers les utopies*"' ['Utopias appear much more attainable than previously thought: How can their definitive accomplishment be avoided? Utopias are achievable. Life is moving towards utopias'], Hölscher, p. 48.

13 The *Oxford English Dictionary* suggests Glenn Negley and J. Max Patrick's *Quest for Utopia* (1952) as the first instance of its use (the *Mundus Alter et Idem* of Joseph Hall is the 'opposite of *eutopia*, the ideal society: it is a *dystopia*, if it is permissible to coin a word'); and Chad Walsh's *From Utopia to Nightmare* (1962) as a more confident treatment of the dystopia as an 'inverted utopia'.

14 The most comprehensive analytic account of the literary-critical categories used to identify and read 'anti-utopian' fictions before and after the advent of the term 'dystopia' is Tom Moylan's chapter, 'New Maps of Hell', in Moylan, *Scraps*

of the Untainted Sky: Science Fiction, Utopia, Dystopia* (Boulder; London: Westview Press, 2000), pp. 111–46.

15 Adorno, 'Aldous Huxley and Utopia', in *Prisms*, trans. Samuel and Shierry Weber (Cambridge, MA: MIT Press, 1983), p. 114: 'The inevitable character of the negative utopia arises from projecting the limitations imposed by the relations of production (the enthronement of the productive apparatus for the sake of profit) as properties of the human and technical productive forces per se.'

16 George Woodcock, 'Utopias in Negative', *Sewanee Review*, 64:1 (Jan.–Mar. 1956), 81–97. It is interesting to note that Woodcock sees the rise of what he then refers to as the 'anti-utopia' as coinciding with the loss of utopian fictions, 'the virtual disappearance of the orthodox Utopia as a literary form. Wells was the last important Utopian', p. 83.

17 Frederic Jameson, *An American Utopia: Dual Power and the Universal Army*, ed. Slavoj Žižek (London; New York: Verso, 2016), p. 1.

18 Mark Bould, 'Dulltopia: On the Dystopian Impulses of Slow Cinema', *The Boston Review / Global Dystopia*, 22 Jan. 2018. http://bostonreview.net/literature-culture-arts-society/mark-bould-dulltopia (accessed 28 January 2022).

19 See Kim S. Robinson's essay 'Dystopias Now: the End of the World Is Over, Now the Real Work Begins', *Commune Magazine*, (2 Nov. 2018) for a description of a contemporary anxiety that dystopias now comfort. https://communemag.com/dystopias-now/ (accessed 23 January 2022).

20 Adorno, 'Trying to Understand *Endgame*' (1961), in Adorno, *Notes to Literature, Vol. 1*, trans. Shierry Weber Nicholsen (New York: Columbia University Press, 1991), p. 245.

21 Cited in ibid., p. 245.

22 Ibid., p. 245.

23 Adorno, 'Commitment' (1962), in Adorno, *Notes to Literature, Vol. II*, trans. Shierry Weber Nicholsen (New York: Columbia University Press, 1992), p. 81.

24 Darko Suvin, *Metamorphoses of Science Fiction: On the Poetics and History of a Literary Genre* (1979) ed. Gerry Canavan (Bern: Peter Lang, 2016), p. 54, original italics.

25 Ibid., p. 68, original italics.

26 Chad Walsh, *From Utopia to Nightmare* (London: Bles, 1962), p. 18.

27 Gregory Claeys, *Dystopia: A Natural History* (Oxford: Oxford University Press, 2017), pp. 273–4.

28 Ibid., p. 18.

29 Adorno, 'Aldous Huxley and Utopia', in *Prisms*, p. 115.

30 A very helpful chapter on the English dystopia's existence in the 1870s and 1880s as part of the mood of military and political apprehension in Europe, and in anticipation of the 'terrain of mass politics' in England itself, is 'Anti-Communism and the Cacotopia', in Beaumont, *Utopia LTD*, pp. 129–68. For the American landscape, see Phillip E. Wegner's chapter, 'Writing the New American (Re)Public', in Wegner, *Imaginary Communities, Utopia, the Nation and the Spatial Histories of Modernity* (Berkeley: Los Angeles; London: University of California Press, 2002).

31 Adorno, 'The Position of the Narrator in the Contemporary Novel' (1954), in *Notes to Literature, Vol. I*, p. 34.
32 Suvin, *Metamorphoses*, p. 80.
33 Legislation passed in 1890 and 1894 prohibited the creation of any building over 80 feet high in London until the 1960s. The London Building Act, Prohibited Buildings was itself provoked by Henry Alers Hankey's creation of Queen Anne's Mansions in Westminster. By 1890, it was 100 feet tall and consisted of twelve storeys. On the outcry this caused, see Richard Dennis, '"Babylonian Flats" in Victorian and Edwardian London', *The London Journal*, 33:3 (2008), 233–47.
34 Adorno, 'The Position of the Narrator in the Contemporary Novel', p. 30.
35 Ibid., p. 30.
36 Ibid., p. 30.
37 Ibid., p. 31.
38 Ibid., p. 31. See also Adorno, *Aesthetic Theory*, p. 308: 'if, in one regard, as a product of the social labor of spirit, art is always implicitly a *fait social*, in becoming bourgeois art its social aspect was made explicit. The object of bourgeois art is the relation of itself as artifact to empirical society; *Don Quixote* stands at the beginning of this development.'
39 Adorno, 'The Position of the Narrator in the Contemporary Novel', p. 32.
40 Ibid., p. 33.
41 Ibid., p. 34.
42 Ibid., p. 35. This is an argument with Lukács which can be traced in more detail in Adorno, 'Extorted Reconciliation', in *Notes to Literature, Vol. II*; see also Fredric Jameson, *Marxism and Form: Twentieth-Century Dialectical Theories of Literature* (Princeton: Princeton University Press, 1974).
43 Adorno, 'The Position of the Narrator in the Contemporary Novel', p. 35.
44 Adorno, 'Commitment', in *Notes to Literature, Vol. II*, p. 78.
45 Suvin, 'SF and the Novum', in *Metamorphoses of Science Fiction*, p. 80.
46 Ibid., p. 80.
47 This does not mean that SF or utopian fictions are not themselves political but that their cognitive universes are wider and deeper. Reflecting on the trajectory of his own work in 2000, Suvin wrote of his work as attempting to 'lay some fundaments for a philosophical history of SF ... [A project] most akin to Walter Benjamin's reconstruction or montage of historical material as philosophy, which also, and supremely means, the philosophy of bodies living together, usually called politics.' See Suvin, 'Afterword: with Sober, Estranged Eyes', in Patrick Parrinder (ed.). *Learning from Other Worlds: Estrangement, Cognition and the Politics of Science Fiction and Utopia* (Liverpool: Liverpool University Press, 2000), p. 239.
48 Aldous Huxley, *Brave New World* (1932) (Harmondsworth: Penguin, 1955), p. 28. Hereafter all quotations from *Brave New World* are referenced in the text in parentheses.
49 Huxley, 'Foreword' (1946), *Brave New World*.

50 On Huxley and 'massification', see the essays in Aldous Huxley, *Music at Night, and Other Essays* (London: Chatto and Windus, 1931), and Huxley, *Ends and Means* (1937) (London: Chatto and Windus, 1946). See also the 'Introduction' to David Bradshaw (ed.) *The Hidden Huxley: Contempt and Compassion for the Masses* (London: Faber and Faber, 1994).

51 Franco Moretti, 'From The Waste Land to the Artificial Paradise' (1983), in *Signs Taken for Wonders: Essays in the Sociology of Literary Forms*, rev. ed. (London; New York: Verso, 1988), p. 233.

52 Claeys, *Dystopia: A Natural History*, p. 364.

53 Ibid., pp. 364–5.

54 Adorno, 'Commitment', in *Aesthetics and Politics*, p. 180.

55 Ibid., p. 177.

56 Adorno, 'Commitment', in *Notes to Literature, Vol. II*, p. 80. Note that Sartre is more sensitive to reading as an activity which places demands, that being 'human' is not something equally distributed, and that a type of writing can compel the recognition of humanity where it would be otherwise denied.

57 Ibid., p. 81.

58 Ibid., p. 80.

59 Ibid., p. 82.

60 Ibid., p. 82.

61 Ibid., p. 82.

62 Adorno, 'Commitment', in *Aesthetics and Politics*, p. 183.

63 Jack London published *Iron Heel* in 1908. The novel frames the rise to power of an oligarchical tyranny in the US through a written account of attempts to defeat it. This internal frame is itself framed by a temporal perspective set centuries in the future, a future when the oligarchy has been overthrown. On London's novel as a 'critical utopia', see Wegner, *Imaginary Communities*, pp. 99–145.

64 On the argument for interpreting *Verfremdungseffekt* as 'estrangement' (rather than the more familiar 'alienation effect'), see Fredric Jameson, Part 1 of Jameson, *Brecht and Method* (London; New York: Verso, 1998).

65 Adorno, 'Commitment' in *Aesthetics and Politics*, p. 185.

66 Suvin, 'The SF Novel as Epic Narration' (1982), in Suvin, *Positions and Presuppositions in Science Fiction* (London: Palgrave Macmillan, 1988), p. 77.

67 Adorno and Max Horkheimer, *Dialectic of Enlightenment*, trans. John Cumming (London: Verso, 1997), p. 87.

68 Suvin, 'SF and the Novum', in *Metamorphoses*, p. 88.

69 Darko Suvin and Marc Angenot, 'Not Only But Also: On Cognition and Ideology in SF and SF Criticism' (1979), in Suvin, *Positions and Presuppositions*, p. 48.

70 Adorno, *Negative Dialectics*, p. 56.

71 Adorno, 'Presuppositions', in *Notes to Literature, Vol. II*, p. 98.

72 Ibid., p. 98.

73 Ibid., p. 97.

74 Ibid., p. 99.

75 Ibid., p. 99.

76 Ibid., p. 99.
77 Ibid., p. 99.
78 Ibid., pp. 100–1.
79 Ibid., p. 99.
80 Adorno, *Aesthetic Theory*, p. 1.

1

Negative commitment at work

To ground the terms introduced in the first chapter, and to give some depth to the difference between the classical dystopias and the dystopias of our own moment, I am going to give a brief reading of one of the earliest of the classical dystopias, E.M. Forster's novella 'The Machine Stops' (1909), then of a dystopia from the mid-century, Frederik Pohl and Cyril M. Kornbluth's *The Space Merchants* (1952), and finish with a recent dystopia, *Red Clocks: A Novel* (2018) by Leni Zumas. Doing these readings in this sequence should provide a way of differentiating where we are now while also substantiating the more abstract definition of dystopia as a genre needed to open up the exploration.

'The Machine Stops'

Forster's 'The Machine Stops' was published first in 1909, four years after H.G. Wells's *A Modern Utopia* (1905). The story can be put to use here to sketch the central aspects of the genre which, over half a century later, came to be called dystopian fiction. The story is set in the future, that much it shares with the utopian fictions, and their anti-utopian variants, of the latter decades of the nineteenth century. The continuities stop there, however. It is not just that Forster's future polity is global – Wells had already outlined why, for a *modern* utopia, '[n]o less than a planet will serve ... [a] World State, therefore ... must be'.[1] It is rather the shape of the story which the reader encounters in the time of the non-place – the dystopian time of the globalised future – rather than mediated by some traveller or sleeper whose own discomfiture and slow familiarisation could sharpen the cognitive route to be taken by the reader. There is no outside place left at all and there is no 'outside' temporality left at all.

In this future globalised system, all live underground, in a 'civilisation' so far 'advanced' that there is no longer any need for human beings to labour. The civilisation is uniform but analogies with hives or with ants are repelled not only by the text's insistence that 'nature' has been abolished, rendered unnecessary by the development of artificial substitutes for everything, but also by the generalisation of leisure as the condition and medium of life. This is a dystopia in which the 'machine' of the title has taken the burden of labour from human beings, releasing them to universal leisure.

In addition to stressing the story's combination of temporal restriction and spatial scope, and the evident anxieties about what happens to humans afflicted with an excess of leisure – all formal premises of the classic dystopia – we need to note Forster's narrative style, a light irony, unfolded in a third-person mode which addresses the reader as humanist. In his own reading of Forster's story and the creation of 'this radically new form', Tom Moylan stresses the central 'function of the narrator' once the novum starts for the reader *in medias res*: 'writing from some third place, the narrator offers a set of social values that implicitly opposes the very society it describes'.[2] It is the structural presence and narrative impossibility of those same 'values' which concerns us here as that contradiction is the ground of negative commitment. There is no shortage of 'values' at work in the story, or in the classic dystopias which follow it. There is a problem with where to house them, however: an older humanism could bewail or celebrate a humanity which if freed from the present or the past could fix those values in itself. In the classic dystopias, though they may be enabled by that same tradition of humanist thought, the object of humanism collapses into and becomes as problematic as 'progress' or 'civilisation' itself, concepts which are at the heart of the problem but are also the place from which the problem has to be named. Moylan sees the 'residual romantic humanism' at work in Forster's story, a humanism which 'collapses all the dimensions of modernity into the single mystifying trope of the Machine', but he does not dwell on what the story's division of humanity, into those who see and those who do not, does to the same humanist position the narrative wants for itself and for its reader.[3]

Embedded in the form of Forster's story is an anti-utopian politics where 'utopia' is shaded by the popularity of the utopian fictions of the late nineteenth century, in particular by the energetically scientific optimism of H.G. Wells and by the more mechanical or bureaucracy-focused industrial future of Edward Bellamy's *Looking Backward, 2000–1887* (1888). The Introduction above noted the constitutive role of the antagonism with utopia (and with the particular forms of 'socialism' which contest 'utopia' in the late nineteenth and early twentieth century) which illuminates or irradiates the early exemplars of the dystopian tradition. Given that the utopian fictions of the period from the mid-nineteenth century were themselves antagonistic – with their antagonistic object being the organisation of capitalism or of gender – the anti-utopianism of the classic dystopia is mobile not static, and, in its movement against utopia, it tends to exceed its own critique of utopian thinking, pushing out into some new thing as it confirms the possibility of the utopia but works to reject its desirability.[4]

For now though, we should examine the narrative world of 'The Machine Stops' in more detail. Part One of this three-part story opens as follows:

> Imagine, if you can, a small room, hexagonal in shape like the cell of a bee. It is lighted neither by window nor by lamp, yet it is filled with a soft radiance. There are no apertures for ventilation, yet the air is fresh. There are no musical instruments, and yet, at the moment that my meditation opens, this room is throbbing with melodious sounds. An arm-chair is in the centre, by its side a reading-desk – that is all the furniture. And in the arm-chair there sits a swaddled lump of flesh – a woman, about five feet high, with a face as white as a fungus. It is to her that the little room belongs.[5]

The 'belonging' here is peculiar: the woman belongs more to the room than it to her. It is her support system but she is its creature. It feeds her, bathes her, brings her to bed, or to communion with others, dispenses medicine, provides light and darkness, all through a myriad 'buttons' which summon the various services, each of which is delivered mechanically. There is, however, no longer any need for a concept of ownership as there is no longer any property. With the overcoming of the conceptual apparatus of owning and getting, Forster's humans collapse: without the compulsion to self-preservation, they 'degenerate' to wasted things, creatures of a borderless leisure, knowing nothing of will or of want.[6]

Everybody lives in cities built underground, each one composed of multitudes of such hexagonal cells, as the surface of the earth is now mere surface, the ceiling of what passes for life underground.[7] That surface is judged hostile to life; whilst travel across it is still possible, it occurs in air-ships with windows closed to blank out whatever may disturb in the vision of earth below and sky above. Underground there is no more night or day, the only temporal rhythms are those of repetition, patterns for which are provided by the meals delivered by the machine or by the schedule of 'lectures' piped into each room. Communication is by 'speaking-tube' and is incessant. So far removed from direct experience – of themselves or of others – are the inhabitants of this machine world, rendered irritable by the lack of anything else, that they clamour for 'ideas', free-floating or decontextualised descriptions of things as they are or once were.

The death of experience which Adorno would later argue was both part of the abstraction of social relations brought to a heightened form in monopoly capitalism, and the historical content of the emptiness of the subject in modernist aesthetics, is registered in Forster's underground-dwellers. Divorced from any experience of their own, for them the world around them is likewise insubstantial, hollow, devoid of meaning or cannot exist in even an objective manner. The 'machine' is no longer the frame or context of existence, it has entered into everything and thinned everything out, including those for whom it was to have existed:

> the machine did not transmit *nuances* of expression. It only gave a general idea of people – an idea that was good enough for all practical purposes ... The imponderable bloom, declared by a discredited philosophy to be the actual essence of intercourse, was rightly ignored by the Machine, just as the imponderable bloom of the grape was ignored by the manufacturers of artificial fruit. Something 'good enough' had long since been accepted by our race. (*TMS*, p. 93)

Forster's story could then seem to trace the outlines of a world in which an instrumentalizing reason has triumphed over even the last remnant of undamaged experience which was memory – a world interpreted by J.M. Bernstein as a world in which

> nothing would or could matter to an individual, in which the course of events was neutral with respect to subjectivity, in which subjects were beyond meaningful change and transformation.[8]

As might be clear already from the 'imponderable bloom' and its 'artificial' opposite named in the quotation from Forster's story above, 'The Machine Stops' wants the world which is not the 'artificial fruit', a world of full experience which the narrator both assumes and uses to chastise the dystopian world in which it has withered. Not science or reason or capitalism is at stake here but humans – 'our race' – who succumb too easily to the mass-mediated proxies offered in place of experience.[9]

Though the 'clumsy system of public gatherings had been long since abandoned' (p. 95), a proto-television system enables lectures to be given without anyone moving from their mechanically operated chairs. These lectures satisfy a bad-tempered appetite for 'ideas' which is endless in the population. The 'ideas' need to be colourless and impersonal:

> First-hand ideas do not really exist. They are but the physical impressions produced by love and fear ... Let your ideas be second-hand, and if possible tenth-hand, for then they will be far removed from that disturbing element – direct observation. (*TMS*, p. 113)

With a population who can no longer experience or observe anything which is not 'machine-made', uniform and expected or standardised to fit 'minds [which have] been prepared beforehand', the inhabitants of the machine world look forward to 'a generation that has got beyond facts, beyond impressions, a generation absolutely colourless,' a generation '*Seraphically free / From taint of personality*' (*TMS*, p. 114).

Nature has not been demythologised here as much as abolished. With it goes the past as history is subjected to a retelling 'not as it happened, but as it would have happened had it taken place in the days of the Machine' (*TMS*, p. 115). In a world in which the machine has come to act as a substitute for the self, where the self is as redundant as property, the family, hunger or want, humans revert to myth. What there is to be known has shrunk and is too well known but Forster positions this knowledge as itself negated by some remnant of a desire to worship. There are no more gods, only the machine, so people worship the machine. At first illicitly, with a mixture of shame and joy, and then officially:

> Those who had long worshipped silently now began to talk. They described the strange feeling of peace that came over them when they handled the Book of the Machine ... 'The Machine', they exclaimed, 'feeds us and clothes us and houses us; through it we speak to one another, through it we see one another, in it we have our being. The Machine is the friend of ideas and the enemy of superstition: the Machine is omnipotent, eternal; blessed is the machine' ... The word 'religion' was sedulously avoided, and in theory the Machine was still the creation and the implement of man. But in practice, all save a few retrogrades, worshipped it as divine (*TMS*, p. 115/6)

Forster's is not a story written to produce terror or even fear simply but one designed rather to appal. The fungal-white, toothless and hairless 'swaddled lump of flesh' (*TMS*, p. 91) is the allegorical surface of a revulsion felt at what happens when leisure is universalised and its subjects disintegrate into the failed flesh of learnt appetites and rote clichés. The machine which will liberate humankind from labour will deliver it to the bondage of an appalling leisure, one machine-made through and through.

The shrunken materialism of the machine age turns into its opposite in 'The Machine Stops'. The machine becomes the giver and taker of human life, its vast operations dispensing with even that type of human life that is management or the bureaucracy of its organisation. The latter leaves as its residue the 'Book of the Machine', an instruction manual which people take to reverently kissing. Once the Book becomes the revelation of the machine's divinity, however, it can no longer be consulted for instructions: the machine itself, now divine, can no longer be interfered with, no longer mended when parts wear out. Over time, they all wear out and the machine collapses, tearing down its own system and killing all within it. A machine needs managers and mechanics more than it needs devotees.

The story dramatises the completion of reification and does so in a way which posits this total reification as neither painful nor restful. Rather it is experienced as a busy thing, as a surrender unto something of selves which are completed in that surrendering, but there remains irritation, a hierarchy of 'advanced' ideas over less 'advanced' ones, and the impatience experienced when the machine itself starts to disintegrate. The frozen dialectic between machine and the subjects who at first created it ends in the destruction of both. That dialectic is completed and made visible only in a glimpse of a future at the story's end, when 'scraps of an untainted sky' appear, opened up by the tearing apart of the roof of the underground city which breaks 'like a honeycomb' as its inhabitants stagger and die. On the surface of the earth, it is suggested, are misfits, those cast out of, or made 'homeless' by, the Machine age because they couldnt adapt: they are '"hiding in the mist and the ferns until our civilisation stops. To-day they are the Homeless – to-morrow –"' (*TMS*, p. 123).

This splitting of the human subject into the many and the few, those who are integrated into the dystopian world and those who cannot or will not be so integrated, provides the political interest and one index of the historicity of dystopian fiction in the first decades of the twentieth century. Rooted in contradictions long dormant within liberalism, these contradictions reached the point of conflict when confronted with political projects to use the state to 'improve' social relations, to plan all those areas of life the fiction of organicism could no longer sustain. The values of this liberalism remain the same and govern the distress that sounds in the fiction: liberty, culture, connection, the individual. They can no longer be treated as universal, however, but are confronted with what becomes in these fictions the 'delirium of acquiescence' (Forster, p. 96). Humans cannot be trusted to be liberal, they surrender themselves, revelling in their own cancellation of resistance even as they celebrate their entrapment. This dilemma of liberalism provides a keynote in the classic dystopias which follow Forster's down the decades of the twentieth century.

Neither its appearance nor its endurance as the premise of a series of tropes about 'the masses' or 'mass society' or, a little later, 'consumer society', can be explained by recourse to the 'anti-utopian' antagonisms which found the classical dystopias. Forster's story allegorises not humankind's domination by the machines they have created nor even that domination's need to cancel nature to fully achieve itself. It is rather the yearning for such domination, the ease with which humans slip into their place or acquiesce in it, which is the topic or the subject of this allegory. This imagination of the end of capitalism as an end which yet leaves human beings in hoc to a world they neither know nor wish to know, a world which has become invisible to subjects too in thrall to it to see it, marks the moment of dystopian fiction proper.

For Wells, a modern utopia was possible and desirable, the dystopia is in part an answer to that: it gives us a world that is possible but not desirable. In the former, the present is wretched and will be overcome, in the latter too much will be lost in that overcoming, too much of what is precious in the present, and those losses will riddle the foundation of the new social formation with such flaws and fissures that it may fall. Both share a deeper sympathy, however, for in both machines, states, and the social orders these two express and regulate, are things in themselves, possessed of their own developmental logic. Nature too is a thing outside of human relationships, to be conquered for Wells, and to be longed for or wept over for Forster.

Both *A Modern Utopia* and 'The Machine Stops' make strenuous efforts to spurn politics in favour of an ontology of how things are, a determined pragmatism about what humans are. It is in the form of Forster's story that we can elicit the aspects of that type of commitment I am terming a 'negative commitment', one which will allow us to approach dystopian fiction more widely not as 'autonomous' literature but yet as doing something interesting enough to merit close attention.

In 'The Machine Stops', as in the dystopias which followed, there is an internal body, a 'misfit', used to carve out a space in which the irrationality of the regime becomes tangible, one in which another mode of perception is concretised and generalised and a language for it found even if only in the ambivalence of glimpses. Kuno, the son of the woman whose cell opens the story, was born muscular but out of some oversight was not destroyed as per the procedure of euthanising infants 'who promised undue strength' (*TMS*, p. 104). This bodily difference provokes difference absolutely and Kuno becomes an individual, a man convinced of the necessity to find 'out a way of my own' (*TMS*, p. 104). To do so, he first reclaims his body for its own movement, and with it reclaims space and the sense thereof. In surrendering that sense to the machine

> We have lost a part of ourselves. I determined to recover it, and I began by walking up and down the platform of the railway outside my room. Up and down, until I was tired, and so did recapture the meaning of 'Near' and 'Far'. 'Near' is a place to which I can get quickly on my feet, not a place to which the train or the air-ship will take me quickly. 'Far' is a place to which I cannot get quickly on my feet ... Man is the measure. That was my first lesson. (*TMMS*, p. 105)

When the machine collapses under the weight of the new contradiction that the return to religion occasioned, Kuno is killed along with all others. His appearance is necessary at two levels, however: formally, it provides the element of conflict without which dystopias could not be narrative fictions but would become mere descriptions; and it ontologises individuality as the form for and of freedom. It is a recognisably romantic mode of individuality and it suffers from its loneliness as much as it gains from it. It is not possible for 'man' to be 'the measure' when there is only one such man and all others are easily functions of the machine. This contradiction is resolved at the level of the narrative style, in the narrative's depersonalised offer of that same individuality to his readers as the reading position from which the dystopia makes sense. The cost of the resolution is not 'progress' itself but rather happiness. That hostility to happiness is by now so familiar it is hard to recognise but it should be seen as being formative for the classical dystopia. In this mode, it can be seen as an anxiety about regression – about what happens to people when they have enough – in ways which echo Adorno's critique of the 'scientific consciousness' which

> was always closely bound up with the reality principle and similarly hostile to happiness. While happiness is supposedly the goal of all domination over nature, it always appears to the reality principle as regression to mere nature. This can be seen even in the highest philosophies, including Kant's and Hegel's. Reason, in whose absolute idea these philosophies have their pathos, is denounced by them as something both pert and disrespectful as soon as it challenges the established system of values.[10]

The Space Merchants

The planet Venus hangs over the busy narrative activity of Frederik Pohl and Cyril Kornbluth's *The Space Merchants* (1952). Venus does not appear and nobody goes there but that somebody has been there, and that it will be colonised, are pivots organising or motivating what there is of a plot in this twisting American dystopia.[11] As an absent organising structure, Venus is told in the text in two ways – through its material properties and effects (sand and smoke, free formaldehyde, ferocious levels of heat and wind, a strange form of light); and through the symbolic shapes and narrative forms that its existence as an exploitable place is pressed into once America has decided it wants Venus as a settler colony, a new frontier.

The novel is ambivalent about the first of these acts of presence. The physical properties of Venus are known to be forbidding, but overcrowding, deforestation, soil erosion and pollution on Earth add a veneer of logic to the contest over who is to 'settle' Venus, and, by the narrative's end, it is the underground revolutionary 'conservation' movement, or 'Consies', who have wrested control of the transport to Venus, though whether that signals the farcical end of the Consies and their politics, or their success, is not clear. The novel is, however, not ambivalent about the second of the acts of presence which establish Venus in the novel: advertising and all the sophisticated machinery of deceit and self-deceit it works through. This machinery awes, enrages and bewilders the novel and it is this – less the presence of a

critique of advertising and more how the novel handles its own critique –
which provides the novel's historical interest for us.

As the novel takes the form of a first-person narration, and the narrator is a senior advertising executive, Mitchell Courtenay of Fowler
Schocken Associates (the largest advertising agency in New York City at
some unspecified point in the mid- to far future), the novel has to work to
open a narrative space capable of disrupting or countering Courtenay's
self-understanding. It does so by positioning him structurally in the place
of the dystopian resister but then denying him any consciousness of the
necessity of resistance. The denial is interesting as, to keep the narrative in a dystopian shape, a moment of resistance is needed: for this novel,
and only momentarily, the situation of the resister and the dystopian
world is inverted. Mitchell Courtenay does not question his world but
that world questions him when it ceases to be one which reflects back to
him his own understanding. In his comments on *The Space Merchants* in
New Maps of Hell (1960), Kingsley Amis points up both the adherence
to the genre and the disruption of the genre such a narrative innovation
brings about:

> After due advantage has been taken of Mitchell's vantage point as a hypno-
> tised supporter of the system, and of the comic possibilities of his consider-
> ing himself a free critical intelligence within it, he is made to change sides ...
> *Mitchell does not begin to hate his society until after it has begun to hate him.*
> In this case it is long after ...[12]

Amis is too quick to elide belief with 'hypnotism' and too quick to totalise
the 'society' which hates. Rather it is the notion itself of a 'free critical intelligence' which is put under strain – and which consequently throws cognition itself into question as what is known unravels into what is believed – in
a social order which insists in a businesslike manner that it is the best and
that it is inevitable. The satire is of the newly prosperous American advertising industry, its confidence concretised by the political success of its
decade-long campaign to see off the threat posed by the New Deal, and the
latter's constitution of consumers as those who may need to be protected
from 'deceptive' advertising, and more widely from the system of free enter-
prise which would generate it.[13] But the satire works through estranging the
notion of cognition itself. Posing the system as one which 'hypnotises' those
caught in it – as Amis does – misses that system's absolute dependence – a
dependence politicised by the anti-communism of the advertising industry
in the late 1940s and early 1950s – on the subject as a *freely* choosing
consumer. 'Curiosity' is trapped in this model of the subject; knowledge
becomes 'information', and everything is placed as not only knowable
but *having to be known* for free choice to be exercised. The advertising

executive believes himself above the 'tricks' of the trade but it is that very belief which signals how tightly he is caught:

> today the curious individual becomes a nihilist. Anything that cannot be recognized, subsumed and verified he rejects as idiocy or ideology, as subjective in the derogatory sense. But what he already knows and can identify becomes valueless in the process, mere repetition, so much wasted time and money. This aporia of mass culture and the science affiliated to it reduces its victims to its own kind of praxis, namely a blunted perseverance.[14]

The 'perseverance' of the advertising executive's sense of himself in the world is what prevents resistance in *The Space Merchants*. Hovering over the realisation that he is being 'had', the advertiser himself – the possessor of the sanctioned 'critical intelligence' of the self-reflexive creator of consumer desires – cannot reject or leave that identity but must wait until it becomes an object of scorn for others before he can step out of the carcass. In the pages which follow, I will analyse how the 'hatred' named by Amis is a social order's antipathy to those it hymns as 'consumers'. The identity of 'the consumer' here signals the defeat of both 'the human' as a unifying identity – as in Forster's story – and also of its political counterpart, 'the citizen'.

Courtney begins to experience his social order's hatred of him once he is kidnapped and downgraded to 'consumer' status from his previous executive perch. His sense of himself is stronger than that of hardship, however, or hardship cannot knock cognitive patterns or the ideology structuring them while that hardship is experienced as temporary or a mistake. That Courtney can know 'the real' from 'below' and yet maintain his own investments in the rightness and credibility of the social order which necessitates that 'below' brings home the dull force or power of forms of thought which can resist even the experiences which should themselves estrange them. The paradoxical force – at once transparently dishonest and yet forcefully persuasive – of advertising as part of the culture industry can be opened up only if we take seriously the impossibility of its job (to sell the present as ripe with promise) and the ease with which it achieves it:

> the culture industry tends to make itself the embodiment of authoritative pronouncements, and thus the irrefutable prophet of the prevailing order. It skilfully steers a winding course between the cliffs of demonstrable misinformation and manifest truth, faithfully reproducing the phenomenon whose opaqueness blocks any insight and installs the ubiquitous and intact phenomenon as ideal. Ideology is split into the photograph of stubborn life and the naked lie about its meaning – which is not expressed but suggested and yet drummed in.[15]

Venus enters the novel – misidentified as a star by the 'talented slovenliness' of a copywriter[16] – in a draft advertising campaign to recruit colonisers. In the executive boardroom of an American-owned advertising company, a 'projected Picasso' fades out to be replaced by a picture of the 'Venus Rocket', 'a thousand-foot monster, the bloated child of the slim V-2s and stubby moon rockets of the past' (*SM*, p. 5).[17] A voiceover describes its mission:

> 'This is the ship that a modern Columbus will drive through the void ... Six and a half million tons of trapped lightning and steel – an ark for eighteen hundred men and women, and everything to make a new world for their home. Who will man it? What fortunate pioneers will tear an empire from the rich, fresh soil of another world?' (*SM*, p. 6)

The accompanying visual narrative turns into a sequence not on space but on the contours of an enclosed domesticity, a horrendous scene of unavoidable proximity and confinement but one which is presented with confidence as tempting:

> On the screen the picture dissolved to a spacious suburban roomette in early morning. On the screen the husband folding the bed into the wall and taking down the partition to the children's nook; the wife dialling breakfast and erecting the table ... they spoke persuasively to each other about how wise and brave they had been to apply for passage in the Venus rocket. (*SM*, p. 6)

There has been a shift here. Forster's cells in 'The Machine Stops' were everyday, familiar, taken for granted. That familiarity contributed to the potency of their estranging effect. In that story, from its opening lines to the rupture which finishes it, there is something openly, inalienably, unarguably wrong about humans living as monads, at least physically. The comfort the inhabitants found in their enclosed and atomised spaces was an index of how wrong their world was, that they could not notice how enclosed their lives were. In *The Space Merchants*, the 'roomette' belongs to the advertised unreal, the spiritualised realm of the desirable and the enviable: it is presented as tempting in the language of contemporary temptation, advertising.

Those who go to Venus will, for generations, have to endure 'life in hermetically sealed cabins ... while working on Venus's unbreathable atmosphere and waterless chemistry' (*SM*, p. 6). This is the 'reality' of Venus, articulated in the language the advertising men share only amongst themselves. It does not go into the marketing campaign but the supposedly charming 'roomette' does. The 'reality' of Venus is inhospitable: the nine-minute commercial being prepared does not deny or dwell on that 'reality'. Yet the desirable version dwelt on by the commercial is not so far removed in terms of space. Only the smiling, happy inhabitants of the miniaturised private realm and the 'highly imaginative' series of a transformed Venus somewhere in the future (all 'verdant valleys, crystal lakes, brilliant mountain vistas' (*SM*, p. 6)) belong seamlessly to the inflated dream language of advertising. The 'spacious suburban roomette' is the oddity which gets in the way of the whole being seamless. Whilst we would expect the verdant valleys and the vistas of mountains and lakes, there more to titillate imagination than to figure any future terraformed Venus, there is something wrong with the lack of imaginative inflation embodied in the spatial dimensions of the 'roomette'. That 'spacious suburban roomette' cannot be glossed over or inflated. It is what it is: one room as a family living space.

This silent insistence on the indelible material limits of living arrangements on the Venus project sounds a note which subtends the novel as a whole: there is always the layer of the material to limit and to shape the brave new realm of the commercial symbolic. The latter may preen itself on having conquered the world but the world so conquered, and the conquest itself, is vulnerable to puncture by the materiality which is its condition and its prize. The dimensions of the 'roomette' should be a warning, an objective limit to desire buried in the small print of the nine-minute advertisement, but it is not as it needs to be there; space requires figuring even in advertisements. The happy family is a meaning or cluster of meanings which require embodiment and such embodiment brings with it the need for bodies to be located in space. The 'material' limit is not the 'reality' of Venus – if it was, the voyage there could not even be considered – but the internal limits to the imagination of advertisers. Impoverished imaginations no matter how well-paid or canny or motivated cannot imagine what they do not know or even suspect – spaciousness, light, ease.

The draft advertisement does not give any of its viewers pause. Seated around the boardroom table of Fowler Schocken Associates, the 'largest advertising agency in the city', a handful of senior managers admire it. Each belongs to his profession and each is well remunerated for so wholly sublating their own self-preservation to the company's. In a social order without spaciousness, however, one in which even imaginative spaciousness is not possible, even the well-paid, the most highly paid functions, live cramped lives. When the company manager reminds everyone of how 'worthwhile' their work is, he notes that there is not a person in the boardroom 'who has less than a two-room apartment ... [e]ven the bachelors' (*SM*, p. 2).[18]

There is an important limit laid down here. The work of advertising and of the marketing and public-relations industries with which it is blended, whether thought of as effective creativity or systematised deceit, has limits. Advertising's self-image in the novel is as indispensable to the 'God of sales'. The executives who are caught up in the positing and perpetuating of this

image are not cynical but believe in what consequently becomes their historic mission of 'reach[ing] into the souls of men and women', a task once
fulfilled by lyric poetry but now inherited by the poet's successors, all those
'people capable of putting together words that stir and move and sing' (*SM*,
p. 41). The novel situates this self-image, this succession of advertising to
the place of lyric poetry, in the development of mass production. Once
markets became 'mass', advertising was needed to teach people literacy in
the market's ways, and in the course of this changed itself:

> From the simple hand-maiden task of selling already-manufactured goods to
> its present role of creating industries and re-designing a world's folkways to
> meet the needs of commerce. (*SM*, p. 7)

'Folkways' was a term coined by the American sociologist William Graham
Sumner in his early work *Folkways* (1907). As Sumner used it, the term
referred to the overlooked or value-free, the customary social conventions
which regulate non-contested behaviours in any social group. Any social
order has as the infrastructure of its everyday interactions 'folkways' which
domesticate need, provide inter-generational bonds and the content of traditions. Folkways are unconscious and collective and powerful:

> Need was the first experience, and it was followed by the blundering effort to
> satisfy it ... all at last adopted the same way for the same purpose; hence the
> ways turned into custom and became mass phenomena. Instincts were devel-
> oped in connection with them. In this way folkways arose.[19]

The professionalisation of advertising which began in the 1880s and was
fully prepared to take advantage of postwar prosperity in the 1940s, was
able to use the vocabularies of social psychology and sociology to depict a
world of systemic social and psychic structures – of folkways – available
for reworking.[20] Such a change positioned advertising – or the self-image
of Madison Avenue – as part and parcel of the mediation of post-Second
World War America itself as 'free' and as the leader of the 'free world'. In
their critique of the centrality and spread of advertising in the twentieth
century, Adorno and Horkheimer are clear on the diminution of competition which serves as the context for advertising's frenzied centrality. As they
were writing, advertising had ceased to be a 'social service ... informing the
buyer about the market'. Rather, when

> the free market is coming to an end, those who control the system are
> entrenching themselves in [advertising]. It strengthens the firm bond between
> the consumers and the big combines. Only those who can pay the exorbitant
> rates charged by the advertising agencies ... only those who are already in a
> position to do so, or are co-opted by the decision of the banks and industrial

capital, can enter the pseudo-market as sellers ... Advertising today is a negative principle, a blocking device: everything that does not bear its stamp is economically suspect.[21]

For many literary scholars, however, Pohl and Kornbluth's novel does not articulate that moment in economic and cultural history when production (and with it the power of ownership) becomes invisible and almost unthinkable. When, simultaneously, language burst out of any obligation to signify and revelled in the ease with which it thrived when so unmoored. Rather the novel is treated as a more or less successful swipe at 'consumer culture'. For Gregory Claeys, for example, *The Space Merchants*

> unfolds a perfectly plausible vision ... A century hence, a vastly overpopulated world is dominated by giant multinational corporations who outwit moronic consumers by subliminal advertising and by lacing foods with habit-forming substances.[22]

We have to object that this 'vision' is *not* plausible: it does exist in the novel but only as a fantasy without a subject. There are too few 'consumers' (scarcity is the mode of life for most) and those who literally do consume – the creators of advertising as those with disposable income – are trapped within that identity. Far from being 'moronic consumers', they articulate the stupidity and venality of a system for which a human being *can only be* a consumer or be one who is shamefully failing to consume. For advertisements – for their industry – a consumer is not a fetish but must be continually created as one. And now the whole world is only graspable through advertising: not political discourse, but all discourse has eliminated the concept of production and with it of labour (and of labour's once opposite – the public). The only mode of address is from advertisers to consumers. The

> most intimate reactions of human beings have been so thoroughly reified that the idea of anything specific to themselves now persists only as an utterly abstract notion ... The triumph of advertising in the culture industry is that consumers feel compelled to buy and use its products even though they see through them.[23]

Forster's dystopia in 1909 gave us the 'Machine' as an externalised thing, the usurper of all the apparatus of social life (family, education, labour, culture, even of, finally, religion). Pohl and Kornbluth bring the machine into language, the arena of language once reserved for poetry or non-instrumentalised language use, now captured for advertising, and direct that language at those whose only – and inescapable – job in relation to it is to consume. The industry's insiders know that '[w]ords and pictures. Sight and sound and smell and taste and touch' are needed to create and to perpetuate the dream of the commodity which needs the consumer or consumption itself to realise itself, but 'the greatest of these is words' (*SM*, p. 41).

The machine is here shrunk to – or expanded to – a libidinal apparatus whose object is the creation and refinement of collective desires where such desires are the psychic cement of individuality as a socially recognisable thing. A consumer or the consumer is deindividualised by definition. As such they can neither consent to nor reject the address advertising makes to them. When a character protests, defiantly, that he just likes a particular brand of clothing, that he is not influenced by advertisements, that he 'never read[s] the ads' (*SM*, p. 40), the company executive responsible for that brand's marketing grins and notes that '"our ultimate triumph is wrapped up in that statement"' (*SM*, p. 40). Any attempt to change his brand will not work. You would wear different clothes only

> 'with a vague, submerged discontent. It's going to work on your libido, because our ads for Starrzelius – even though you say you don't read them – have convinced you that it isn't quite virile to trade with any other firm. Your self-esteem will suffer, deep down you'll *know* that you're not wearing the best. Your subconscious won't stand up under much of that.' (*SM*, p. 40, original italics)

We need to slow down here before concluding that the paean to *advertising* sung by the advertising executives provides a guide as to how to read this novel or even provides the dystopian meaning or vision of this particular dystopia. Advertising is a machine and the libido is indeed what it likes to figure for itself as its raw material to produce sales. Yet, for the novel, it is not clear at all that advertising works anywhere outside the self-image of the advertising companies. And neither is it clear that that self-image is spontaneous or organic to their work as a 'creative industry'.

When one advertising executive cannot bear the olfactory work done by a rival firm's advertisement for an anti-perspirant, he throws up. Sitting on a plane, he could not escape the advertisement. His body revolted. When his seatmate comments that 'some of those ads are enough to make anybody sick', he comes dangerously close to breaching a taboo. A particular advertisement may be found wanting in finesse or depth but advertising itself would be criticised only by those whose views were politically 'unsound':

> Well, I couldn't let that get by. 'Exactly what do you mean by that remark?' I asked evenly. It frightened him. 'I only meant that it smelled a little strong … Just that particular ad. I didn't mean ads in general. There's nothing wrong with me, my friend … I'm perfectly sound, friend. I come from a good family. I went to a good school … see? I'm perfectly sound!' (*SM*, p. 61)

There is no doubt that the attempt to claim the 'subconscious' or access to it for advertising articulates a generalised and deep unease with advertising as an excessive and deceitful source of power in the world. This was the era of popular books which purported to anatomise that power – Vance Packard had published *The Hidden Persuaders* in 1957 – but the novel does not allow the claim any realisation. Two things stand in its way – scarcity and coercion. If we take the latter first, the novel becomes not a critique of 'consumerism' but something more striated and historically dense. Its satiric target is not Madison Avenue but the damaged consciousness of those who know and yet do not know that there is no such thing as a consumer. America is the imperial usurper of European dreams of colonisation. With only a rump political apparatus at local and federal level, and privatised security forces selling legitimate and sophisticated forms of violence to the highest bidder, 'America' is the space occupied by a few monopolistic concerns whose reach extends across the planet.

Starrzelius Verily owns an India which is no longer India but 'Indiastries … The first spherical trust. Merging a whole subcontinent into a single manufacturing complex' (*SM*, p. 3).[24] Ensuring the fiction of competition is maintained, one advertising agency feuds with another but each works for identical concerns. The consumer posited by both cannot be trusted even here to 'choose' one over the other so teams of industrial anthropologists design methods to get the right branded packaging on to the right lunches in 'all primary schools east of the Mississippi' – your own company's colours for 'the candy, ice-cream, and Kiddiebutt cigarette ration', your rival's for the 'soyaburgers and regenerated steak' (*SM*, p. 3).

Commerce owns the world and the market is free to regulate all worldly relations. India, a continent, became a factory and a corporation selling that factory's products. The Chlorella Corporation has an ersatz-meat processing plant in Costa Rica. The annual budget of Costa Rica is $185 billion; the taxes paid by Chlorella (by its workers) amount to $180 billion per year. Hence, 'the government – *and courts* – of Costa Rica do just about what Chlorella wants done' (*SM*, p. 74, original italics). In North America, senators are no longer elected by geographically specific constituencies but by corporations – the 'senator from Du Pont chemicals … the Senator from Nash Kelvinator' (*SM*, p. 8). This political triumph of capital – its success in absorbing fully the liberal or state- and public-centred form of politics – is marked by the disappearance of the bourgeois class, the class of owners of capital, and by the disappearance of that class's classic antagonist, the working class.

Adorno analysed this historical moment in his 'Reflections on Class Theory', an essay written in 1942 when Adorno was in America. Using the shift from the 'market economy' of a liberal order to the market's operations in 'monopoly capitalism', Adorno argues that in the former the 'untrue aspect of the concept of [the bourgeois] class was latent'. That untrue aspect was the concept's treatment of the bourgeoisie as a unity: when set against its antagonist, the nineteenth-century proletariat, the bourgeois class acted as a unity but were also internally subject to competition and to the hierarchy of the larger against the smaller owners of capital. The then bourgeoisie presented itself as a universal class, as not a class at all. Nineteenth-century theory needed then to denounce 'the bourgeois class as a unity, a class against the proletariat, in order to expose the fact that the universal interest it claimed to represent possesses a particularist dimension'.[25]

Its particularist unity at that time was more visible and more pressing than the internal disunity of the bourgeoisie, its internal hierarchy and its sectoral conflicts. During the classic moment of liberal capitalism, the 'egalitarian form of the class serves as an instrument to protect the privilege of the dominant segment over its supporters while concealing it'.[26] When using the concept of the bourgeois class, Adorno insists on a recognition of both facets of the concept – its articulation of the particularist unity which is the reality of the dominating class, and which necessarily punctures the claim to universal interest posited by that class – *and* the concept's hiding or concealment of the equally particularist disunity of that same class. The concept's truth rests with the former, its untruth with the latter. If the use of the concept is to have any critical momentum in the altered historical circumstances of the mid-twentieth century, the theorist must grasp both. The concept of class is both 'as true and as false as the liberal system' itself was:

> [the concept's] truth is its critical aspect: it designates the unity in which particular bourgeois interest are made real. Its untruth lies in the non-unity of the class. Its immanent determination by the state of power relations is the tribute it is forced to pay to its own particularity, which its unity benefits. Its real non-unity is veiled by its no less real unity.[27]

The concept of the 'consumer' – attempted usurper of the concept of 'class' – has inherited that dialectic but in an altered form. Our novel and Adorno's anatomy of the fortunes of the concept of class in the twentieth century meet at this point: in both, the forms taken by large capital articulate a new historical conjuncture for class relations, one in which the concept of class itself revolves, its formerly latent aspect now foremost, and its once truth now buried over. In

> the market economy, the untrue aspect of the concept of class was latent: in monopoly capitalism it has become as visible as its own truth – the survival of classes – has become invisible.[28]

The form and function of the corporations which operate across the pages of *The Space Merchants* can brook no opposition from rivals smaller than themselves. They absorb or quash them. The only rivalry left – a parody of the free market – is a competition between 'equals' where all else has been extinguished. The remaining two behemoths compete for market dominance not by innovating or with imaginative marketing but by state-sanctioned commercial 'feuds'. The use of the older term 'feuds' here is neatly designed. When our narrator suspects that he may be caught up in one such feud, he is worried for his life but his boss trusts to the code by which such feuds operate, a gentleman's agreement scaled up so that there are rules for appropriate and inappropriate commercial executions. A rival firm is 'cheap, they're crooked but they know the rules of the game. Killing in an industrial feud is a misdemeanour. Killing *without* notification is a *commercial offence*' (SM, p. 38, original italics).

These 'feuds' are elaborate but are ultimately personal. There is nothing to differentiate the feuding entities: equally matched, neither can win. When Mitchell Courtenay is kidnapped by Taunton's, he is prepared for torture by its head, B.J. Taunton. This man speaks the script Fowler Schocken also spoke:

> 'Essentially,' he brooded, 'essentially an artist. A dreamer of dreams; a weaver of visions.' It gave me an uncanny sense of double vision. I seemed to see Fowler Schocken sitting there instead of his rival, the man who stood against everything that Fowler Schocken stood for. (SM, p. 115)

There are no more small enterprises, no entrepreneurs, no market openings, no market competition except the appearance of such maintained by the great concerns which have divided up the world between them:

> 'There's an old saying, men. "The world is our oyster." We've made it come true. But, we've eaten that oyster ... We've eaten it,' he repeated. 'We've actually and literally conquered the world. Like Alexander, we weep for new worlds to conquer.' (SM, p. 7)

This is the tip on the sign of the disunity of the bourgeois class in the mid-twentieth century. The larger capitalists no longer need to make common ground with the totality of capital. They are too big to need any such commonality politically, and could be damaged by it only economically. For Adorno this was a conjuncture in which the very idea of a ruling class was simultaneously realised and erased. Capital becomes too big to see the same moment as its owners become invisible as owners:

> Theory's prognosis of a few owners and an overwhelming mass of the expropriated has come true, but instead of becoming glaringly obvious, this has

been conjured out of existence by the mass society in which class society has culminated. The ruling class disappears behind the concentration of capital. This latter has reached a magnitude and acquired a weight of its own that enables capital to present itself as an institution, as the expression of society as a whole. By virtue of its omnipotence, the particular is able to usurp the totality.[29]

It is from within this conjuncture that Pohl and Kornbluth's decision to name workers 'consumers' in *The Space Merchants* starts to make sense. For 'consumers' in the novel barely consume. They are too poor, there is too much scarcity. What they do is work. Cars, the most iconic of the symbols of mass or ordinary consumption in the 1950s, are absent. Oil is too scarce to be used for individual transport. Cars have been replaced by 'pedicabs': when Fowler Schocken goes '"out for a spin, I pedal a Cadillac. The wolf is a long way from the door"' (*SM*, p. 3). Household items – white goods or consumer durables, and décor or furnishings for design and style – are likewise absent, as are houses. Members of the executive class live in one or two-room apartments and bear the 'battle scars of life in a city apartment': 'You set up the bed at night, you took it down in the morning, you set up the table for breakfast, you took it down to get to the door' (*SM*, p. 46). There appear to be no interiors at all for those who live below the executive class line and who are called 'consumers'. In chapter 17, very near the novel's end, a scene opens in the headquarters of Taunton's – Fowler Schockens' rivals – at night. Access to the building is via the 'night-dweller entrance' (*SM*, p. 166). A 'night-dweller' is someone who rents a step on the internal stairways of the building to sleep. Signs in the undersized pay elevator describe their condition:

> 'Night-dwellers are responsible for their own policing. Management assumes no responsibility for thefts, assaults or rapes.'
> 'Night-dwellers will note that barriers are upped at 22:10 nightly and arrange their calls of nature accordingly.'
> 'Rent is due and payable nightly in advance at the autoclerk.'
> 'Management reserves the right to refuse rental to patrons of Starrzelius products.' (*SM*, p. 167)

The night-time scene in Taunton Towers – a scene of many anonymous bodies 'squirming uneasily, trying to find some comfort on the steps before the barriers upped' (*SM*, p. 167) – is brief and illustrative only. It plays no part in the plot, unlike the other moment in the novel where time is spent with 'consumers' rather than managers.

Plot-wise the shift to a place of work is motivated by the kidnapping of our narrator, Mitch Courtenay. His identity is forcibly altered and he is sent back into existence as 'simply a lower-class consumer' rather than a 'star-class copysmith' (*SM*, p. 67). The reader subsequently discovers that his lover, unbeknownst to Courtenay a member of the Consies, had organised his 'shanghai-ing' as she had wanted him 'to get a taste of the consumer's life': 'I thought – I don't know. I thought you'd see how fouled-up things have become. It's hard to see when you're star class. From the bottom it's easier to see' (*SM*, p. 135). He does not 'see', however. The time the executive spends as a worker on a plantation in Costa Rica is not sufficient and could never be sufficient to jolt his consciousness out of consumption as it is not 'easier' to see 'from the bottom'. Courtenay fails to 'rebel' and spends his time inveigling to get back to his former life. When he does reject that life, it is almost as an afterthought – the novel's rather than the character's – in a scene which seems designed to summon up and parody the draft advertisement which opened the novel. On a spaceship to Venus, cramped, airless and uncomfortable, Courtenay kisses his lover, their kiss less a resolution to the plot than it is a shrug at how inevitable such a reconciliation has to be in a plot-system which brooks no opposition.

Red Clocks

'Domestic violence' – a phrase that might have been coined to keep 'the family' as a concept free of its taint – has a peculiarly significant role in Leni Zumas's novel *Red Clocks* (2018). In this dystopian fiction, there is no challenge mounted to the dystopian regime but there is a challenge mounted to one of its expressions, or, better, there are two such challenges mounted, one in a legal context, and one political. Both challenges turn on individual cases but neither is individualised. In a novel which blurs the borders between private and public, and homologously between past and present, domestic violence is only a small part of the network or tissue of connections tying together nodes of suffering or of pain. 'Domestic' violence, or violence considered to be domestic because it takes place in the intimate heart of the private realm, is visited upon one partner or ex-partner by another, plays little part in dystopia's history. In the melodramatic narratives of capitalism's overcoming or undoing, narratives like Ignatius Donnelly's *Caesar's Column* (1890) or London's *Iron Heel* (1908), white women – beautiful, genteel and young – are 'trafficked' into sexual slavery because this form of capitalism cannot help but proceed by corrupting all that should lie outside it. By the time of the classic dystopia, however, violence against women is a function of the state, and acts as a sign and symptom of the centralised or 'planned' state's excessiveness, its capacity and desire to usurp or to absorb the private sphere.

In *Red Clocks*, the state is present only in terms of its effects, its laws and its manner of implementing them – the juridical, administrative and carceral structures tasked with executing them. These all have largely only an abstract narrative presence yet they possess a power of determination denied to other narrative elements. This abstract presence is shaped around women's bodies, in particular the fertility of those bodies. If pregnant, a woman is host to an entity with rights. Those rights are compatible with the woman's only as long as she continues as a host and surrenders herself to being fully such a host. She cannot choose not to be such a host. Two years before the dystopia's story

> the United States Congress ratified the Personhood Amendment, which gives the constitutional right to life, liberty, and property to a fertilised egg at the moment of conception. Abortion is now illegal in all fifty states. Abortion providers can be charged with second-degree murder, abortion seekers with conspiracy to commit murder. In vitro fertilisation, too, is federally banned, because the amendment outlaws the transfer of embryos from laboratory to uterus (the embryos can't give their consent to be moved.)[30]

Zumas's *Red Clocks* was reviewed initially as part of a wave of broadly feminist novels using the dystopian form to pinpoint the peculiar threats to women's autonomy posed by political movements in the twenty-first century. Coinciding with the popular success of Hulu's television adaptation of *The Handmaid's Tale*, and with the narrative shifts in that adaptation's attention to resistance, particularly to the stylisation of collective forms of resistance, these novels were and are part of a revitalisation of forms of feminism in American (and English-language more generally) popular culture.[31] Reviewed alongside Louise Erdrich's *Future Home of the Living God* (2017), Christina Dalcher's *Vox* (2018), Joanne Ramos's *The Farm* (2019) and Naomi Alderman's *The Power* (2016), *Red Clocks* was, alongside these fictions, treated as expressing both a renewed anxiety about the security of women's rights, and the centrality of female friendship or allyship to either the endurance of the regime or to resistance to it. In *The Atlantic* magazine, Sophie Gilbert reviewed Zumas's book as 'a thoughtful, complicated picture of womanhood – and a fierce argument for individual choice'. The novel's focus on personal lives rather than political events was admired:

> *Red Clocks* … is deeply, intentionally personal. Rather than trafficking in sweeping generalizations or one-size-fits-all dictates, it focuses on the uniqueness of all of its characters, who are nevertheless linked by the immutability of their bodies.[32]

In Silvia Martinez-Falquina's essay 'Feminist Dystopia and Reality', Zumas's novel was read alongside Erdrich's *Future Home of the Living God*, and both novels were likewise praised for presenting an 'activist' call for

> fluidity and relationality as essential values in the recovery of a voice for women. By blurring the borders between dystopia and the current reality, these novels raise a call to take action against the loss of women's reproductive rights and environmental destruction. Further, their rootedness in reality and emphasis on relationality, reciprocity and solidarity show a move towards a new transmodern ethics.[33]

The focus of our brief exploration here will, however, not be on how the text articulates and treats its political moment but on the collapse of the novum in that articulation. The novum collapses by shrinking inwards in time: it is stretched so thinly across a present which expands to greet it that nothing of a future is visible or tangible. There is just now. Such precise attention is paid to the present that estrangement is rendered redundant. As readers, we look so closely at what is there, and what is there is so ordinary yet so tenuous, so hard-fought-for yet so unwanted, that it becomes difficult to see where dystopia is at all. If the world has always been like this, if there is no chance of it ever not being like this, how is it possible to measure how bad this present is? With the shrinking of the novum, the political distinctiveness of a negative commitment is also altered: this novel has no unspoken commitment to the present, it seems to have no commitment at all. There just is what is there, and the people who endure it, day by day.

Red Clocks can be used here as a sharp example of the distinctiveness of contemporary dystopias: they have sloughed off the structural need for distance or are denied it by the dailiness of the situations they trace. I will not here open up fully the problem of how to interpret this new mutation in the morphospace of the dystopia. That is a job embarked upon in the final chapter. What we can do with *Red Clocks* is delineate the contours of the mutation, in particular the new presence of ordinariness in the space mapped out by those contours. With *Red Clocks*, we can first elucidate how its narrative form works, and what that work does to render unnecessary or even 'outdate' the dialectic of cognition and estrangement once constitutive of the novum.

In *Red Clocks*, a 'near future' dystopia, time shrinks but its depths fill out. The novel has as much to say, in its sideways, glancing way, about the past as about the specificity of the present world. In building that world, it relies more on character, on the experiences of five women whose stories thicken and absorb time as the connections and differences between them are slowly woven. The plot requires scenes in which the state is present (interrogation at the border, a prison cell, a court house), and in which a formally organised and politicised opposition is outlined (the Polyphony Collective and the network of organisations hinted at in the posters on its walls (*RCs*, p. 315)). Additionally, it is the passing and implementation of a particular piece of legislation – the Twenty-Eighth Amendment or Personhood Amendment – which organises the political temporality of the novel. The dominant temporality of this dystopia is not the one organised by these political forces, however. It is ordinary time, daily time – the logic of a recognisably twenty-first-century experiential time – which provides the novel's temporal scope. This is a use of time which refuses the estrangement of any future even as it is set in the future. The focus of *Red Clocks* is relentlessly private and yet – possibly because of the rigour of that focus – the novel deprivatises the domestic sphere, rendering it instead as a scene of capture or of refuge.

The state is an absent cause in its removal of the right to access legal abortions or in its insistence that only couples can adopt. But these are measures which interrupt and reshape a private sphere which long predates them. Domestic violence shapes one woman's experience of home life; a suffocating marriage another's; one woman longs to be pregnant so pays for infertility procedures she cannot afford; one young woman is terrified by a pregnancy she does not want but cannot legally end. Bodies, families and homes are the key spaces of this dystopia. There is a public realm, the realm of those antagonisms which constitute formal political acts and actors, but it is remote and dispersed rather than total or totalising.

With this receding of the state-centred public sphere, and a refusal to centre the commercial grotesque as the generator of deprivation, deceit and pain, the private realm expands and becomes the loci of its own horrors as well as of small pleasures. This inversion of the attention distributed between private and public alters the shape of the dystopia. Individual lives come to hold unhappiness in a myriad muted forms rather than being the object of an apparatus whose consequence their unhappiness is. This does *not* domesticate dystopia but it does render it everyday, ordinary, temporally of a here and now which is too plainly quotidian to ever be capable of shocking. The shock comes more slowly: that the quotidian, the everyday is so hard, so unnecessarily hard.

The novel is composed of excerpts from the life stories of five women. Each woman is given sufficient biographical detail and depth for her character to be specific, too concrete to translate into an allegorical figure. They are each given proper names and inhabit networks of personal relations via those names. But for the novel itself, each character is known via an abstraction from those networks: the Biographer, the Mender, the Daughter, the Wife. Only the fifth woman, the woman whose presence in the novel is most fugitive as she belongs to the nineteenth century and little about her is known, gets no abstracted name but remains doubly and triply mediated in order to have any presence at all. Each section is titled with the abstracted name of one of the four – the Biographer, the Mender, the Daughter, the Wife – and each section is followed by the untitled page (or infrequently pages) detailing some aspect of the telling of or the erasure of the life of the nineteenth-century polar explorer EivØr Mínervudottír.

The text's structure is one of a formal repetition, a cycling through instances from the lives of each of these women, each separate but proximate, building over the duration of the text to a counterpoint which holds both isolation and connection in the equilibrium of stasis. There are no first-person narrative voices in the novel. Rather a free-indirect-style dependent narrative is the medium of them all, a medium of a designed and contained ambivalence. That narrative voice provides the element of a continuity which is thickened cumulatively by the reiteration of shared spatial and social detail. Each of the four contemporary women lives in the fictional town of Newville, a beautiful, isolated and poor fishing town on the coast of Oregon, two hours' drive from Salem. Two years before the story opens, the United States had elected a new President: the Twenty-Eighth Amendment, the 'Personhood Amendment', had followed, as had a federal ban on IVF, the restriction of adoption to married couples, the defunding of Planned Parenthood, and a more general stress on a 'mission' to 'restore' *dignity, strength and prosperity to American families'* (*RCs*, p. 32, original italics).

There is no positive political materialisation of this regime in the text. It exists as a series of barriers impacting on individual lives but it has no narrative of its own, no space from which a rationale or apologia could be articulated. The 'Biographer' watches television with a friend but they watch only 'Masterpiece mysteries' in the friend's 'little house with its rose-dotted wallpaper and stone fireplace and wool rugs, rain pattering on the oriel windows' (*RCs*, p. 84). These are the murder mysteries typical of genteel England's public sense of itself in the mid-twentieth century, consciously anachronistic now, that is why they are enjoyed. The friend, Penny, is an unpublished novelist. She writes 'entertainments', romance novels which are

> soap operas valorizing romantic love as the sole telos of a female life. Penny has written nine of them, all waiting for cover art showing bulge-groined men relieving bulge-chested women of their bodices. She intends to be a published author by her seventieth birthday. Three years to make it happen. (*RCs*, p. 85)

As with the absence of televised news, and the absence of print news texts, the cell phones which are used in the novel are curiously mute about the twenty-first century. They make and take calls only, the internet with all the chaotic speech of social media is not present at all. This careful sculpting *out* of technological features and anxieties helps the novel organise its own sense of place and time as local, centred on the rhythms of the sea and the seasons. It is as background to that calm that the political events take on a sharp profile even as they stay in the background; and it is in the foreground of that calm that individual lives expose their own pain. It is not only the reifications of political history which take place behind people's backs but their own lives too.

For the Biographer, the coming of the new President took place when she wasn't looking:

> She was just quietly teaching history when it happened. Woke up one morning to a president elect she hadn't voted for. This man thought women who mis-carried should pay for funerals for the fetal tissue and thought a lab techni-cian who accidentally dropped an embryo during in vitro transfer was guilty of manslaughter. She had heard there was glee on the lawns of her father's Orlando retirement village. Marching in the streets of Portland. In Newville: brackish calm. (*RCs*, p. 31)

The geographical distribution of attention to the criminalisation of abor-tion here is also a dispersal of the political weight of the state and its figures. This President was elected, the policies his administration enacts are welcomed or supported as much as contested across the country. Beliefs – their material and cultural nexus as much if not more than their conscious possession – here occupy the structural position the older or classic model of dystopia gave to the regime. The novel, however, does not substitute the former for the latter, does not draft an indictment of an ideological bloc which might keep the structural dynamic of narrative and counter-narrative in play. Rather this narrative dynamic is undone formally whilst the need for it is maintained thematically. The formal undoing emerges as the slow probing and unravelling (something too gentle and gradual to be called an interrogation, too unfinished and uncertain to be called a judgement) of the family as an unavoidable structure of biographical narrative as much as of gendered existence.

This is a formal undoing only as the family stories of the five women stretch before and beyond the four or five months which frame the con-temporary time of the novel. That temporality is undone from the inside of their stories, splits and is split again by memory and by research, by regret and longing, dissatisfaction and hope, and by fear and by anger. Amidst all of this affective life, the state shrinks: becomes only one more absent cause. The novel is stylistically organised to take full advantage of the resulting temporal fluidity. Nothing is resolved as the narrative things do not exist as discrete events happening to or experienced by delimited monads.

I will return to the possible meanings of the text's stylistic choices at the end of this section. There is in those choices something of the aesthetic ambition of an older modernism – the easy refusal of linearity and embrace of an intrasubjectivity which flows – but there is also a falling short of modernist openness. This condition or tension may have something to tell us of the historicity of the contemporary dystopia's relation to literature. For now however, we must spend some time examining how the text achieves its contemporaneity. It is not just a matter of shrugging off the need to figure the state or the work of capital as centralising and centripetal forces. The state is in the novel, as is capital: the former most forcefully in the restrictions on women's reproductive choices,[34] the latter in the private or commercial fertility clinics which promise to use science to open up those choices for women who pay to have their fertility 'repaired' and given back to them.[35] The Biographer's very first section in the novel takes place in a private clinic, in a 'room for women whose bodies are broken' (*RCs*, p. 2). Her doctor examines her: seeing only the metrics he uses to assess the progress of her treatment, he cannot see her:

> he slides in the ultrasound wand … and presses it up against her cervix. 'your lining's nice and thin,' he says. 'Four point five. Right where we want it.' On the monitor, the lining of the Biographer's uterus is a sash of white chalk in a black swell, hardly enough of a thing, it seems, to measure, but Kalbfleisch is a trained professional in whose expertise she is putting her trust. And her money – so much money that the numbers seem virtual, mythical, details from a story about money rather than money anyone actually has. The Biographer, for example, does not have it. She's using credit cards. (*RCs*, pp. 3–4)

But neither the state nor capital nor any relation between them dominates or defines the novel's dystopian space. The family does, the relations through which family life is lived and left or endured. Friendship is an important adjunct to this prioritisation of family life but it does not have either the spatial specificity or historical expansiveness that the latter has. Family life – endured, abandoned, desired – cannot be described as a centre to this dystopia however as it does not have such an institutional or even relational centre. Homes largely organise the character space of the novel but not its meanings.

These meanings are multiple and divergent but have in common a quality of ordinariness. Unhappiness here is ordinary, is a property of ordinary life. No immediately political practice is responsible for or 'causes' this unhappiness until abortion is banned. Neither the banning of abortion nor the illegal overcoming of that ban through the work of the Polyphony Collective touches that unhappiness. Though there are significant events dotted throughout the novel, punctuating and mediating the threads of the dishevelled plot, these do not organise the text's unhappiness. The latter is comprised of ripples which radiate out from events significantly not part of the novel. Again there is not a direct causal momentum to these ripples. The affects – pervasive and permanent yet tenuous and half-buried – are iterated in such a way that they take on a life of their own, become life rather than its consequences.

Two or three examples may help sharpen the paradoxical specificity of a generalised unhappiness in the novel. First, the Biographer's brother, Archie. A heroin addict, he had died long before the novel opens with the Biographer's struggle to conceive. Archie is only the faintest presence in the novel. Heroin addiction, death from an overdose, is too ordinary to require explanation even if this novel was interested in explanation. He exists in recall, fragments of memory which float in and out of the Biographer's own daily thoughts. She misses him and thinks of him often but these are thoughts which do not have a clear object. Saturated with sadness and love, thoughts of his death are wrapped up in thoughts of his life, and all are embedded in thoughts of or about her own life and the options for having a child close to her as the novel draws to a close: the Biographer

> climbs to the top of the East stairwell. Sits down against a wall.
> The excitement she once felt about a nineteen-year old biology major's sperm, her willingness to drink a foul but magical tea, her wild hope on that run to Mattie's house –
> Gone.
> She picks at the lace of her sneakers.
> All the doors have closed.
> The ones, at least, she tried to open.
> How much of her ferocious longing is cellular instinct, and how much is socially installed? Whose urges is she listening to? Her life, like anyone's, could go a way she never wanted, never planned and turn out marvellous.
> Fingering her shoelaces, she hears the first bell.
> Thinks of her brother getting into his first-choice college and gloating, 'I'm set.' (*RCs*, p. 330)

He was not 'set' – a term or concept which has no positive presence in the novel at all but which we could gloss as 'set fair', 'set to achieve', 'set-up-for-life', where 'life' has the fantastic meaning of good, 'a good life'. The Biographer is a history teacher. When one of her teenage students becomes pregnant, the Biographer longs to ask the student to let her be the baby's mother but instead drives the student to the underground abortion clinic and stays with her through the termination procedure. Later,

> She did not tell Mattie that even though Archie graduated with honors from his first-choice college, he was not set.
> She did not tell Mattie about finding him, eight years ago, in the kitchen of his apartment. He wore black jeans and no shirt. Lips blue, cheeks flat and

white. On the counter was a half-eaten bowl of cereal, bearful of honey, burnt
spoon, lighter, glassine packet. The needle lay on the floor beside him. (*RCs*,
pp. 330–1)

The juxtaposition of the cheerful comestibles and the scene of death and
the manner of that death is not jarring or designed to be. This is a dystopia
which is comfortable locating some of its horrors in domesticity, indeed
insists on that location but insists with equally quiet emphasis that location is not a structure of relationality, much less one of causation. The
plastic honeybear and bowl of cereal might be denied any investment in the
signification of breakfast as only a beginning – one involving sun, cheer,
busyness – but they do not therefore take on any sinister or mocking echoes.
They are just there – as family life is there, a structure which appears as
unavoidable and as unmoveable.

Mattie, the teenager who is the Daughter, seeks the Biographer's help
to end her pregnancy. She is also a character whose thoughts twirl around
an earlier loss. Herself adopted and unaware that her birth mother (the
Mender) lives in the same small town as her, Mattie (or the Daughter)
has parents who love her deeply. They support the new Constitutional
Amendment but this is not why Mattie does not tell them she is pregnant.

[The father:] 'When someone decides to murder a fellow human with a gun,
we put them in jail, don't we?'
   'Not if they're a cop.'
   'Think of all the families waiting for a child, Think of me and your mom,
how long we waited.'
   'But – '
   'An embryo is a living being.' (*RCs*, p. 120)

The Daughter does not tell her parents she is pregnant at least in part
because she cannot bear the idea of having a baby and putting that baby up
for adoption:

She doesn't want the kid to wonder why he wasn't kept.
   And she doesn't want to wonder what happened to him. Was he given to
parents like hers or parents who scream and are bigots and don't take him to
the doctor enough. (*RCs*, p. 121)

The figure of loss in the Daughter's thoughts is her birth mother. She has
no thoughts of her birth father. She is also racked with another loss, the
loss of a friend who gave herself a homemade abortion when she became
pregnant a month after the Federal abortion ban had gone into effect (*RCs*,
p. 72). The friend, Yasmine, never appears in the novel. She is incarcerated.
She exists in a suspended tense in the Daughter's memories as the latter
misses her,

... Yasmine.

The self-scraper. The mutilator.

Yasmine, who was the first person the daughter became blood sisters with (second grade).

Yasmine, who was the first person the daughter ever kissed (fourth grade).

Yasmine, who made him wear a condom but got pregnant anyway. (*RCs*, p. 49)

Yasmine did not die but lost so much blood she had to be hospitalised. She was not yet sixteen. Her

uterus was so badly damaged it had to be removed.

The cops came while she was still in the hospital. (*RCs*, p. 259)

Yasmine is black. Her mother the only woman of colour in the Oregon State legislature (*RCs*, p. 245).[36] Yasmine blames the Daughter for calling for medical help. As her own pregnancy develops, the Daughter's thoughts revolve around her absent friend as much as they do the 'clump' (p. 194) growing inside her:

She has to get her body clean. Stop being seasick. Stop the blue veins from branching across her tightening breasts. *Don't be the free milk*.[37]

Terribly she misses Yasmine.

Bolt River Youth Correctional Facility is a medium-security state prison for females twelve to twenty years old.

Numbers of letters, cards and care packages the Daughter mailed to Bolt River the first year Yasmine was inside: sixty-four.

Number of words she heard back from Yasmine: Zero.

Whenever she phoned the front office, she was told, 'the offender is refusing your call.'

Yasmine's mother said, 'I've got no idea, Matts. I simply don't.'

After a year, the Daughter stopped trying. (*RCs*, p. 285, original italics)

As with the Biographer's absent brother, the Daughter's absent friend opens up a prehistory to the novel's present, one which thickens that present, levers it open from the back so that the world before the Twenty-Eighth Amendment, and the reversal of *Roe* v. *Wade* (*RCs*, p. 49), has institutions and rhythms among their relations, has a shape beyond the availability of abortion in fifty states.

The Mender, a non-heroicised figure of self-sufficiency in the novel, is surrounded but not shaped by the experience of her mother's leaving her, and by the death of the aunt who then took care of her at eight years old. These losses are relatively straightforward in the novel's dominant register of ambivalence and uncertainty. The Mender may have loved her mother but she does not miss her. Before her aunt Temple when her mother forgot to buy food, the Mender cooked ketchup, mustard, and mayonnaise into a hot crust.

Before Temple, she put herself to bed.

Before Temple, she took a lot of aspirin, because regular doctors were too expensive and the ER staff knew the Mender's mother only too well.

Before Temple, she had never been to the movies. (*RCs*, p. 130)

These are not scenes of a dystopian unhappiness, they are ordinary scenes or scenes from ordinary life. This is a dystopia – in a way which is arguably peculiar to contemporary dystopias though not pervasive across the genre at all – which rejects the future as its novum even as it formally places itself there. The material enabling this rejection is the present, the text's circling around the repetitions and routines of daily life in the present, the things which make that life liveable and which simultaneously make it unbearable.

In the 'Introduction' to *Full Surrogacy Now: Feminism against Family*, Sophie Lewis reads Margaret Atwood's *The Handmaid's Tale* as neatly reproducing a

> wishful scenario at least as old as feminism itself. Cisgender womanhood, united without regard to class, race or colonialism, can blame all its woes on evil fundamentalists with guns.[38]

Noting both the 'downplaying' of the 'class dynamics of fascism' as well as its 'deraced slave narrative', Lewis reads Atwood's novel as one which satisfies a craving for solidarity without solidarity:

> we are not yet living in *The Handmaid's Tale*. People's eagerness to assert that we are betokens nothing so much as wishful thinking. What do I mean by this? That, inasmuch as it promises that a 'universal' (trans-erasive) feminist solidarity would automatically flourish in the worst of all possible worlds, the dystopia functions as a kind of utopia: a vision of the vast majority of women finally seeing the light and counting themselves as feminist because society has started systematically treating them all – not just black women – like chattel.[39]

If we flip this reading – one which is arguably more directly applicable as a critique of the television form of *The Handmaid's Tale* where resistance and solidarity are thematised – we can see that it might be applied to the classic dystopia as a form: not that all such dystopias generalise the need for resistance – they do not – but that for their readers they posit oppression as something which will hurt all equally and which will come from outside, from civil strife or political alterations but something which is not at work already in the very heart of ordinary life.

In its determination to render the crises of ordinary life, to open up the systemic pains of just 'family life', Zumas's novel suggests that the classic dystopia either no longer can or no longer wishes to explore a future worse than the present.[40] For this novel, as for one thread in the weave which constitutes contemporary dystopian fictions, the present is the consequence of the past and is inexplicable without that past. History has returned and it is history also as 'ordinary', as the daily rhythms of work and of domesticity and their systemic hurts, just as much as it is history as the imperialism and extractive logics of the nineteenth century which on a wider scale burnt out of the present any chance it could generate a future different to that past.

Notes

1 H.G. Wells (1905) *A Modern Utopia*, in Wells, *The First Men in the Moon, and A Modern Utopia* (Ware: Wordsworth Classics, 2017), p. 210. Wells makes clear the reasons why the 'whole trend of modern thought is against the permanence' of those enclosures (the mountain valley or island) which had structured previous utopias as places withdrawn from the world. Foremost amongst those reasons are the development of the technologies of war which mean that no place is safe from those same technologies. Whilst once the physical features of a place may have rendered it isolated enough for it to 'maintain itself intact from outward force ... Now perhaps you might still guard a rocky coast or a narrow pass; but what of that near tomorrow when the flying machine soars overhead ... That leaves no room for a modern Utopia in Central Africa, or in South America ... We need a planet.' *A Modern Utopia*, p. 210.

2 Tom Moylan, *Scraps of the Untainted Sky: Science Fiction, Utopia, Dystopia* (Boulder; London: Westview Press, 2000), p. 159. For Moylan, it is a 'third place' when put alongside the novum's centralised mechanical world, and the space of those exiled from it, the unnamed homeless inhabitants of the surface.

3 Ibid., p. 111.

4 That the utopian fictions of the late nineteenth century were designed less to offer images of a full and rich socialised form of freedom, and more to indicate the idiocy of living poorly when the means of living well were so possible, is made clear most bluntly by Wells in *A Modern Utopia*. In his 'Note to the Reader', he is short: a utopia is a 'state of affairs at once possible and more desirable than the world in which I live'. Wells, *A Modern Utopia*, p. 201.

5 E.M. Forster (1909) 'The Machine Stops', in E.M. Forster, *Selected Stories* (London: Penguin, 2001), p. 91. Hereafter, all quotations from Forster's story are referenced in parentheses in the text.

6 On the widespread influence of imperial anxieties about 'degeneration' as the reversal of 'progress', see William M. Greenslade's *Degeneration, Culture and the Novel: 1880–1940* (Cambridge: Cambridge University Press, 2010). A too literal reading but one useful for noting the centrality of 'degeneration' to Forster's story can be found in Mark Decker's use of Max Nordau's *Degeneration* (1892) to read 'The Machine Stops' as a 'rhetorical parable

designed to argue that modernity was weakening not only Britain's ability to produce the soldiers it needed to maintain its empire, but also the British people's ability to reproduce at rates that would maintain their unique identity'. Mark Decker, 'Biomedical Imaginaries: the Case of "The Machine Stops"', in Donald M. Hassler and Clyde Wilcox (eds), *New Boundaries in Political Science Fiction* (Columbia: University of South Carolina Press, 2008), p. 54.

7 We should note the frequency of the 'underground' to figures of dystopian space before Forster's. It is the hidden visibility or topos of the unseemly, the wretched, the threatening which stretches from Dostoevsky, in *Notes from the Underground* (1864), to the site of those who have access to Vril in Edward Bulwer Lytton's *The Coming Race* (1871), and the site of the silent devourers of the ease of the leisured class, the Morlocks, in Wells's *The Time Machine* (1895), and in Fritz Lang's film *Metropolis* (1927). By the 1950s, however, the 'underground' has become what it became during the Second World War and in the anti-colonial struggles which followed: the site of the resistance, the physical space which is not directly subject to power, and the name for those who inhabit and prolong such a space. This is the meaning it takes in *The Space Merchants* (1952), in *The Handmaid's Tale* (1985) and which it still has in such recent iterations as Atwood's sequel to *The Handmaid's Tale*, *The Testaments* (2019), in *Red Clocks* (2018), and in the many young-adult dystopias. The political meanings of the dystopian underground are thrown into more complexity in Boots Riley's film *Sorry to Bother You* (2018), and in Jordan Peele's film *Us* (2019), however. The shift and reason for it deserve closer attention than I can give here.

8 J.M. Bernstein, *Adorno: Disenchantment and Ethics* (Cambridge: Cambridge University Press, 2001), p. 114.

9 I will refrain from comparing the dystopian texts we are exploring with Adorno's treatment of Beckett as it is not a comparison which is fair to either, but the following quotation is both too productively relevant and too beautiful to pass over. Writing of how Beckett achieved a 'realism' by spurning the illusory remnants of realism, Adorno notes that Beckett's 'narratives, which he sardonically calls novels, no more offer objective descriptions of social reality than – as the widespread misunderstanding supposes – they present the reduction of life to basic human relationships ... The narratives are marked as much by an objectively motivated loss of the object as by its correlative, the impoverishment of the subject ... The more total society becomes, the more completely it contracts to a unanimous system, and all the more do the artworks in which this experience is sedimented become the other of this society ... New art is as abstract as social relations have in truth become. In like manner, the concepts of the realistic and the symbolic are put out of service.' Adorno, *Aesthetic Theory* (1970) trans. Robert Hullot-Kentor (London: Bloomsbury, 2013), p. 42.

10 Theodor Adorno, 'The Essay as Form' (written 1954–58, first published as 'Der Essay als Form', *Nota zur Literatur*, I (1958)), in *The Adorno Reader*, ed. Brian O'Connor, (Oxford: Blackwell, 2000), p. 108.

11 On the political bonds, artistic disagreements and long history of Pohl and
    Kornbluth's writing partnership, see David Seed, 'Take-Over Bids: the Power
    Fantasies of Frederik Pohl and Cyril Kornbluth', in *Foundation*, 0:42 (Fall
    1993), 42–58. In 1984, Pohl published his single-authored sequel to *The Space
    Merchants*, *The Merchants' War*.
12 Kingsley Amis, *New Maps of Hell: A Survey of Science Fiction* (1960) (London:
    Penguin, 2012), p. 97, my ellipses.
13 On the campaign to create and to make a political force out of the Advertising
    Council of America, see Robert Griffith, 'The Selling of America: the Advertising
    Council and American Politics, 1942–1960', *The Business History Review*, 57:3
    (Autumn 1983), 388–412. The commitment to public power, progressive forms
    of taxation, labour rights and regulation of the advertisement industries of the
    New Deal era combined with anti-communism to make 1938's Wheeler-Lea
    Amendment (which gave the Federal Trade Commission oversight of and the
    power to prohibit 'deceptive' advertisements in certain sectors) a harbinger
    of dark days to come for the industry. By the early 1950s, the Advertising
    Council, created to beat back any prospect of a renewed 'New Deal' order after
    the Second World War, had solidified a 'unique relationship' with the various
    branches of the federal government, and had successfully positioned advertis-
    ing, marketing and public relations as integral to the public interest (Griffith,
    'The Selling of America', p. 392). See also chapter 1, 'Persuaders in the Public
    Interest', of Dawn Spring, *Advertising in the Age of Persuasion: Building Brand
    America, 1941–1961* (New York: Palgrave Macmillan, 2011), pp. 9–28.
14 Theodor Adorno, 'The Schema of Mass Culture', in Theodor Adorno, *The
    Culture Industry: Selected Essays on Mass Culture*, ed. J.M. Bernstein (London;
    New York: Routledge, 1991), p. 73.
15 Adorno and Horkheimer, 'The Culture Industry: Enlightenment as Mass
    Deception,' in *Dialectic of Enlightenment*, p. 147.
16 Frederik Pohl and C.M. Kornbluth, *The Space Merchants* (1952) (London:
    Orion, 2003), p. 6. Hereafter all quotations are referenced in the text. The
    novel began its life as a serial, 'Gravy Planet', in the American magazine for
    'social science fiction' founded in 1950, *Galaxy*. On the tendency within *Galaxy*
    and its world for 'social science fiction', see Malisa Kurtz's chapter 'After the
    War, 1945–65', in Roger Luckhurst (ed.), *Science Fiction: A Literary History*
    (London: British Library, 2017), pp. 137–43.
17 It should be noted that Kornbluth and Pohl's frictionless subsumption of the
    imagery of science fiction to the deceit of advertising was part of a longer critique
    they made of how a love of gimmicks contributed to science fiction's disregard
    for both science and its reader. In a lecture he delivered in 1957, Kornbluth iron-
    ised the result: 'We are suspending reality, you and I. By the signs of the rocket
    ship and the ray gun and the time machine we indicate that the relationship
    between us has nothing to do with the real world. By writing the stuff and by
    reading it we abdicate from action, we give free play to our unconscious drives
    and symbols, we write and read not about the real world but about ourselves
    and the things within ourselves.' Kornbluth, 'The Failure of the Science Fiction

Novel as Social Criticism', in Basil Davenport (ed.), *The Science Fiction Novel: Imagination and Social Criticism*, 3rd ed. (Chicago: Advent, 1969), p. 50. See Seed, 'Take-Over Bids', pp. 42–4, for a discussion of how this commitment to a socially 'critical' science fiction plays out in *The Space Merchants*.

18 Just how cramped living conditions are in this American future is evident most powerfully in how eyes have become used to seeing only what is in front of them, literally but also imaginatively. There is a passage when two characters visit the site where the Venus rocket is being made. The area around the site (in Arizona) is clear of buildings and of any other structures. It is this clearness or emptiness which strikes them: 'Oddly, the most impressive thing about it to me was not the rocket itself but the wide swathe around it. For a full mile the land was cleared ... Partly security, partly radiation. The gleaming sand cut by irriga-tion pipes looked strange. There probably wasn't another sight like it in North America. It troubled my eyes. Not for years had I focused them more than a few yards' (*SM*, p. 49).

19 W.G. Sumner, 'Folkways: a Study of the Sociological Importance of Usages, Manners, Customs, Mores and Morals' (1907), in Philip D. Manning (ed.) *On Folkways and Mores: William Graham Sumner Then and Now* (Abingdon; New York: Routledge, 2015), pp. 77/78.

20 One of the best short pieces on the alterations within the advertising indus-try as they relate to the development of what Adorno would have termed the monopoly phase of late capitalism is still Raymond Williams, 'Advertising: the Magic System', in Williams, *Problems in Materialism and Culture* (London: Verso, 1980). It is not only advertising's internal alterations which need to be considered but the functions to which advertisements were put in a recomposi-tion of how commodities circulated in a 'mass market': modern advertising came of age in the Great War when not a market but a nation needed to be both controlled and inspired: 'it was in the war itself, when now not a market but a nation had to be controlled and organised, yet in democratic conditions and without some of the older compulsions that new kinds of persuasion were devel-oped and applied' (Williams, 'Advertising', p. 180). In her unpublished thesis, Mary Elizabeth Davis reads *The Space Merchants* as a 'weak critique' of adver-tisements' obfuscation of the processes of labour and extraction which make up production. See Mary Elizabeth Davis, 'On Advertising's Terms: Influence of Spatial Logic on the Weak Critiques of Consumer Capitalism in *Player Piano, Fahrenheit 451*, and *The Space Merchants*' (PhD, Indiana University of Pennsylvania, May 2010). Proquest Digital Dissertations. Web, December 2020.

21 Adorno and Horkheimer, 'The Culture Industry: Enlightenment as Mass Deception', in *Dialectic of Enlightenment*, p. 162.

22 Claeys, *Dystopia*, p. 455.

23 Adorno and Horkheimer, 'The Culture Industry: Enlightenment as Mass Deception', in *Dialectic of Enlightenment*, p. 167.

24 An aeroplane touching down at 'Little America' (once the Antarctic) 'was Indian ... That ship, from nose to tail, was Indiastry built. The crewmen were Indiastry-trained and Indiastry-employed. The passengers, walking and sleeping,

paid tribute minute by minute to Indiastry. And Indiastry paid tribute to Fowler Schocken Associates' (*TSM*, p. 61). Advertising is an excrescence, a growth, not a condition or cause, of this stage of capitalism.

25 Adorno, 'Reflections on Class Theory' (1942), trans. Rodney Livingstone, in Adorno, *Can One Live after Auschwitz?: A Philosophical Reader*, ed. Rolf Tiedemann (Stanford: Stanford University Press, 2003), p. 98.

26 Ibid., p. 98.

27 Ibid., p. 99.

28 Ibid., p. 99.

29 Ibid., p. 99.

30 Leni Zumas, *Red Clocks: A Novel* (2018) (London: The Borough Press/ HarperCollins, 2019), pp. 30–1. Hereafter, all references to the novel are included in the text in parentheses.

31 Hulu broadcast the first episode of Series One on 26 April 2017. At the time of writing, a fourth series has been broadcast. The text's commitment to thematise resistance as much as oppression is marked in the first series' finale: June's line that 'They shouldn't have given us uniforms if they didn't want us to be an army', is useful as a measure both of the collectivisation of resistance in the TV series and of the difference this makes between the series and the source text in the novel. For a critical account of the types of feminism articulated in dystopias conscious of Trump, see Sarah Dillon, 'Who Rules the World? Reimagining the Contemporary Feminist Dystopia', in Jennifer Cooke (ed.), *The New Feminist Literary Studies* (Cambridge: Cambridge University Press, 2020), pp. 169–81.

32 Sophie Gilbert, '*Red Clocks* Imagines America without Abortion', *The Atlantic*, 7 Feb. 2018. www.theatlantic.com/entertainment/archive/2018/02/leni-zumas-red-clocks-review/552464/ (accessed 23 January 2022). See also Gilbert's essay 'The Remarkable Rise of the Feminist Dystopia', *The Atlantic*, 4 Oct. 2018. www.theatlantic.com/entertainment/archive/2018/10/feminist-speculative-fiction-2018/571822/ (accessed 22 January 2022).

33 Silvia Martínez-Falquina, 'Feminist Dystopia and Reality in Louise Erdrich's *Future Home of the Living God* and Leni Zumas's *Red Clocks*', *The European Legacy*, 26:3–4 (2021), 286.

34 Not only there but also in the conditions which made the Twenty-Eighth amendment possible, in the consensus which underpins the state's co-optation of consensus as the ground of its own sovereignty. This is shadowed practically in the juvenile correction facility. This state locks up children in a grotesque parody of its own paternalism. The novel imagines a teenager of colour who is locked up because she accessed an illegal abortion. But the facility to which she was committed was one which already existed and exists. On carceral rates for children in America, see Erica R. Meiners, 'Trouble with the Child in the Carceral State', *Social Justice*, 41:3 (2015), 120–44. On mass-incarceration in America more generally, specifically the racialised composition of prison populations in the 'new Jim Crow', see Reuben Jonathan Miller and Amanda Alexander, 'The Price of Carceral Citizenship: Punishment, Surveillance and Social Welfare Policy in an Age of Carceral Expansion', *Michigan Journal of Race and Law*,

21:2 (2016), 291–314. On how certain forms of feminism lent themselves to the legitimation of incarceration as social policy, see Kristin Bumiller, *In an Abusive State: How Neoliberalism Appropriated the Feminist Movement against Sexual Violence* (Durham, NC: Duke University Press, 2008).

35 The novel's treatment of reproductive technologies is ambivalent about the technologies themselves but unambivalent about the clinic's transformation of a woman's body into the bits she pays to repair or improve. That the Biographer's doctor does not diagnose the PCOS which renders her fertility treatments next to useless is only the most pointed illustration of how commercial reproductive techniques 'see' the parts of a body they're paid to look at.

36 In school, Yasmine works harder than her peers. When she gets pregnant, her mother's professional position – the burden of her colour on her position – plays out in her decision to attempt her own abortion: 'Yasmine said she didn't intend to be anyone's stereotype. Black teen mother slurping welfare of the backs of hardworking citizens, etc. ... She didn't intend to jeopardise her mother's career. She gave herself a homemade abortion' (*RCs*, p. 245).

37 When the Daughter or Mattie tries to cross 'the Pink Wall' and get into Canada for a termination, she is stopped by a border guard who is kindly and sends her back rather than arresting her: 'I've got two daughters aboot your age. Let's say I've got a soft spot.' The last words he says to her are 'Like I tell my daughters: be the cow they have to buy ... Don't be the free milk' (*RCs*, p. 246).

38 Sophie Lewis, *Full Surrogacy Now: Feminism against Family* (London; New York: Verso, 2019), p 10.

39 Ibid., p. 11.

40 For the concept of 'crisis ordinariness', see Lauren Berlant, *Cruel Optimism* (Durham, NC: Duke University Press, 2011), pp. 8–11, 51–93.

2

Orwell and the classic dystopia

Introduction

I want to use this chapter to read George Orwell's *Nineteen Eighty-Four* (1949) as an example of the 'classic dystopia', a central form in the genre's history, the one against which or with which other variations work. As a classic dystopia, perhaps the most influential of them all so far, *Nineteen Eighty-Four* belongs in this book both because of its trace presence in later dystopian fictions and because of its wider presence in the reception and interpretation not only of dystopias but of political events and the language used to apprehend and oppose or support them.

To read *Nineteen Eighty-Four* is difficult, however, as, despite the large scholarship which exists, it is arguably not so much a text read at all as one agreed with. Where it receives critical readings, Orwell rather than the novel is frequently what is puzzled over as scholars strive to prise his politics and reputation out of the grip of those who would honour his prose style, and the values sedimented in his insistence on that style, and leave his commitment to socialism silent.

The focus of the reading which follows is what the novel makes of 'history'. The argument is that whilst *Nineteen Eighty-Four* can be used to model the workings of both the novum, and hence of the political work done by a negative commitment, it is also useful as a way into seeing how cut off from the past the classic dystopia must be – how it must cut itself off from its own past so as to create its novum and commit to the present. *Nineteen Eighty-Four* can be read as an anti-utopian text, arguably it must be. But reading it in the terms of a negative commitment make clear that the grounds of its ideological potency are also what it fights against. This anti-utopian novel is one in search of 'hope' even as its form locks it into construing hope only as 'an endless, hopeless effort to get back into the past'.[1] My aim overall in this chapter is to use this reading of *Nineteen Eighty-Four* to fill the idea of negative commitment with an initial layer of meaning at the level of the genre.

'Reason, left to work alone, creates monsters,' wrote Adorno and Horkheimer in *Dialectic of Enlightenment*, 'while imagination unalloyed by the power of reason gives rise to futile ideas'.[2] Orwell's dystopian fiction is one in which three centralised super-states use reason very imaginatively to render all of life monstrous, in a novel which imagines such a world yet holds to reason in so doing. Orwell's work – not only in *Nineteen Eighty-Four* but arguably as the governing passions of his life's work, on the one hand the existence of intolerable, unnecessary suffering, on the other the erosion of political and intellectual liberty – may seem as if his understanding of the catastrophes of the first half of the twentieth century align with if they do not overlap with the understanding of the present articulated in *Dialectic of Enlightenment*. But they are incompatible to the point of being mutually exclusive in terms of their understanding of those catastrophes even as they might share a recognition of the shape of some of the dangers.

Reason for Orwell was an individual capacity, to be realised with education and to be nurtured by freedom from interference. Language might interfere with reason but only from the outside, twisting its operations as it entered words which had been damaged or deranged by political or economic forces.[3] When Fredric Jameson discusses Adorno's project to desubjectify thinking about aesthetics, he relates that project to a wider conjunction in the middle decades of the twentieth century, the turn of philosophy 'away from what are now known as "philosophies of the subject" – that is to say, from the earlier modern attempt to ground truth in consciousness'.[4] This 'turn' for Adorno, a 'radical turn from and against subjectivity', can be related to a historical narrative against whose contours we can see, at least momentarily, the figure of Orwell as well as that of Adorno. Jameson describes it thus – a historical period in which the 'tendencies and interests of the modern state and of monopoly capitalism' appear to no longer be willing to uphold the fiction of the autonomous self but

> can be seen as having a stake in the planification of the individual, the reduction of individual and subjective choice in the era of organised society, the penetration and colonisation of the older autonomous ego, but also of the Unconscious and desire, by the forces of the market.[5]

Jameson is concerned to explicate the position of Adorno's work by, and in, the 1990s, and notes the 'objectively ambiguous' position of any desubjectifying project for aesthetics in that context. Here, we can take desubjectification as the name for a fear Orwell worked out of, one he would have related to capitalism, in for example, the 'money-god's' taking up residence in culture and in the conditions of romance in *Keep the Aspidistra Flying* (1936) or to the profits to be made out of total war

in *Coming Up for Air* (1939). *Nineteen Eighty-Four* took 'totalitarianism' as its object however and it is as a fear of a totalising political project
that *Nineteen Eighty-Four's* fears of the planned subject are read. This is
desubjectification as part of what Orwell saw as the world of monopoly and
of bureaucracy, the forces *Nineteen Eighty-Four* dramatises as 'the barren
world of monopoly industry and centralised government', which composed
the final moments of Oceania's pre-history (*NEF*, p. 235).

    Where Adorno worked to understand the individual as constituted – to
her cost – by the historical compulsions of a self-preservation which scorned
its own social being, Orwell held on to the individual self as ontological
ground, as weapon and as goal. For some scholars, Orwell's commitment
to empiricism continues and perpetuates an older tradition of English hostility to abstraction.[6] And it does, but to see only the continuity is to miss
how strained and distorted that commitment to empiricism becomes with
Orwell. Less so in his non-fiction where he writes as if there were still places
outside history but frequently in his fiction, Orwell has nowhere to put
'truth' except in subjective apprehension of it. Anxious not to relativise, he
mutates 'truth' into 'fact', something which hits the body with the force of
a weight, and which cannot be argued with.

    He is as a thinker, and more so as a novelist, caught at the painful end of
one moment of identity thinking, the older liberal moment of experiencing
the subject as sovereign, with privacy as its right and rightful space, and
the newer realisation, frequently articulated as an appalled fear of any hint
of what becomes an all-encompassing 'collectivism', that subjects can be
'created' by social forces. Adorno describes the alteration thus:

> Identity thinking, screen-image of the dominant dichotomy, in the age of
> subjective impotence no longer poses as the absolutisation of the subject.
> Instead what is taking shape is a type of seemingly anti-subjectivist, scientifi-
> cally objective identity thinking ... The ideal of depersonalising knowledge for
> the sake of objectivity retains nothing but *the caput mortuum* of objectivity.[7]

The situation of Orwell in the interwar years was not one which pushed
him to advocate for the objectivity of knowledge as his conceptualisation
of the subject still allowed for or depended on knowledge to be precisely
that: his conception of the subject, that is, should have been able to assume
or posit a knowledge which was knowledge of the object without any
tremor or whisper of the subject troubling it. It is that conceptualisation
which becomes strained and brittle, however, as this subject is at once, for
Orwell, itself true or real and yet everywhere dissolving into what he would
have perceived as the undoing of the self in 'orthodoxy' or 'cant'. Orwell's
notion of the individual self bears the scars of the work he makes it do in
a context where desubjectification was perceived as a threat, as a thing to

come (whether from 'collectivisation' of the Stalinist sort or the equally des-ubjectifying depredations of a universalising culture industry) rather than understood as a revelation of an older history at work in new ways. Brittle in form, and existentially thin or repetitive, their isolation their definitive mark and constitutive force as early as *Burmese Days* (1934), Orwell's fictional protagonists become progressively more negative, defined largely by the fixations they feel themselves against, unable to exist without the worldliness and strength of their antagonisms.

I will argue in the pages that follow that part of the terrible inevitability of Winston Smith's defeat in *Nineteen Eighty-Four* has to be understood as part of its narrative logic: totalitarianism is most terrifying not because it can destroy the individual but because it reveals the individual as not individual at all. Before entering the novel, it may be well to model Orwell's understanding less of the individual than of the most lethal of the forces arrayed against it, language. For whilst the protagonists of his novels can be used to resist the shrinking and corresponding rigidifying of the space of individuality, the writer's person as practised in the non-fiction seems to swing wholly the other way, proffering an image of the individual who just needs courage and decency, needs to 'dare to be a Daniel'.[8]

A moment in *The Road to Wigan Pier* (1937) may help here to crystal-lise the constellation Orwell made out of reason, the self, and those social tendencies aggressively preventing their double or dual integrity. When Orwell moves from the 'reportage' of the first half of the volume to the more autobiographical account of its second part, he starts immediately in his brisk, no-nonsense manner to set about defining socialism through the prism of class differences:

> For before you can be sure whether you are genuinely in favour of Socialism, you have got to decide whether things are tolerable or not tolerable, and you have got to take up a definite attitude on the terribly difficult issue of class.

Once he has described his own position in the nether regions of the upper-middle class – 'the layer of society lying between £2,000 and £300 [*sic*]'[9] – he goes on to insist on what is presented as a fact, what has to be a fact if it is to serve as the key pivot and guarantor of the objectivity of class differ-ences, and for the objectivity of their absurdity, without having to enter the treacherous waters of understanding those differences in any language more abstract than just the name of the revulsion they produce:

> the real secret of class distinctions in the West – the real reason why a European of bourgeois upbringing, even when he calls himself a Communist, cannot without a hard effort think of a working man as his equal ... *The lower classes smell.*[10]

It is central here that the 'fact' is not any smell at all but *a belief*, even more accurately an ideological understanding of working-class people as without any inclination to cleanliness. Orwell will not use the term 'ideology', however: he holds on to his grim 'fact' as the only ground on which his knowledge of class will appear as not his knowledge at all but as certain and as definite as any smell. The silent desperation of this reach for a fact is hidden in the certainty of the 'fact' itself once this has been brought to the surface of the prose.

That to all above them, the 'lower classes smell' is one way of materialising class differences, of inoculating them from the purported abstractions which would dilute or distort the essential 'fact', something which can be caught in language but which, being so physical, is not dependent on that slippery realm of language for its meaning:

> That was what we were taught – the lower classes smell. And here, obviously, you are at an impassable barrier. For no feeling of like or dislike is quite so fundamental as a *physical* feeling. Race hatred, religious hatred, differences of education, of temperament, of intellect, even differences of moral code, can be got over; but physical repulsion cannot.[11]

This rhetorical habit of factualising an argument, and of dramatising that fact as a physical thing, is here neatly embodied. This fact which is not a fact serves as a metonymy for a whole set of interlocking structures generating rhythms of life and of behaviour, of values, tastes, 'prejudices', without ever having to go near the difficulty of naming, evaluating or explaining. An honest gaze and plain speaking can cut through to the bare bones of the matter when the bare bones of the matter are themselves posited by that gaze, which seems flexible but cannot look away lest the bones disappear with it, leaving only the linguistic rubble of expectations, hope, fear and ideological habit.

Reason, which Orwell will insist on as part of what enables one to get 'outside the class racket',[12] or outside the 'empire-racket',[13] is triumphant but only at the expense of being externalised as part of the logic of the world rather than an immanent capacity of the individual, of being objectified and figured as a fact. All 'the horrible jargon' that the 'middle-class socialists' think it necessary to employ, 'phrases like "bourgeois ideology" and "proletarian solidarity" and "expropriation of the expropriators"' do not inspire but disgust the 'ordinary person': 'Even the single word "Comrade" has done its dirty little bit towards discrediting the Socialist movement.'[14] You cannot overcome 'facts' with thought, and it is facts which need to be faced if the ordinary middle-class person is to be moved to stand with socialists against fascism, to see the world as it really is. To fully understand Orwell's desperate need for facts, we would have to make a study of the disenchantment of the world, as seen not through the eyes of Orwell (where it is given a punctual and temporary existence, setting in after the brutality of the First World War and ceasing some time around 1930) but through the wider and longer lens of anxieties about language, the falling away of expression from emotion, of social or objective meaning from subjective value, which are frequently associated with modernism,[15] but which when added to anxieties about how the technologies of mass cultural reproduction ensure an ease of circulation for meanings hardened into familiarity by repetition, could help us see Orwell's insistence on fact as a struggle rather than a style.

That is outside my scope, however: here this excursus into Orwell's need to get a soul into a fact can serve to prefigure my focus in what follows on how that same need works in the classic dystopia to make its stand against totalitarianism a definite yet utterly negative one. I have divided my reading in what follows into three sections. The first explores why Smith's diary is not used as a textual space for personal history, for Smith's own contemporary history, his memories, nightmares and dreams, for the 'interminable restless monologue that had been running inside his head, literally for years' but rather becomes the space where that 'monologue had dried up' (*NEF*, p. 10). The second explores the very different history presented in 'The Theory and Practice of Oligarchical Collectivism' and its treatment by the novel as having real explanatory purchase on the past. My final section brings these two modes of history together to see why their separation – the separation of the personal or private from the public or political – was necessary to the dystopian form. It is my contention here that Orwell's dystopia is, however different, committed to that same crip pling polarisation 'of subjective and objective' that Adorno noted in *Brave New World*, a separation 'reified to a rigid alternative', and one which leaves no room for history (now only possible as a looming threat outside the individual).[16] The question is why.

History and the last man

'It was a bright cold day in April, and the clocks were striking thirteen.' This is the sentence which begins *Nineteen Eighty-Four*, preceding the sentence in which Winston Smith himself enters, 'his chin nuzzled into his breast in an effort to escape the vile wind'. Much commentary on the novel pays most attention to Winston Smith, perhaps understandably so as he is one of the two main textual mediators of the regime: its observer, interpreter, critic and victim (the Book and O'Brien, its possible author, are the second). Smith is structurally central as the breach in the regime which makes it visible or casts it into legibility. Raffaella Baccolini and Tom Moylan have described this narrative structuring of regime and opposition as central to the classic dystopia. They describe the ways in which this agonistic structure is not the duality before reconciliation of realism but is a function of

> a deeper and more totalizing agenda in the dystopian form insofar as the text
> is built around the construction of a narrative of the hegemonic order and a
> counter-narrative of resistance.[17]

As such an agent of resistance, Smith is 'the last man', an odd version of a figure as old as Frankenstein's monster and one which increased in incidence as the nineteenth century turned over.[18] I want to pay some attention to the narrative style which delivers him, however. That style was described by Orwell as 'naturalist',[19] perhaps because of the dystopia's ambition to totalise, to figure the entirety of the social order which forms its subject, and perhaps because of Orwell's insistence on stressing as squalid the things which remain the same even in this future-world so different from the world of the 1940s: the smells, the meanness of the food, the alcohol, the vistas of 'rotting nineteenth-century houses' outside (*NEF*, p. 5), the lifts which do not work inside. And most of all, the bodies and their ills and ageing, from the varicose vein above the right ankle on the 'meagreness of [Smith's] body' (*NEF*, p. 4) to the 'enormous wreck of a woman, aged about sixty, with great tumbling breasts and thick coils of white hair' who is thrown into the holding cell with an arrested Smith, and who vomits 'copiously on the floor' just in front of him (*NEF*, pp. 261–2).

Naturalism however is or was more than a totalising interpretive horizon and an empiricising insistence: it should be able to use the latter to fill the former, to be rich with the detail which comes from describing relationships as much as things.[20] There are few relationships *in Nineteen Eighty-Four* which are not necessary for the plot and those that do enter – the Parsons family, the gossips and fighters in the 'prole-district' streets and pub, the woman with brawny arms who sings outside the window of the flat above Charrington's shop – are there to exemplify something which exists abstractly and independently of their particular existences: the entry of the state into the family as children become spies; the proles' absorption in the routines of their own lives, an absorption which divorces them from history as surely as the Party divorces history from truth; that in the bodies of the proles, their brawny physicality, there may yet be hope for a different future.

Our third-person narrator is fixed on Smith, that 'bright cold day in April' sets him in time as his slipping 'through the doors of Victory Mansions' sets him in space, and it is as the object of the narrative that the style pursues Smith, literalising the experience of the regime – and of opposition to it – through the immediate engagement of 'Sight, hearing, feeling and smell … Winston's senses; it is his fatigue as he climbs the stairs'.[21] For Roger Fowler, Orwell's style 'has dual characteristics: it is both "realistic" and "psychological"', with the latter tying Orwell's seven novels to 'the modern mode of fiction':

> the use of conventions such as stream of consciousness, free direct and free indirect thought, verbs of perception and of mental process, to highlight the character as source of experience and of thought.[22]

In a novel torn between the reality and even sanctity of individual interiority, of the individual mind or psyche as *real*, and the simultaneous and equal necessity of the external world as factual, Orwell's style registers a tension. For 'two plus two' to equal four, there must be a mind capable of apprehending it as such; for there to be a mind capable of apprehending it as such, two plus two must remain equal to four. Smith is not an unusual type of character in Orwell's fiction: from Flory of *Burmese Days* to Comstock and Bowling of *Keep the Aspidistra Flying* and *Coming Up for Air*, Orwell uses as a focaliser, an outsider-figure, unhappy but disillusionedly so, objective or objectivising.

None of these earlier characters needed to act as the point of resistance for a regime resting on the premise that not only the past but the person is mutable, changeable not from within but from without. The earlier protagonists changed, or failed to change and despised themselves for it, 'organically', as part of their adjustment to a social order they saw no alternative to but adjustment. Their integration was willed and in willing it each self held on to some core of autonomy even as autonomy's appearance had to be sacrificed to the always gendered conventions of a social life hell-bent on ensuring that the private realm, the realm of a feminised 'respectability' if done right, acts as the end-point for a model of the subject as autonomous.

Thrown into opposition to the regime (rather than allowed to will a surrender to it), to act as the narrative structure which can tell of the regime, reveal it to be not a normality but an edifice, Smith's very ordinariness becomes exaggerated, the reliance on his sensibility more 'modernist' in Fowler's terms than the other novels' protagonists yet pushed always to empiricise, to become external even in his pain. The surprising emptiness of the diary, introduced in the very first few pages of the text, and its disappearance from Part Two and Part Three, suggest something of the realm of experience the novel's style cannot tolerate.

In the dystopias from the first half of the twentieth century, books, or more specifically the reading of them, have a dual purpose: to register the unnaturalness of the regime in some form, and to provide information on how the regime casts itself as normative: how it relies on some immanent force in history or in human nature as its premise, either blotting out that premise and thereby altering human nature, or pandering to that premise and thereby sustaining itself.

There are two books given a function in Oceania: 'The Theory and Practice of Oligarchical Collectivism', and the strange fitful entries in the second book, Smith's diary. Here I want to use the latter to bring to the surface some of the more knotty problems to do with language and consciousness, and the barriers to making these 'values' hostile to the regime. 'Totalitarianism' relies on these as much as Smith does, and for both history is the goal. The Party wants it textualised and that text to be hyper-mobile, erased and rewritten at will; Smith wants it less law-like than bone-like, dense with an immoveable reality which can yet be used to tell the terrible present of its falseness.

For both, language and thought are the mediators between subject and structure, between experience and knowledge. The Party goes to war on language with Newspeak, the narrative goes to war on the Party with plain speak. For the former, 'doublethink' names and erases the mutability of the past and of the present. For the narrative, 'facts' oppose doublethink in the sense of revealing it at work though they fail to ground an opposition to it as that opposition would have to be epistemological; and where the Party has 'doublethink', Smith refuses an epistemology because a way of seeing – the novum's desired way – not only reliant on facts but composed of facts, cannot tangle too intimately with a subject lest it become *only* a way of seeing.

The diary is both old and beautiful, its 'smooth creamy paper, a little yellowed by age … of a kind that had not been manufactured for at least forty years past' (*NEF*, p. 8). It is the first thing Smith buys from what he later discovers to be Charrington's shop. It is a luxury item, illicit to own – as is the buying of it ('"dealing on the free market", it was called') and expensive at the price of $2.50. As an old thing and a beautiful thing, the book which becomes the diary bears the imprint of the past, unknowable and yet there, materially present in its ineffable and unspeaking form. And that form resolves itself into the act of writing, a much older act by the time Smith takes up his pen to write 'April 4th, 1984':

> The pen was an archaic instrument, seldom used even for signatures, and he had procured one, furtively and with some difficulty, simply because of a feeling that the beautiful creamy paper deserved to be written on with a real nib instead of being scratched with an ink-pencil … To mark the paper was the decisive act. (*NEF*, p. 9)

Mark it he does, and goes on to discover in marking it an answer to his question: for 'whom … was he writing this diary?' By the time he closes his first entry, he can write:

To the future or to the past, to a time when thought is free, when men are different from one another and do not live alone – to a time when truth exists and what is done cannot be undone.

From the age of uniformity, from the age of solitude, from the age of Big Brother, from the age of doublethink – greetings!' (*NEF*, p. 32)

The introduction of the diary should have been a key moment for the function of Winston Smith in the novel, the introduction of a space for some temporal and experiential heterogeneity. Through writing it, through it becoming a form for his subjectivity, the novel could have provided Smith with a place where he interpellated himself, spreading out as first-person experience the fear and the frustrations, the hate and the doubt felt as a subject of this unwanted world. The entries in the diary are few and are as sparse as Smith's own body, however. By Part Two the diary has disappeared, its role taken by Julia who now acts as interlocutor, the union with Smith a space where both can be subjectively free and honest for however little time there is left to them. In Part Three, Julia's place is taken in turn by O'Brien and freedom finishes in the torture and the breaking of Smith.

In the eight chapters which make up Part One, the diary is written in four times, in the eighth chapter, it is opened but not written in. The first entry is the description not of Smith's feelings or even his thoughts but of the scenes from the war film he had watched the previous evening, and the response of the 'woman down in the prole part of the house ... kicking up a fuss and shouting they didnt oughter of showed it not in front of kids they didnt it aint right not in front of kids' (*NEF*, p. 11) before she is turned out by the police.

The novel then returns to the third person as Smith wonders 'what had made him pour out this stream of rubbish', and the text gives to the third person the narration of the important memory of the 'Two Minutes Hate' from his morning in the Ministry. The memory is important as it establishes more detail about the regime, introducing Goldstein, the supposed resistance, and the love of Big Brother. The ease with which hatred is whipped up when directed and collective, and the simultaneous ease with which the object of hatred twitches and flicks (from Goldstein to Big Brother, to Julia) is important both in the novel and to later readings of the novel but it is not dwelt upon here. Instead the two-minute hate is narrated as the setting, the informative and detailed scenic occasion for the memory Smith is recalling, the momentary catching of O'Brien's eye:

For a second, two seconds, they had exchanged an equivocal glance, and that was the end of the story. But even that was a memorable event in the locked loneliness in which one had to live. (*NEF*, p. 21)

Following the memory, Smith does write but what he writes is a slogan: 'DOWN WITH BIG BROTHER' (*NEF*, p. 21), repeated four more times. This is writing which happened 'as though by automatic action'. The act of memory is given to the third-person narrator, the act of opposition to Smith's almost 'automatic' self. By the time the first diary entry has finished, Smith is writing '[t]o the future or to the past' (*NEF*, p. 32), the diary not a repository for his self but a reaching outward to a reader not from the age of uniformity and of solitude.

The only significant entry in the diary in terms of an increase and intensification of subjectivity is the entry in chapter VI which tells of Smith's memory of the purchase of sex from a 'prole' woman, a not infrequent 'lapse' during the nearly eleven years he has been separated from his wife. This is the first diary entry to make use of the 'I', to centre Smith as subject of his own telling.[23] The diary entry is itself sparse, the contextualisation and interpretation of the event left to the third-person narrator. For example:

> It was three years ago. It was on a dark evening, in a narrow side-street near one of the big railway stations. She was standing near a doorway in the wall, under a street lamp that hardly gave any light. She had a young face, painted very thick. It was really the paint that appealed to me, the whiteness of it, like a mask, and the bright red lips. Party women never paint their faces. There was nobody else in the street, and no telescreens. She said two dollars. I –
> For the moment it was too difficult to go on. He shut his eyes and pressed his fingers against them, trying to squeeze out the vision that kept recurring ... Your worst enemy, he reflected, was your own nervous system. (*NEF*, p. 73)

The diary entry continues in this vein, each fragment of an entry breaking off as Smith cannot go on, to end with the reason he finds it difficult to write, the woman was 'old' and he is ashamed: 'When I saw her in the light she was quite an old woman, fifty years old at least. But I went ahead and did it just the same' (*NEF*, p. 79). The fierce empiricism with which his repulsion is narrated, the cycling through the sequence of his horror at the prole woman's smell ('an odour compounded of bugs and dirty clothes and villainous cheap scent'), to his horror of his wife Katharine's beauty, stupidity, orthodoxy and rigidity during sex, is all taken outside the diary entry. Where there should be subjectivity, there are only facts, where there is subjectivity, it too is a fact, the externalised details of an almost physicalised sensibility, a sensibility at one remove from its owner: 'He saw himself standing there in the dim lamplight, with the smell of bugs and cheap scent in his nostrils, and in his heart a feeling of defeat and resentment which even at that moment was mixed up with the thought of Katharine's white body, frozen for ever by the hypnotic power of the Party' (*NEF*, pp. 78–9).

History in 'The Theory and Practice of Oligarchical Collectivism'

The diary opens a space for the subject to have his own history, for the present to meet the past in personal recall or the temporal fluidity of memory, but this space is only opened. It is not used. The urgency and wide political significance of memory are established elsewhere, with means other than a subjectivity. There are two possible reasons for why Orwell chose to leave the diary so empty of Smith's self. Thematically, memory, even at the subconscious level of musing or day-dreaming, is dependent on the collective resources of the extant language. The Smith of the diary entries is descriptive or angry or exclamatory: his language spurts out of him rather than unfolding any interior landscapes of unease, longing and mourning. The latter are given textual weight, just not in the diary.

It is the task of the depersonalised and depersonalising third-person narrative to establish – or even better *to fix* – subjective meaning, not the task of the subject himself. Smith does not have access to that level of language, to give the resources of memory to a self, to a subjectivity with all the explosiveness of memory's volatility and the uncontrollable depths of fantasy and wishes. That explosiveness of memory and its shaky reaching for truths enriched or troubled by 'Mother', by longing and need, are all taken outside of Smith's interiority and are given back to him with their arbitrariness or volatility ruled out.

That there is no definite narrative given to the events of Smith's childhood and to the fate of his mother lends the novel a depth of sadness which is summoned up almost without textual effort. That the past is so remote, so lost to him, lends Smith an ineradicable aura of existential pain and suffering, one which needs little in the way of comment or even of consciousness. But the lostness of that past means that, for the narration, it can work as a repository of more than private lives or the possibilities of private lives however. One dream of Smith's, the early dream of his Mother, ends with Julia – at this point known only as the 'girl with the dark hair' – throwing her clothes aside, a bodily freedom which

> seemed to annihilate a whole culture, a whole system of thought, as though Big Brother and the Party and the Thought Police could all be swept into nothingness by a single splendid movement of the arm. That too was a gesture belonging to the ancient time. Winston woke up with the word 'Shakespeare' on his lips. (*NEF*, p. 36)

Unless Orwell is here parodying Huxley's *Brave New World*, the narrative overshoots itself. The addition of 'Shakespeare' to Smith's lips draws attention to just how much the 'dream' is not presented as much as it is interpreted, used as a place to project all the novel's understanding of the 'ancient time' closed to Smith.

Secondly, though 'Orwellian' has become a term associated with the description of power exercised in a particular way (all-encompassing or threatening to be, dishonest, coercive, intrusive) and of the ideological positions used to defend or legitimise such uses of power, Orwell himself as a writer has a peculiar aversion to using the term 'ideology'. In *Nineteen Eighty-Four* itself, there is a consistent squeezing out of room for ambiguity by the novel's own style, a push to render even emotions as thing-like, if not factual then carrying some force akin to factuality in its establishment of an objectivity in no need of interpretation.[24] Smith's body is one such externalising instrument, the slowness with which it moves up the stairs of Victory Mansions witness to his unhappiness and ill health, or the initial hesitations in his response to Julia's body an awkward voicing of his bewildered pride and shock at what is happening.[25] This reliance on the body as a speaking device makes the scenes of torture all the more unbearable as even that is taken from Smith, broken just as his mind was.

This I think is why the 'Book' is present and is given such a cohering task by the novel: it provides a non-subjective mode of presentation of change and its causes as if these were historical laws. Oceania becomes inevitable instead of inexplicable. The history which enters the novel through the readings of two chapters from 'The Theory and Practice of Oligarchical Collectivism' presents history itself as only empirical, known by its results. As such, there is no polemic here, no argument or interpretation, but a record of events, their causes and their consequences. This is 'the Book' which is purportedly to serve as the unifying text of the opposition, the underground organisation called 'the Brotherhood'. Yet there is no opposition in it: the Party and those who wish to overthrow it agree on the meanings and the shape of the historical 'cycles' that have brought both to be where they are. 'The Book' in other words is just history, history in some pure sense as knowledge. As this knowledge is banned in Oceania, its value is incalculable, the book is as precious as encounters with it are rare.[26]

Reaching far behind the regime of Ingsoc and its counterparts, the Book describes the historiographic discovery that that history is cyclical, and the description of a dilemma for this cyclical law in the shape of something which would arrest the cycle's movement and initiate a new history: this is what is promised and threatened by 'progress'. The latter, in the form of 'science and technology' (*NEF*, p. 218), has made scarcity itself redundant. Technological developments – 'the machine' (*NEF*, p. 219) – have enabled the production of such a surplus of goods that now plenty, and with it what the text understands as equality, are within reach. This is the premise of the

Party's existence, to prevent the realisation of that promise, to stop that new history from beginning.

The level of industrialisation reached by the late nineteenth century had already interrupted the cyclical rhythm of historical change. The absence of agents in the quotation which follows (so unlike the prose of Trotsky to whose position Goldstein's is frequently compared) is notable but not surprising:

> The primary aim of modern warfare ... is to use up the products of the machine without raising the general standard of living. Ever since the end of the nineteenth century, the problem of what to do with the surplus of consumption goods has been latent in industrial society ... From the moment when the machine first made its appearance it was clear to all thinking people that the need for human drudgery, and therefore to a great extent for human inequality, had disappeared. (*NEF*, pp. 218–19)[27]

Oceania, and its sister 'super-states', Eastasia and Eurasia, are states beyond yet incorporate ideology; well beyond capital but have abstracted and retained the mode of exploitation peculiar to capital but without market competition, the 'free' selling of labour power by a majority working-class population. Each super-state possesses a state apparatus which is identical with a political party and which owns everything, and which uses that everything to wage a war which has as its immediate purpose the prolongation of war, and the prevention of an 'equality' materially in reach. As states, they are machines for rationalising life. Now, however, rationalisation has as its purpose the destruction rather than the creation of value – 'to use up the products of the machine'.

> The problem was how to keep the wheels of industry turning without increasing the real wealth of the world. Goods must be produced but they must not be distributed. And in practice the only way of achieving this was by continuous warfare. (*NEF*, p. 220)

War is the most efficient destroyer of labour time and is simultaneously the most efficient producer of the fear and rage seemingly necessary to ensure the acceptance of a social order permanently on a war-footing. The three super-states which organise the whole are without differentiating beliefs or values themselves: 'the three philosophies are barely distinguishable, and the social systems which they support are not distinguishable at all' (*NEF*, p. 226).

In one combination or another,

> these three super-states are permanently at war ... It is a warfare of limited aims between combatants who are unable to destroy one another, have no material cause for fighting and are not divided by any genuine ideological

difference. This is not to say that either the conduct of war, or the prevailing attitude towards it, has become less bloodthirsty or more chivalrous. On the contrary, war hysteria is continuous and universal in all countries ... But in a physical sense war involves very small numbers of people, mostly highly trained specialists, and causes comparatively few casualties. (*NEF*, p. 215)

Each state possesses nuclear weapons but by an unspoken agreement knows that they will never be used. The 'atomic war of the nineteen-fifties' was sufficient to persuade the respective rulers that permanent warfare requires less lethal weapons (*NEF*, p. 218). For this book inside the novel, there is a logic to the presentation of these super-states – not to their non-'philosophies' but to their emergence and their securing of what is called here 'power'. The logic is a comparative one premised on what the new rulers learned from history: the ancient and enduring division of humanity into 'the High, the Middle and the Low'; the irreconcilable 'aims' of each group; the regular eruption of the 'Middle, who enlist the Low on their side by pretending to them that they are fighting for liberty and justice' (*NEF*, p. 231); and the return to equilibrium as the once-Middle become the new High for a period, and the Low, perpetually credulous and perpetually disappointed, are returned to their old position of servitude. By the beginning of the twentieth century, 'equality', so long the veil for duping 'the Low', had become 'technically possible'. By ensuring that its possibility was perpetually postponed, the new 'High' group could ensure the arrest of history and the continuity of their own domination.

> As early as the beginning of the twentieth century, human equality had become technically possible ... there was no longer any real need for class distinctions or for large differences of wealth. In earlier ages, class distinctions had been not only inevitable but desirable. Inequality was the price of civilisation. With the development of machine production, however, the case was altered ... [F]rom the point of view of the new groups who were on the point of seizing power, human equality was no longer an ideal to be striven after, but a danger to be averted. (*NEF*, p. 234)

By the early twentieth century, 'all the main currents of political thought were authoritarian': there was a decade of war and revolution across the globe, the victors of which were the movements of Ingsoc and its counterparts in Eastasia and Eurasia (*NEF*, p. 234).[28] Across the world, the new 'High' took their places and set about ensuring that they would never leave them, that the 'hierarchical society' no historical formation had ever been without would live on for ever. The new 'High' are without ideology of their own, are without any thirst for wealth or status or prestige. Compared with the ruling classes of previous epochs, they are 'hungrier for pure power, and, above all, more conscious of what they were doing and more intent on crushing opposition' (*NEF*, p. 235). This 'new aristocracy' is an eccentric assemblage of the emergent professions of the early twentieth century: 'made up for the most part of bureaucrats, scientists, technicians, trade-union organisers, publicity experts, sociologists, teachers, journalists and professional politicians' (*NEF*, p. 235). Apart from their non-organic composition as a class, their negative unity, what consolidates this group is their determination to wipe the concept of equality and with it any possibility of opposition out of the English language.

Smith's reading of the book ends just as the text he is reading embarks on an explanation of 'why': 'why should human equality be averted? … What is the motive for this huge, accurately planned effort to freeze history at a particular moment of time?' (*NEF*, p. 246). The Book is no more detailed than this but it is enough. Upon reading it, Smith is reassured: he understands 'how' the world operates. It is no longer inexplicable. That now is the novel's premise. This is the present, that was the past. A 'why' is peeled away from the knowledge given but it is in effect unnecessary, its answer buried in the possibility of the regime itself. Even though it leaves him asking 'why', the Book has 'systematised the knowledge that he possessed already', situating his sanity as his opposition to this regime, and situating the reader as knowing now the truth of the regime, *how* it works, a truth impossible to resist within the confines of the text's vocabulary except on Smith's subjectively skeletal terms. Upon reading the Book, Smith 'knew better than before that he was not mad … There was truth and there was untruth, and if you clung to the truth even against the whole world, you were not mad' (*NEF*, p. 247). The 'truth' however is that the world of Oceania exists, that it was not just possible but realised in the terrible events of the twentieth century.

Before going on to conclude by exploring the narrative consequences of excluding memory and including history as a summary, in other words before moving to interpret the dystopia's *peculiar attachment to history simultaneously with its erasure of history*, it should be pointed out that the question of 'why', although put in a positivist manner which assumes that it could have been answered by the chronicle given in 'the Book' if Smith had had the opportunity of reading further, is answered only when O'Brien enters the text in Part Three, his explication there fusing personal and chronicle narratives, the Book becoming more real somehow as its logic is repeated and ornamented by O'Brien's dialogic defeat of Smith in the scenes which blend torture and conversation. The answer to the 'why' question is performed by O'Brien himself – never individual, always the voice of the Party yet he individualises the Party, makes it possible in narrative terms – and is as powerful as his dramatisation of cruelty is but is still no answer at all: 'power-hunger', an end in itself, a pathology. What the novel calls 'totalitarianism' is a system of rule which is pathological, which is inexplicable without this and yet remains inexplicable with this:

> The Party seeks power entirely for its own sake. We are not interested in the good of others; we are interested solely in power. Not wealth or luxury or long life or happiness: only power, pure power ... Power is not a means, it is an end. One does not establish a dictatorship in order to safeguard a revolution; one makes the revolution in order to establish the dictatorship. The object of persecution is persecution. The object of torture is torture. The object of power is power. (*NEF*, pp. 301–2)

What makes the regime of the Party possible is the state, the modern centralised state, but, for the novel, power is not something to be historicised or even questioned but which just is, a terrible thing, an atrocious thing but thing-like all the same.[29] There has always been a group in 'power', 'power' there has always been. What power is other than power over 'the Low' and 'the Middle' is of no importance. The Party took 'power' and will use this power to perpetuate power for ever. This mystification of power should make the novel incomprehensible but the combined naturalism of its style and the incorporation of a historical narrative which posits the party and oligarchical collectivism itself as the inheritance of Communism, ensures a potent legibility.

Conclusion: negative commitment

Writing in 1984 of Orwell's novel, Raymond Williams noted the 'peculiar unreality of the projection' of a world divided into three super-states permanently at war and permanently in power.[30] His task in this essay on Orwell, a late continuation of an argument with Orwell Williams began as early as the 1956 essay, 'Science Fiction', was to reassess both Orwell's 'vision' and the legacy of the novel. Grappling with the 'difficulty of the form' of *Nineteen Eighty-Four*, William identifies three narrative layers at work. Firstly, the naturalistic level of the world as experienced by Smith, the 'infrastructure, immediately recognisable from Orwell's other fiction, in which the hero-victim moves through a squalid world'; secondly, the level of the Book, one described by Williams as the method of a 'historical and political essay' which gives a 'structure of argument, indeed of anticipations'; and finally, the 'superstructure ... in which, by a method ranging from fantasy to satire and parody, the cruelty and repression of the society are made to appear at once ludicrous and savagely absurd'.[31]

Williams spends most of his essay unpacking the second layer, the 'central structure of argument, this element of reasoned anticipation', articulated in distilled form in the Book and in the novel's 'Appendix' but generative of certainties throughout the novel. I agree with Williams's emphasis on the centrality of this textual register, this central structure 'on which, at the level of ideas, the book is founded'.[32] But it cannot be right to thread those ideas through Orwell's own extra-textual 'ideas of how the world was going and could go'. For Williams, that is, the formal (and political) difficulties introduced into the novel by the presence of the Book's structure of ideas about historical change, require that a critical reading detour into Orwell's earlier or contemporaneous work – critically his engagement with James Burnham – before returning to why the novel's structure of ideas so fatally occluded not only the historicity but the possibility of all those, including Orwell himself, who fought for better worlds, keeping 'the strength to imagine, as well as to work for, human dignity, freedom and peace'.[33]

Whilst not disagreeing with Williams's wider analysis of Orwell's understanding of Burnham's miserable theses in particular, I do not think it useful to supplement *Nineteen Eighty-Four* with Orwell. To do so is in effect to miss – by covering over – the novel's ideological power, the potency of the radical ambivalence which its overall narrative structure of negative commitment creates: a commitment to a 'truth' which cannot be filled with any positive content but which can because of this be mobilised to enable positive readings from political positions as different as Friedrich Hayek's and Storm Jameson's.[34]

If we strip out Orwell from the process of interpretation, however, we cannot have recourse to the ways in which Orwell did not believe the premises, explicit and tacit, of the history presented in *Nineteen Eighty-Four*. One of the sentences chosen by Williams as indicating something Orwell clearly 'did not believe' can work here to provide a way into an interpretation of the novel's narrative as a whole when Orwell is removed from it. The Book's Chapter 1, 'Ignorance Is Strength', contains the most direct exposition of the Book's (and arguably the novel's) philosophy of history. It begins with a conscious echo of and rejection of the argument of *The Communist Manifesto*'s opening chapter:

> Throughout recorded time, and probably since the end of the Neolithic Age, there have been three kinds of people in the world, the High, the Middle, and the Low … Even after enormous upheavals and seemingly irrevocable changes, the same pattern has always reasserted itself, just as a gyroscope will always return to equilibrium, however far it is pushed one way or the other. (*NEF*, p. 231)[35]

In the recurrent struggles between these three groups, a singular 'struggle which is the same in its main outlines recur[ring] over and over again' (*NEF*, p. 210), the Low function as ballast, as weight tempted to fall in behind one side or the other but never moving upward from their own posi-tion. It is not the static or de-historicising nature of this movement which Williams objects to but the removal of any progress towards equality in the processes of the movement:

> 'No advance in wealth, no softening of manners, no reform or revolution has ever brought human equality a millimetre nearer.'
>   This is, as written, such obvious nonsense that the status of the whole argument becomes questionable. If this were really true, there would be no basis for calling Ingsoc a 'perversion'; it would be yet one more example of an inevitable, even innate process. Clearly Orwell did not believe this.[36]

It matters not whether Orwell believed it, however. This novel dramatises such a lack of 'equality': equality's only existence in the past is a fairy-story to tempt those who believe in it into some movement. Its existence in the present – the textual present of the Book – an abstract possibility of realisa-tion now that industrial modes of production have made the realm of plenty a feasible proposition. As with *Brave New World*, there is a buried utopia in *Nineteen Eighty-Four* but the cost of its existing at all – as historical yet never realised promise (that, 'as early as the beginning of the twenti-eth century, human equality had become technically possible') – is that it should stay buried, not just one more value or mode of life made impossible by the dystopian regime but the negative reason for the regime's existence.[37] Technically, there is 'no basis' for calling Ingsoc a perversion in terms of its structural existence as a hierarchical society. It is a 'perversion' only in the methods it deploys, and they are deployed to stop history – the regime is itself historical in so far as it imitates the typical cycle of usurpation to found itself but to keep itself, to secure itself against any new cycle, against any change, it becomes totalitarian.

If Orwell's own political position (as internally contradictory as that was) is removed from the interpretation, there is no argument – nor any possibility of an argument given the airlessness of the Book's insistence on an expository style which brooks no opposition – in *Nineteen Eighty-Four*'s internal Book. Additionally, the meaning of 'equality' used by the Book has only the negative meaning of the absence of a 'hierarchical society'. As history has been only a succession of hierarchies, and as history is now frozen, there has indeed been no 'equality'. The fuller paragraph from which Williams excerpts may be useful here:

> Of the three groups, only the Low are never even temporarily successful in achieving their aims. It would be an exaggeration to say that throughout history there has been no progress of a material kind. Even today, in a period of decline, the average human being is physically better off than he was a few centuries ago. But no advance in wealth, no softening of manners, no reform

or revolution has ever brought human equality a millimetre nearer. From the point of view of the Low, no historic change has ever meant much more than a change in the name of their masters. (*NEF*, p. 232)

Williams's interpretation is one which struggles, in the moment of the 'celebrations' of Orwell in Britain in 1984, to pull the novel out of the embrace of those who saw in it only an anti-socialism. In the process of his reassessment, however, the genre is lost. The novel must be read but when Orwell is the interpretative key, when his non-fictional works are used to smooth out the novel's strangeness and harshness, what it is as a dystopia is lost. Take the notion of 'equality' Williams puzzles over: its possible realisation haunts the classic dystopia as a genre because the genre began in an era when the premise of utopian thinking was that an end to the era of material scarcity had come into view. This was a development of technological and of industrial capacity but was one which also found political expression in both utopian movements, and in the forms of international Socialism. Alongside alterations in the state's relationship with civil society before the First World War, and the emergence of a culture industry which also revealed the porosity of the borders between private and public spheres, the socialisation or deprivatisation of leisure time, this moment or conjuncture was one which could create a sort of slow panic in intellectuals. An increased scope for the state could only be thought of as threatening catastrophe. As E.M. Forster pithily encapsulated the perceived potential of any centralised planning or collective models to collapse into tyranny, '[p]rogrammes mean pogroms'.[38]

Orwell's novel commits to a world in which the possibility of 'equality' has been defeated. The forces which make 'equality' theoretically or even 'technically' possible are the same forces which generate political or intellectual patterns and habits which will deny that possibility. That Orwell makes the latter so much more visible, forceful than the former, that the former is barely visible at all, is why his commitment can be termed 'negative' and what any exploration of the novel needs to work towards understanding. That negative commitment in *Nineteen Eighty-Four* takes the form of an anti-socialism which for Orwell may have been a way of disentangling a clean or 'democratic' form of socialism from Stalinism but for the novel is just an anti-socialism without its antagonist as necessary partner:

Socialism, a theory which appeared in the early nineteenth century and was the last link in a chain of thought stretching back to the slave rebellions of antiquity, was still deeply infected by the Utopianism of past ages. But in each variant of Socialism that appeared from about 1900 onwards the aim of establishing liberty and equality was more and more openly abandoned. (*NEF*, p. 233)

Abandoned, that is, when, viewed as a merely technical possibility, it had become realisable. Negative commitment is that commitment – not to the things lost or destroyed – but to those which become unimaginable in the dystopia. The world put forward is wrong because it has defeated the possibility of something which has never had any historical existence, and because it abolishes a truth which the novel itself cannot name except as the hard limits of fact.

Orwell wrote a novel in which his commitment to warning of the vulnerability of truth, its tendency to dissolve when subjected to political contests, overcame his own political commitment to democratic socialism. The novel has only the negative commitment enabled or demanded by the regime it despises. Stalinism (and fascism) take their place in the prehistory of Oceania as the naive oligarchies of the past, stumbling backwards towards that total regime change only the Party clear-sightedly wills and implements: the 'German Nazis and the Russian Communists came very close to us in their methods, but they never had the courage to recognise their own motives' (*NEF* p. 302). Behind them lie the tumult of successive opportunistic revolutions, the modern ideals of equality and freedom only ever partly believed in by emergent rulers who yet always successfully instrumentalised those ideals to move the Earth to their needs. Socialism, in this understanding of historical change or the constituent processes involved in large-scale social change, is only the dream of defeated reformers, specified only to the extent that it is absent in a regime designed to be 'the exact opposite of the stupid hedonistic Utopias that the old reformers imagined' (*NEF*, p. 306).

These 'Utopian' dreams cannot however be set down beside Oceania as some alternative to it. As abstract as they are, they too are tainted by the intellectual rejection of liberty and equality that the novel selects as the critical forerunner to the political elimination of even the promise of both: the variants of socialism the novel identifies as having abandoned equality and liberty are given a precise historical period – from about 1900 onwards – the period in which international and national socialist movements began to reach out to parliamentary power or to push for or achieve revolutionary power.

Capitalism has an even fainter presence in the text than any socialist movement, its absence indeed renders these latter phantasmagorical. Capitalism is entirely removed from any causal or structural role in the movements which shape history: these movements are themselves without antagonists as the structure of society has been static in all its guises, hierarchical always, open only to one 'class' usurping another at semi-regular intervals: the 'class' at the top is all that changes, the structure does not, and the upheaval which must be necessary to bring about even this limited replacement is passed over in silence.

The novel is anti-'totalitarian', that is its commitment. It casts that whole elaborate world into being – gives it all the definite details for such a world to exist as a fully fledged fiction – so as to set its face, and its readers, against it. What holds it and us against it is the strength of the novel's anger and despair, and these exist only locked on to the brutality which is the regime. The formal structures of the novel lock the shape of its antagonism into the revolt of Winston Smith against the regime. The negativity of the novel does not lie in the absoluteness of Smith's defeat, however, but in his own imagination of his own defeat, the inevitability of it. Negative commitment is here the shape of this opposition: on one side the regime, its success, on the other, the man, just him, his rage and pain and despair. There is nothing outside of him which can be figured in any positive way. He does not stand for truth or freedom or equality but against their absence or elimination. The novel has no content to give to his rebellion except the sheer fact of it.

There is a moment in Part One which comes close to widening Smith's pain, to materialising it as intolerable suffering, a socially wide and deep suffering, and a suffering which is not necessary. Sitting in the filthy canteen of the Ministry of Truth, with only inadequate food and sour drink in his belly, and a broken cigarette in his hand, Smiths listens to the 'fabulous statistics' which pour out of the telescreen. Production of all goods is up, everything is increasing – food, clothing, housing, furniture, everything 'except disease, crime and insanity' (*NEF*, p. 68).

With the unavoidable babble of lies in his ears, staring at the muck left on the table he sits at, Smith meditates 'on the physical texture of life':

> Had it always been like this? Had food always tasted like this? ... Always in your stomach and in your skin there was a sort of protest, a feeling that you had been cheated of something that you had a right to. It was true that he had no memories of anything greatly different ... And though, of course, it grew worse as one's body aged, was it not a sign that this was *not* the natural order of things, if one's heart sickened at the discomfort and dirt and scarcity ...?
> (*NEF*, p. 69 – original italics)

Smith here suffers or reflects on his own suffering and knows it to be wrong. You do not need the past to know present pains. The daily deprivations felt by his body an index not so much of the falsities of the official statistics but of their utter irrelevance. Suffering is always historical but it does not need history to know itself as suffering. Orwell switches the tracks, however, and directs Smith's consciousness of suffering back not only to memory but to the collective mute memories, the necessarily unconscious memories the text will later embody in 'the proles': 'Why should one feel it to be intolerable unless one had some kind of ancestral memory that things had once

been different?' (*NEF*, p. 69). The 'proles', the 'disregarded', have the force
to alter history but not the mind. They can open history up to change again
and they have captured in the very bones of their bodies a time from before
the regime:

> *If there is hope*, wrote Winston, *it lies in the proles*.
>   If there was hope, it *must* lie in the proles, because only there, in those
> swarming disregarded masses, 85 per cent of the population of Oceania, could
> the force to destroy the Party ever be generated. (*NEF*, p. 80, original italics)

They themselves are outside of history, however, with no way in: 'until they
become conscious they will never rebel, and until after they have rebelled,
they cannot become conscious.' (*NEF*, p. 81). Being outside of history, they
retain the power to feel, to act on instinct or impulse, to be without orthodoxy: they were

> governed by private loyalties which they did not question ... They were not
> loyal to a party or a country or an idea, they were loyal to one another ... The
> proles had stayed human. They had not become hardened inside. They had
> held on to the primitive emotions which he himself had to re-learn by con-
> scious effort. (*NEF*, p. 191)

It is not their class but their humanity, a remnant rather than a force, which
over-distinguishes 'the proles'. They are not the middle term which might
mediate between the text's almost cartoonishly rigid polarity of self and
social order, overturning by dynamising the self, allowing the social that is
within the self, the suffering which defines it and the potential to recognise
that suffering immanent within it, to express itself in recognition or even
in solidarity. The 'proles' are confined to act as a repository for something
only abstractly collective – the price of which is being outside the social
movement of history altogether – something 'primitive' or 'ancestral' or
ancient. What that is is buried deep in their collective flesh, in their fecun-
dity and strength, in their joy in food and drink and carousing. These are
'people who had never learned to think but who were storing up in their
hearts and bellies and muscles the power that would one day overturn the
world' (*NEF*, p. 251).

> The birds sang, the proles sang, the Party did not sing. All round the world, in
> London and New York, in Africa and Brazil and in the mysterious, forbidden
> lands beyond the frontiers, in the streets of Paris and Berlin, in the villages of
> the endless Russian plain, in the bazaars of China and Japan – everywhere
> stood the same solid unconquerable figure, made monstrous by work and
> childbearing, toiling from birth to death and still singing.
>   Out of those mighty loins a race of conscious beings must one day come.
> You were the dead: theirs was the future.

But you could share in that future if you kept alive the mind as they kept alive the body, and passed on the secret doctrine that two plus two makes four. (*NEF*, p. 252)

Between the empiricism which dramatises Smith's refusal to acquiesce – his reliance on a truth which can be presented only as an immediately comprehensible fact or a transparent recording of such a fact – and the instrumentalised yet oddly absolute idealism of O'Brien – 'Reality exists in the human mind, and nowhere else' (*NEF*, p. 285) – mind itself as a concept is stretched to the point where it breaks off all contact with either an externalised reality or the ideal forms from which the former is estranged, and becomes a monadic territory, itself empty but there to be fought over and won or lost. Language and thought suffer the same fate. Newspeak is the name of the damage done to a language which is posited as being once – before the fall – without any silences or erasures of its own, without any historicity, before being so degraded. 'Doublethink' describes the same process in the sphere of thought – a mode of thinking – which must once have been also outside history if it was to be so rational and objective, so clear of history's hierarchies and battles.

Orwell's novel surrenders truth to fact because it cannot bear admitting the social and historical antinomies of belief and of value into a realm of truth which, because it has to be protected from them, has become so vulnerably brittle. The bearer of belief and of value – Smith himself – is a hollow man, not because history has emptied him of some authentic or organic selfhood to fill him with mechanised social 'instincts' but because the economy of the text cannot spare him subjective space: reality cannot be relativised. The fear of talking to others which is a product of the regime is reproduced in the emptiness of the diary, the fear of Smith talking to himself. Even memory for Smith is not granted to him but experienced by him and by the reader as 'involuntary ... outside oneself' (*NEF*, p. 285)

Orwell tries to press prose into having the sensuous particularity of the single human body. The only reliable element Smith has is his body even though he knows it only as so many sites of pain or discomfort. It is not so much that it is his when so much is not as this body is always watched, and as a watched thing can betray him, but rather that it feels things which are undeniable, feels things which are as metaphorical as the text will allow. This body is less a map of the possible – a belly can be full, a cigarette or a glass of gin can be good even if bad, a body can be satisfied in sex or in solitude – than it is important as a sort of history book itself, its pains a register of wrongness, of suffering which suggests that things should not be so. The proles, who are all body, fleshy, fertile, appetitive, should be able to generalise the work that Smith's body does. But they do not: in their bodies too there is history but, absent mind, it is a history unreadable by them.

Notes

1 George Orwell, *Nineteen Eighty-Four* (1949) (London: Penguin, 1987/2003), p. 88. Hereafter quotations from the novel are referenced in the text in parentheses. We should note that the 'endless, hopeless effort to get back into the past' describes not Winston Smith but an earlier, much fainter character, Rutherford, one of the three men identified as being part of the 'original leader[ship] of the Revolution' 'wiped out' by the 'great purges' of the 1960s (*NEF*, p. 87). They are now 'outlaws, enemies, untouchables, doomed to extinction' but they drink in the Chestnut Tree Café. Rutherford, once a 'famous caricaturist, whose brutal cartoons had helped to inflame popular opinion before and during the Revolution', still creates cartoons but these are lifeless.
2 Adorno and Horkheimer, *Dialectic of Enlightenment*, p. 90.
3 For an exploration of Orwell's understanding of language as part of an 'empiricist politics' which had to privilege a shared 'common sense', see Christopher Norris, 'Language, Truth and Ideology: Orwell and the Post-War Left', in Christopher Norris (ed.), *Inside the Myth. Orwell: Views from the Left* (London: Lawrence and Wishart, 1984), p. 244.
4 Jameson, *Late Marxism: Adorno or the Persistence of the Dialectic* (1990) (London; New York: Verso, 2007), p. 123.
5 Ibid., p. 124.
6 For Orwell's empiricism in the context of a specifically British tradition, see Stefan Collini, *Absent Minds: Intellectuals in Britain* (Oxford: Oxford University Press, 2006), pp. 350–74; Neil McLaughlin, 'Orwell, the Academy and the Intellectuals', in John Rodden (ed.), *The Cambridge Companion to George Orwell* (Cambridge: Cambridge University Press, 2007); and David Dwan, *Liberty, Equality, and Humbug: Orwell's Political Ideals* (Oxford: Oxford University Press, 2018), pp 134–56. For readings which complicate what 'empiricism' means for Orwell, see John Michael Roberts, 'Reading Orwell through Deleuze', *Deleuze Studies*, 4:3 (2010), 356–80; and Alex Woloch, *Or Orwell: Writing and Democratic Socialism* (Cambridge, MA: Harvard University Press, 2016).
7 Adorno, 'On Subject and Object' (first published 1969), in Adorno, *Critical Models: Interventions and Catchwords*, trans. Henry W. Pickford (New York: Columbia University Press, 2005), pp. 252–3.
8 'Dare to be a Daniel / Dare to stand alone; / Dare to have a purpose firm, / Dare to make it known' runs the Revivalist hymn Orwell quotes in his 1946 essay, published in *Polemic*, 'The Prevention of Literature'. Orwell, 'The Prevention of Literature', in Sonia Orwell and Ian Angus (eds) *The Collected Essays, Journalism and Letters of George Orwell. Vol. IV In Front of Your Nose, 1945–1950* (London: Secker and Warburg, 1968), pp. 60–1.

9 George Orwell, *The Road to Wigan Pier* (1937) (London: Penguin, 1989), p. 113. For detail on the scope and internal and historical stratification of the English 'middle class' after 1918, see Ross McKibbin, *Classes and Cultures: England 1918–1951* (Oxford: Oxford University Press, 1998), pp. 70–98.
10 Ibid., p. 119. Original italics.
11 Ibid., p. 119. Original italics.
12 Ibid., p. 145.
13 Ibid., p. 147.
14 Ibid., p. 208.
15 See, for example, the classic essay by Franco Moretti on the alienation from language as experienced or studied by a generation of thinkers and writers in the early twentieth century, 'From The Waste Land to the Artificial Paradise' (1983), in Moretti, *Signs Taken for Wonders: Essays in the Sociology of Literary Forms*, trans. Susan Fischer, David Forgacs and David Miller (London; New York: Verso, 1988), pp. 209–39.
16 Theodor Adorno, 'Aldous Huxley and Utopia', *Prisms* (1967), trans. Samuel and Shierry Weber (Cambridge, M: MIT Press, 1983).
17 Raffaella Baccolini and Tom Moylan (eds), *Dark Horizons: Science Fiction and the Dystopian Imagination* (London; New York: Routledge, 2003), p. 5.
18 The novel had as its original title *The Last Man in Europe*. One useful source for this is Bernard Crick's discussion of a 1944 'outline' sketched in one of Orwell's notebooks, in Appendix A of Crick, *George Orwell: A Life* (London: Secker and Warburg, 1980), pp. 407–9. The figure of the 'last man' is not a private one but a pervasive figure across a variety of discursive positions generated by or in anxieties about modernity's 'massifying' tendencies in the late nineteenth and early twentieth centuries. See especially Ishay Landa's chapter 2, 'The Rise of the Last Humans II: the Opposition to Mass Society', in Landa, *Fascism and the Masses: The Revolt against the Last Humans, 1848–1945* (London: Routledge, 2018).
19 Orwell, letter to F.J. Warburg (31 May, 1947), describing the book he was working on as a 'novel about the future – that is, it is in a sense a fantasy, but in the form of a naturalistic novel'. *Collected Essays, Journalism and Letters of George Orwell: Vol. IV In Front of your Nose, 1945–1950* (London: Secker and Warburg, 1968), pp. 329–30.
20 In *The Political Unconscious*, Fredric Jameson describes the 'threefold imperatives' of naturalism as 'authorial depersonalisation, unity of point of view, and restriction to scenic representation' (pp. 90–1). These all could work to define the style of *NEF* but for the unity of the point of view being made out of the split perspectives of the regime and Smith. Because the latter is largely mediated by the third-person anonymising or depersonalising style, that unity is an asymmetric one. Compare Orwell on Gissing, in particular how easy he makes Gissing's style appear: as an author Gissing does not 'commit the faults that really matter. It is always clear what he means, he never "writes for effect", he knows how to keep the balance between *récit* and dialogue and how to make dialogue sound probable while not contrasting too sharply with the prose that surrounds it.' In 'content' he is limited because of 'the smallness of his range of experience' but

his form works perfectly, Orwell, 'George Gissing' (1948) in *Vol. IV In Front of Your Nose*, p. 434.

21 Roger Fowler, *The Language of George Orwell* (Basingstoke; London: Macmillan, 1995), p. 186.

22 Ibid., p. 185, see also pp. 138–9.

23 In the odd first diary entry, the refusal to use an 'I' is almost pointed: 'Last night to the flicks. All war films. One very good one of a ship full of refugees being bombed … Audience much amused by shots of a great huge fat man trying to swim away with a helicopter after him, first you saw him wallowing along in the water like a porpoise, then you saw him through the helicopters gunsights, then he was full of holes …. Then you saw a lifeboat full of children …' (*NEF*, p. 11). It is not until the final movement of the entry's long sentence that Smith refers to himself rather than to the audience he was a part of.

24 Note Orwell's reference to the unpleasant term 'interpret' in his review of Lewis Mumford's 1929 biography of Herman Melville. Orwell writes that Mumford has 'altogether too keen an eye for the inner meaning'. When it comes to *Moby-Dick* in particular, it 'were much better to have discoursed simply on the form, which is the stuff of poetry, and left the "meaning" alone'. What Orwell objects to is 'interpretation' – done 'with absolute thoroughness, it would cause art itself to vanish … For one can only "interpret" a poem by reducing it to an allegory – which is like eating the apple for the pips.' Orwell, 'Review', *New Adelphi*, Mar.–May 1930, in Sonia Orwell and Ian Angus (eds) *The Collected Essays, Journalism and Letters of George Orwell. Vol. 1 An Age Like This, 1920–1940*, p. 19. Orwell's desire to resist or to prohibit interpretation might be one way of reading *Nineteen Eighty-Four*'s rage for objectivity but that such a drive to objectify is so extreme, so brittle, that it ends up turning into its opposite. As we shall see, it is ambivalence which ultimately characterises the novum of this dystopia, not certainty.

25 All the bodies in *Nineteen Eighty-Four* are made to speak for or of things not themselves: Julia gets undressed by tearing her clothes off 'and when she flung them aside it was with that same magnificent gesture by which a whole civilisation seemed to be annihilated' (*NEF*, p. 142); O'Brien's eyes speak to Smith in chapter 1: 'It was as though their two minds had opened and the thoughts were flowing from one into the other through their eyes. "I am with you," O'Brien seemed to be saying to him' (*NEF*, p. 20); but the heaviest investment in bodies comes with description of 'prole' bodies. These do not speak of themselves but are densely packed, univocal, historical scripts which are read by the text.

26 In the political geography of the dystopia's novum, Oceania 'comprises the Americas, the Atlantic islands including the British Isles, Australasia and the Southern portion of Africa' (*NEF*, p. 215). Along with Eurasia and Eastasia, the three 'great super-states' rule the world and the majority of its peoples: the 'splitting up of the world into three great super-states was an event which could be and indeed was foreseen before the middle of the twentieth century. With the absorption of Europe by Russia and of the British Empire by the United States,

two of the three existing powers, Eurasia and Oceania, were already effectively in being' (*NEF*, p. 214). 'Ingsoc' is usually translated as an abbreviation which points to 'English Socialism': the novel describes it thus: in 'Oceania the prevailing philosophy is called Ingsoc, in Eurasia it is called Neo-Bolshevism, and it Eastasia it is called by a Chinese name usually translated as Death-Worship, but perhaps better rendered as Obliteration of the Self ... Actually the three philosophies are barely distinguishable, and the social systems which they support are not distinguishable at all' (*NEF*, p. 226).

27 Only 'overwork' distances the Book's description of social ills from those targeted by William Beveridge's 1942 Report, a founding document of the ideal form of the British welfare state. Beveridge's 'five giants on the road to reconstruction' were want, ignorance, disease, idleness and squalor. Beveridge, *Social Insurance and Allied Services*: Sir William Beveridge *Social Insurance and Allied Services, Command papers Cmd. 6404, Cmd. 6405* (London: HMSO, 1942). The Report's summary is accessible online here: http://filestore.nationalarchives. gov.uk/pdfs/small/cab-66-31-wp-42-547-27.pdf (accessed 22 January 2022).

28 The key movement in the establishment of the regime is given little space; the expropriation of capital is not present as any sort of cause or causal aspect (it could not be an accidental consequence) of any of the 'national wars, civil wars, revolutions and counter-revolutions' that characterised the decade roughly coterminous with the 1940s (if the limited atomic warfare is to have taken place in the 1950s). The Book does mention it but only obliquely: the 'so-called "abolition of private property" which took place in the middle years of the century meant, in effect, the concentration of property in far fewer hands than before: but with this difference, that the new owners were a group instead of a mass of individuals' (*NEF*, p. 236). A 'mass of individuals' is an odd phrase but that uncertainty is a mark of Orwell's writing not about class but about capitalism – itself or its relation to class differences or its existence in imperial forms. Thomas Pynchon notes, in his 2003 introduction to a Penguin reprint of the 1989 edition of the novel, that the 'regime in Oceania seems immune to the lure of wealth' (*NEF*, p. xx). It is hard to resist the temptation to see this as Orwell's immunity, an immunity which though it may have defined his personal life can in his writing be seen as an indifference to what capitalism is, how it works and what is necessary to abolish it. In *Nineteen Eighty-Four*, capitalism no longer exists, 'unquestionably the capitalists had been expropriated' (*NEF*, p. 236) but there is no sign that it had ever existed, not because those signs have been blotted out or written over consciously but because, for the novel as a whole, they are just not important, capitalism does not signify as power does. A similar absence – the end of capitalism but without any transition – is to be found in the classic dystopias of the first half of the twentieth century though not in those dystopian fictions which pull their temporal scene into a much closer proximity to their present – Jack London, Sinclair Lewis or even Rose Macaulay's newly rediscovered 1918 'prophetic comedy', *What Not* (Bath: Handheld Press, 2019).

29 The entry of the state into what would have been thought of as the essentially private (not familial but including domesticity) realm of civil society, a process

or series of processes which cross and recross the political and social developments of 'planning' and the consolidation of these processes in the formalisation
of a 'welfare-state democracy' in the later 1940s, is a motivating factor in the
development of the genre of the dystopia. As with capitalism as a system, Orwell
presumes a consensus in his readers about what the state is, and does not register
in any explicit or sustained way its changing modes of presence in everyday life
in Britain. In his discussion of *Nineteen Eighty-Four*, Phillip E. Wegner touches
on this in his discussion of 'the attenuation of older forms of national class struggle, within the first world at least, that came hand-in-hand with the institution
of a widespread capital-labor *détente* and the emergence of new extensive forms
of consumerism – processes that together form that key aspect of late modernist
culture and society that has been described as the regime of high "Fordism"',
Wegner, *Imaginary Communities: Utopia, the Nation, and the Spatial Histories
of Modernity*, p. 220.
30 Raymond Williams, 'Afterword: *Nineteen Eighty-Four* in 1984', *Orwell*
    (London: Fontana, 1971/ 1984), p. 109.
31 Williams, *Orwell*, p. 96.
32 Williams, *Orwell*, p. 99. It is not fully clear here if Williams is referring to the
    novel itself or to its internal 'Book'. I have chosen to interpret his reference to
    'the book' in this quotation as meaning the novel itself as Williams capitalises
    the Book elsewhere.
33 Williams, *Orwell*, p. 126. On Orwell's engagement with James Burnham, an
    American ex-Trotskyist who theorised a 'realist' approach to power, see Dwan,
    Liberty, Equality, and Humbug: Orwell's Political Ideals, pp. 20–2, and Ian
    Hall, 'A "Shallow Piece of Naughtiness": George Orwell on Political Realism',
    Millennium, 36:2 (2008), 191–215.
34 In the 1956 'Foreword' to a new edition of *The Road to Serfdom* (1944), Hayek
    wrote of how, when his book was initially published, it had 'seemed to many
    almost sacrilege to suggest that fascism and communism are merely variants
    of the same totalitarianism which central control of all economic activity has
    come to produce, [but that] this has now become almost a commonplace.' For
    the change in public opinion, Hayek points to 'the lessons of events and more
    popular discussions of the problem': he names as the 'most effective' of these
    latter as 'undoubtedly George Orwell's *1984: A Novel*'. F.A. Hayek, *The Road
    to Serfdom: Collected Works of F.A. Hayek*, vol. II (Chicago: University of
    Chicago Press, 2007), p. 43. Storm Jameson, the socialist-feminist writer Orwell
    knew in the 1930s, wrote to him on the publication of *Nineteen Eighty-Four* to
    say that the novel was one which, in its sense of disaster, the sense of the abyss,
    'should stand for our age'. Jameson, Letter to Orwell, cited in Bernard Crick
    (ed.), 'Introduction', *Nineteen Eighty-Four* (Oxford: Clarendon Press, 1984),
    p. 96. The array of political positions the novel has been cited to bolster or to
    attack is staggering. A taste of the variety can be found in the recent 'biography'
    of the novel by Dorian Lynskey, *The Ministry of Truth: A Biography of George
    Orwell's 1984* (London: Picador, 2019).

35 The opening paragraphs from *The Communist Manifesto* should be read for comparison here. It will be seen that, apart from cleaving to a cyclical understanding of history or historical 'gyroscope', the novel's mobilising obsession – fear and hope entwined – is the existence of some interim 'class', the middles, and in particular, that emergent fraction of new professions, a class of people who live by their brains. The existence of this class fraction, Burnham's 'managerial class', seems to fascinate Orwell, in particular its non-organic relation to the world (to England), to language and to taste.

36 Williams, *Orwell*, p. 112.

37 In *Brave New World*, experiments are tried with 'equality' as they are tried with a shortening of the working day. These do not work and their failure to work cements the purported benevolence of the regime: it exists to secure happiness as 'human nature' itself is not suited to either freedom or equality.

38 E.M. Forster, 'George Orwell' (1950), in *Two Cheers for Democracy* (Harmondsworth: Penguin, 1965), p. 70. The Introduction above considered some of the ways in which the classic dystopia was crystallised within this conjuncture, not just a response to the looming catastrophes of the types of organised slaughter of the world wars, but an intervention into both plans and dreams of reform and revolution from the late nineteenth century on, an intervention centred on a fear of the state (well before the appearance of any clear form of welfare state) as much as it is also centred on fears of 'the machine' or of technological usurpation of human capacities.

3

Dystopia and the past

Introduction: From the 'hollow space' to fiction

> Undoubtedly there is much that is neurotic in the relation to the past: defen-
> sive postures where one is not attacked, intense affects where they are hardly
> warranted by the situation, an absence of affect in the face of the gravest
> matters, not seldom simply a repression of what is known or half-known.[1]

The above lines from Adorno's essay on the project in postwar Germany to
'work through' the past refer to the then recent past of Germany, to the
atrocity fascism wreaked on the Jews of Germany and of Europe. We
cannot extrapolate from his words any directly applicable theory or set of
principles to guide how to think historically to protect the present and the
future. And we cannot use his words to simply fix or to ascertain the role of
fictions in helping or damaging what the present needs of history.[2] What I
take from the essay quoted above is a phrase and the question it allows us
to pose. The phrase is 'a hollow space' and it appears as a way of describing
how remembering the past can be a way of forgetting it – with 'an empty
and cold forgetting' – that ways of not knowing and not remembering exist
within formal modes of remembrance:

> Thus we often found in group experiments in the Institute for Social
> Research that mitigating expressions and euphemistic circumlocutions were
> chosen in the reminiscences of deportation and mass murder, or that a hollow
> space formed in the discourse; the universally adopted, almost good-natured
> expression *Kristallnacht*, designating the pogrom of November 1938, attests
> to this inclination.[3]

It is possible to see the English-language dystopias of the first part of the
twentieth century as part of one such 'hollow space' in so far as they make
it impossible to think of either the past and present of the British Empire,
or of slavery in the United States, or of the systems which needed both.
This is a claim about the genre, about the forgetting it has to structurally
instantiate to throw designed oppression, unnecessary suffering, and all

the deformations of life which come with it, into an imagined future. The forgetting itself was not unusual or was a set of practices which could be described as busy, outside the genre. Hence what is remarkable is not that the classic dystopia's critically negative look at the future blanks out the past but that it should pay so much attention to the value of history – right down to the historicity of particular words – in so doing. Orwell's 'Appendix' to *Nineteen Eighty-Four* is only the most condensed of the pleas to protect history – which is to protect a language capable of holding it – from the depredations, political and cultural, of a present which threatened it: when

> Oldspeak had been once and for all superseded, the last link with the past would have been severed. History had already been rewritten, but fragments of the literature of the past survived here and there, imperfectly censored, and so long as one retained one's knowledge of Oldspeak it was possible to read them. In the future such fragments, even if they chanced to survive, would be unintelligible and untranslatable.[4]

Orwell had written in *Burmese Days* – a novel which is not a dystopia only because Burma *was* a colony of the British Empire – of a diegetic world in which truth was not possible: lies are necessary to maintain individual and social identity. The lies can be despised but they cannot be stepped outside of as there is nowhere to step except to know: 'the lie that we're here to uplift our poor black brothers instead of to rob them ... a natural enough lie. But it corrupts us, it corrupts us in ways you can't imagine.'[5] And yet *Nineteen Eighty-Four* posits a language from such a past, 'Oldspeak', which can be trusted not to lie. This is as odd or as paradoxical as the novel's treatment of the press – *The Times* – as if, before the Ministry of Truth, there had been just truth, and the conscription of the press in two world wars had not happened.

The dystopian fictions of the first half of the twentieth century accuse the future of warping language, and with it memory and history. For the permanence of their new regimes to be enabled, language has to be cleansed of terms that can trouble meaning, and history has to be purged as it too might trouble the meanings of the dystopian present. When we pull away from the nova they offer to us, the nova they need us for, we are faced with a conundrum, however. How was it possible for these novels to speak so fluently of the horrors involved in such danger to language and to the past, and yet themselves to stay silent on the past of their own present moments? The novum of the classic dystopia is a hollow space, one which formalises a need for history – for historical consciousness – without any historical content beyond the signifiers of a 'culture' high enough not to need any explanation of its value, one whose absence or censorship is consequently the greatest sign of an untrue order, a twisted or 'unnatural' regime. It is when this 'culture' itself falters in significance in the 1970s and 1980s that the formal need of history can no longer be taken for granted in the genre. The dystopian fictions of the 1980s belong to a moment when history itself seems to falter in dystopian nova, becoming not less meaningful or even present as history but less stable and less certain.

Memory, because it is the only way left of accessing the past, continues in importance throughout the dystopias of the 1980s. But, as we will see later in this chapter, with the exception of Atwood's novel it is a much withered memory, a depleted source. Not because any state form is determined to overwrite it (as in *Nineteen Eighty-Four*) or because it is to be censored along with the past (as in *Brave New World* or *We* or *Fahrenheit 451*) but because it is no longer needed existentially by the inhabitants of the 1980s dystopias. For the subjects of these later dystopias, for Ballard and for Gibson, memory does not need to be crushed as it has, with history or any sense of the past, just leaked out of the present leaving the present all there is and all there ever was. This leakage greatly dissipates also the existential importance of individuality and the importance of this latter for the narrative form dystopias take. If there is nothing left to fight for, it is in part because there is no individual left to fight. The prospect of a non-individual or trans-individual, newly collective, mode of resistance, which was already a defining feature of the 'critical utopias' generated by their very different orientation to the past, will not appear in the classic dystopia until the early years of the twenty-first century.[6]

The Handmaid's Tale

'We slept in what had once been the gymnasium' runs the first sentence of Margaret Atwood's 1985 novel.[7] Of the three novels to be explored in this chapter, Atwood's appears to be working most from the model of the classical dystopia that gave the genre its name and tradition. The state is totalitarian, its reach aspiring to be absolute, to control everything from clothing to survival, education, reproduction and morality. There are militarised borders and wars with enemies to legitimise those borders. This is the type of totalitarianism popularised as an understanding of Nazism and Stalinism in the postwar era, and theorised by Hannah Arendt as 'total domination'.[8] Strict hierarchies determine social place and social function. The myth of meritocracy has been violently dissolved: whatever limited mobility exists, upwards or downwards, is as a consequence, reward or punishment, for skills in performing obedience. Behind obedience, either as the daily uniform of individuals or the regime's own self-image, there are the spaces which prevent absolutism from being absolute. These are spaces not of resistance but of potential resistance, spaces not wholly absorbed by the regime. They are structurally necessary to crystallise the dystopia's capacity – as a fiction – to narrate the limits of the regime. These spaces have roughly two forms: the objective or political form of resistance as organised and social (the Female Road, the 'Mayday' underground cells and networks which organise this, the passwords and looks which hint at these), and the interior forms of unhappiness, an unhappiness which thrives on memory and which is oriented to a personal past and a hatred of the present.

The latter forms belong to the primary mediator of the world of the dystopia that is Gilead, the narrative of Offred, the woman who as 'Handmaid' to a powerful regime Commander belongs to the regime as property or as resource. Offred's first-person narrative comprises the majority of the text but it is important to keep in mind the few pages included as a quasi-appendix, the 'Historical Notes on The Handmaid's Tale', dated 2195, some two hundred years after the events recounted by Offred. This brief appendix closes the novel with an excerpt from an academic historians' conference which hears a paper speculating on the nature and history of the regime and Offred's possible escape and survival. It is not clear from the appendix what finished the regime – if indeed it is finished – it is clear only that an academic relationship to the past has survived both Gilead and its possible undoing.

To give over the bulk of the narrative space to a single interiority is not an exceptional move for a dystopian fiction but it is – by the 1980s – still a relatively unusual one.[9] Offred's is not a written account, a diary or a series of letters but a later transcription into print of a number of audiotapes made by Offred once she had – possibly – escaped. By giving the narrative voice to a Handmaid, Atwood insists on gender not merely as the regime's primary mode of reproducing itself but also as the mode through which the regime is experienced. Gilead, the theocratic state ruled by those who had mounted a coup against the US as a republic, has nationalised female fertility. This is less a departure from than it is a refinement of previous dystopian depictions of the potential reach of the state. By using a Handmaid as narrator, however, herself a nationalised resource, Atwood filters the state – its arrival and its operations – through a consciousness unable to depart from the body that defines her.

As not all women or only a few women are fertile, a Handmaid's experience is local, one link in the mesh that is formally symmetrical with the hierarchy of males but substantively different in every detail with that same hierarchy. There are working-class women, Marthas, who work as servants to the regime's elite; there are other women who are termed 'econo-wives', the (presumably infertile) wives of working-class men; there are the wives of the Commanders (top officials in the bureaucracy or the army), themselves 'barren', who are confined to domestic spheres, spheres in which they rule grimly over the Handmaids and the ('their') Marthas; there are the 'Aunts', the Biblical fundamentalists charged with 're-educating' and disciplining the captured fertile women who are destined to become Handmaids; and there are the 'unwomen', those 'difficult' women who, too unruly or too old or too wedded to a different interpretation of religion, are sent as labour to the colonies, or to the 'Jezebel' clubs to service the sexual needs of powerful men until their bodies give out.

'Woman' has been disaggregated, her several social roles reorganised as individually rather than collectively constitutive so that one may be or has to be a wife but not give birth, give birth but not be a mother, be a 'lover' but not a wife, clean and cook or 'housewife' for the country but not be a mother or an 'aunt'. To be deemed unfit to fulfil any of these now segregated roles is to be no-body at all, an 'unwoman.' Gilead is a white supremacist as well as a male supremacist state: all African-Americans are rounded up and sent to internal 'Homelands'; all Jews are forced to convert or emigrate to Israel.[10] The social system as a whole is dependent on the Handmaids but as a material resource. The Handmaids themselves, as women rather than as wombs, occupy a position of slavery but one in which their work is sexual and biological – conceiving, carrying to term, birthing. Outside of this they have no value and are used for nothing but the symbolic labour of being there, self-sacrificing but red, shamed and shameful somehow.

Where *The Handmaid's Tale* does depart from the classic dystopia is in its narrative style and it is this stylistic specificity – the dystopia's textual form – that needs to be read for its historicity. *The Handmaid's Tale* needed those earlier dystopias to be written, needed the catastrophic instrumentalisation of labour, technology and politics, the tenets of sociobiology and social Darwinism rehearsed from Zamyatin's *We* (1923) to Anthony Burgess's *Clockwork Orange* (1963), to be imaginable, but in its form it signals a shift towards a new, a particularly late twentieth-century way of imagining what dystopia loses, what it crushes, and why.

The 'we' who open the text in the sentence 'We slept in what had once been the gymnasium' are Handmaids in training. The 'gymnasium' is an old High School gym, a place that still holds the smells and sounds of the vanquished past: 'faintly like an afterimage, the pungent scent of sweat, shot through with the sweet taint of chewing gum and perfume ... Dances would have been held there; the musk lingered, a palimpsest of unheard sound, style upon style' (*HT*, p. 13).

I have argued that the commitment made by the classic dystopias is to a present they cannot speak of. That negative form of commitment does not accommodate 'nostalgia' as the latter is too necessarily sensuous and too dispersed or fugitive to have a significant presence or a formal presence in a dystopia which must estrange the present to create itself. In *The Handmaid's Tale*, there is nostalgia, however. With Atwood it is not a nostalgia for the past as much as it is a nostalgia for the futures that past once promised: 'We yearned for the future,' the narrator recalls, 'How did we learn it, that talent for insatiability? It was in the air' (*HT*, p. 13). Fredric Jameson once described as 'the most haunting feature' of *Nineteen Eighty-Four* 'the elegiac sense of the loss of the past, and the uncertainty of memory'.[11] Atwood expands this elegiac sense to encompass both personal or private and collective pasts, the former barely memorable, the latter dependent on objects or texts which themselves need disappearing interpretative codes to be made meaningful. The pasts mourned in *Nineteen Eighty-Four* do not include being able to dream of the future, wanting a future, being future-oriented. Offred's narrative of her past pre-Gilead is saturated with such yearnings, and they too are personal – her own youth and its openness, the openness of women in the 1960s and 1970s, her child, her dreams with her partner about buying a house –

> an old big house, fixing it up. We would have a garden, swings for the children. We would have children. Although we knew it wasn't too likely we could ever afford it, it was something to talk about, a game for Sundays. Such freedom now seems almost weightless. (*HT*, p. 33)

Weightless because unlikely but yet possible, freedom even if only the freedom to daydream. The yearnings for a time when the future was open are also more than personal. Not only does the text specify the vectors of Offred's own life pre-Gilead – attendance at college for women, books in college dorms 'open face down, this way and that, extravagantly', the disciplines of 'Psychology, English, Economics' not only open to women but open to papers on 'date rape', (*HT*, pp. 47–8) but also the historicity of these vectors in the women's movement. The latter opens up in the memory of a collective dream of the future: it is political (the burning of pornographic magazines) but also more generally social – men and women 'tr[ying] each other on, casually, like suits, rejecting whatever did not fit' (*HT*, p. 61).

The remembered openness of the past to a future is not without antagonism and is ambivalent in its presentation. We could see in the remembered openness to a future not yet determined some articulation of a Blochian joy, a glimpse of a Utopian 'not yet', if it was not so clear that some of those future yearnings did achieve realisation. These were the yearnings for a return to domesticity and chaste femininity of the 'moral majority' (women and men) who found the then present intolerable in its openness, got rid of it and erected Gilead in its place.[12]

The question put by the Japanese tourists to the Handmaids, 'Are you happy?' (*HT*, p. 39), is one impossible to put to the women of a pre-Gilead era given what Gilead has done to them but the previous openness of their lives to a future is just as much a reality as Gilead and should not be collapsed into Gilead. This openness is historical, it is 'Western',[13] it is young, it is feminist, it is experimental, and it is, the text suggests, mortally limited. The shape the narrative takes is a personal one: Offred is a Handmaid and this is her 'tale', her story or testimony. This is what happened to her. This story gives us the shape of the regime but is not the story of the regime – of its origins, its internal tensions, its trade or economic relations – or of one of its functionaries or ideologues. Offred is a professional of sorts – she has been trained to be a Handmaid, 're-educated' – but she is a professional of an inverted and unfree private life, a private sphere grown absolute, for women, with the state at its centre even as 'family life' (without children) gives that sphere its form and daily rhythms.

But the narrator's mode of address is as much a collective as a personal one. She uses the 'we' form as much as she uses an 'I' form, about the past as much as about the present she now inhabits. As readers, we never find out her name pre-Gilead, or that of her mother or her young daughter. Her recollections of that past – of the time before Gilead, a time necessarily one of 'freedom' but also of fear and of tensions, of the abrupt eruption of the coup and the political energies it mobilised to found Gilead – are memories delivered in fragments, fleeting impressions returned to and returned to so that they build up over the time of the text not so much into empirical history but into a structure of feeling. That structure of feeling was future-oriented, and perhaps the greatest of the dystopian aspects of this text is that that structure of feeling is not just destroyed but pin-pointed as culpable in its own destruction.

'I'm a refugee from the past,' our narrator tells us at one point, 'and like other refugees I go over the customs and habits of being I've left or been forced to leave behind me' (*HT*, p. 239). What she remembers is a freedom made out of an embrace of a peculiarly limited, a stringently personal, sphere of autonomy and of mutability, of a mode of self-fashioning which sees itself as beyond politics – historically no longer in need of politics – and beyond history; having no such secular or temporal constraints it is 'free':

> It's strange to remember how we used to think, as if everything were available to us, as if there were no contingencies, no boundaries; as if we were free to shape and reshape forever the ever-expanding perimeters of our lives. I was like that too, I did that too. (*HT*, p. 239)

Gilead has shrunk unbearably the perimeters of female lives, foreshortening them to the chance of a biology recast as destiny (and this only where the industrial toxins in the air have not yet colonised that body and destroyed that fertility, chance of another sort). Yet while the openness of the past to multiple possible futures, to self-fashioning and to the proliferation of appetites, is remembered with melancholy, it is also remembered as contradictory:

> If you don't like it, change it, we said, to each other and to ourselves. And so we would change the man, for another one. Change, we were sure, was for the better always. We were revisionists; what we revised was ourselves. (*HT*, p. 239)

The 'we' of the narrative, when it turns to the past, is distinguished generationally from the women of Offred's mother's age, feminists who fought.[14] The structure of feeling articulated by Offred herself can thus be described, paradoxically, as 'post-feminist', one thread in a larger postmodernist sensibility which did not see Gilead coming. The 'we' of the narrative is distinguished politically also, however: there are two groups of political women of Offred's generation, each of which occupied different positions in both the past and the present: feminists and the anti-feminists of Reaganite America. Offred's position is outside of each but it is her narration which creates a triangulated conjuncture which in turn figures 1980s America as poised on the threshold of new terrors and new freedoms. Critically, however, Atwood's insistence on collectivising the subject of the narrative alters its mode of address: for the classic dystopias, only the individual was legible as antagonistic to the regime. The regime held collectivism, individuality was its necessary opponent.

'We is from God, while I is from the Devil' in Zamyatin's *We*, is taken up in countless warnings of the only ever always cruel dangers of collectivisation across the 1930s to the 1950s.[15] The state and the forms it takes the Party, the nation – or articulates – the people, the 'race' – are the place holder for organisation as inherently totalitarian, necessarily a structure hostile to individual autonomy. This structural antagonism mutates in the 1950s and 1960s as the locus of oppression shifts to the corporation, to commerce and the machinery of its symbolic efficiency in advertising and marketing. It is harder here to keep the antagonism between collective and individual stable and persuasive as that machinery runs on the simulation of individual desires and powers, creates a subjectivity powerfully alienated from the real subjects it haunts (these latter barely subjects now and barely capable of individuality) yet also powerfully alluring if not addictive.[16] In the feminist- and anti-racist creation of critical utopias in the science fiction of the 1960s and 1970s, new forms of intersubjective solidarity and agency suggest an overcoming of the older paralysed antagonistic model of collective/individual.[17]

In Atwood, the state returns and with it the hijacking of the collective as the will of the state: 'the same platitudes, the same slogans, the same

phrases: the torch of the future, the cradle of the race, the task before us'
(*HT*, pp. 286–7). But it is set in opposition not to a unique 'I' but to a
mobile, fluid incorporation of past and present collectivities into that 'I' and
to the latter's incorporation into the realities of multiple ways of being collective. This all has consequences for the novum and hence for the reader:
the distance which was a consequence of the doomed individualism of the
classical dystopian protagonist (the 'last man') is undermined here: Offred,
perhaps precisely because she has the function of narrating, of being in the
first person yet speaking of things outside or beyond the personal, possesses
no individualism in the classic sense. She is confused, accommodating,
rebellious, passive, complicit and infrequently full of rage or of shame. The
line of consistency in her is the determination to narrate, to insist that an
interlocutor is imaginable and is hence possible:

> I keep on going with this sad and hungry and sordid, this limping and muti-
> lated story, because after all I want you to hear it, as I will hear yours too if I
> ever get the chance, if I meet you or if you escape, in the future or in Heaven
> or in prison or underground, some other place. What they have in common is
> that they're not here. By telling you anything at all I'm at least believing in
> you, I believe you're there, I believe you into being. Because I'm telling you this
> story I will your existence. I tell, therefore you are. (*HT*, p. 279)

It is narration finally that keeps this dystopia from reproducing the classic
form: both the use of a first-person narrative mode and then the pulling of that
mode into the content, the insistence that, if a tale is told, that very telling
opens the possibility of it being heard, of its being understood. Our narrator
remembers because there is no other mode of resistance imaginable for her.

Hello America[18]

Feminism rather than history, the intersubjective politics of her feminism
rather than the pressures of the 1980s, prevents Atwood completing in
her dystopia the model of the classical antagonism. But it is history that is
embedded in her dystopia's mourning for pasts when different futures were
possible. In the narrative work it does to emphasise memory, the difficulty
and the political value of remembering a different time, Atwood gave to her
dystopia the signature of the 1980s as an era in which the 'end of history'
was becoming visible as a potential source of terror. Just over four decades
earlier, Adorno and Horkheimer had written of the social engineering of a
past 'preserved as the destruction of the past', giving critical theory the task
not of conserving 'the past, but of the redemption of the hopes of the past'.[19]
For the dystopias of the 1980s, the past is both elusive and Janus-faced:

precious because it tells of a time which dreamt not of a utopian future but of a future at all, of a time different to the present; corrupt and to be despised because it produced this dystopian present, delivered the world and all in it to the non-time of a world without history.

Atwood's dystopia is recognisably the world of the 1980s, not the world later codified by postmodernism but a world as posited by the liberal humanism which most nearly defines Atwood's political position. The deprivations wreaked by Gilead are deprivations wreaked on private life: the sphere of personal autonomy, including bodily autonomy, provide the horror. What's remembered in the past is all the apparatus of individual lives lived through personal relations, professions, plans and dreams.[20] That all that is left of utopian hope are the relics of an easily vanquished past (whether vanquished by the regime's rewriting of the past or by the appendix's gloomy look at the absorption of even rebellion into the useless etiquette of scholarly knowledge) poses a dilemma for critical theory: how can the hopes of the past be redeemed if they cannot first be found?

An exploration of two other dystopian novels from the 1980s will provide ways to more closely historicise what should then become a more visible layer of the dystopian novum in the late twentieth century. These two novels jettison the cultural baggage of liberal humanism, and, with it, the key narrative structures of the older dystopian form. That they could do so as easily as they do – dispensing not just with the private sphere but with the model of subjectivity supposed to inhabit it, self-regulating and self-transparent, a model of selfhood which was, when left alone, capable of being the normative model of autonomy – itself tells us something about the end of the postwar settlement, and with it the end of its fears and the emergence of new ones. The world lost the private sphere even as an ideal but did not notice its passing.

In a short story first published in 1981, 'The Gernsback Continuum', William Gibson describes the cultural circulation of semiotic ghosts in an America denuded of even past futures: 'the future had come to America first, but had finally passed it by'. The narrator has been haunted by

> semiotic phantoms, bits of deep cultural imagery that have split off and taken on a life of their own, like the Jules Verne airships that those old Kansas farmers were always seeing ... part of the mass unconscious once.[21]

There is a life-cycle to popular or to commercial culture here: historical moments produce differentiated articulations of alienated creativities as a series of desires the potency of which resides in their contemporary recognis-ability, their immediate and deep – though transient – legibility. That very potency endures in a weakened, a phantom, form even as its contemporary moment disappears; it endures as a second-order type of living, organising, for Gibson, if not experience directly then the hopes that make that experience tolerable even as those impossible past desires are designed never to be realised. Both J.G. Ballard and Gibson call on the detritus of past cultural forms to index the grim failure of the present to have any sense of a future different from itself. The two novels at issue here – Ballard's *Hello America* and Gibson's *Neuromancer* – are both set in the future but both spend their time mapping the absence of any sense of a future. This is an invocation not of some apocalypse to come but of a world in which time – the possibility of temporal change – has been overcome. There is only ever going to be the present, this miserable present, a novum which has no succour for the reader.

Both novels invert the classic dystopia's model of a high culture resisting the depredations, the organised lying and smoothing into inevitability of the present, of 'mass culture'. For these two novelists, popular culture[22] is the last site where the rhythms of history, the memories of the past, and of that past's dreams of a different future, are still faintly visible or tangible. They treat the realm of commercial culture not as a homogenous, continuous regime of alienation and manipulation but as, inadvertently, the most sensitive historical register of the forces securing both continuity and, critically, change in the technological ordering of life in late capitalism.

For Ballard, despite official pronouncements or NASA spectacles dramatising a continuing commitment to 'progress', the Space Age had ended in 1974, its collapse heralded before it arrived by a diminution in popular 'dreams of jetliners and airport lounges'.[23] Whereas postwar ideas of the future had been mediated by fantasies of space colonisation and adventure, the equivalent dreams of the 1960s were of an expansion into 'interior space' in drug-assisted explorations of consciousness or attempts to found communities which enabled 'authentic' forms less of living than of exploring the consciousness of living.

The older dreams do not biodegrade, however, but hang illegibly around, like static interrupting the otherwise pristine broadcasts of new narratives pretending they were always there. That is the critical function of the memories encoded in yellowed, broken, discarded fragments of past cultural moments. Now just so much rubbish, they are testimony at one and the same time to the myth of permanence, and to the sadness of continuity. Neither Ballard nor Gibson allows these fragments any utopian charge. In the context of the 1980s, it is sufficient that they are there as they mark the limits of a time that pronounced itself as limitless.

The 'semiotic phantoms' that haunt the protagonist of Gibson's short story, a commercial photographer commissioned to produce images for a book on American architecture of the 1930s, are phantoms of once-dreamt-of commercial utopias. For the book, *The Airstream Futuropolis: The Tomorrow that Never Was*, the unnamed photographer seeks in the post-industrial waste lands of contemporary America the remains of that once-tomorrow. He photographs buildings figured like 'spray-paint pulp utopias ... look[ing] as though ... designed for people who wore white togas and Lucite sandals', finds designs for huge airliners that would never fly, rendered too heavy by the inclusion of ballrooms and squash courts: 'the designers were populists, you see; they were trying to give the public what it wanted. What the public wanted was the future.'[24]

They are the manufactured utopias of an age of industrial design, transparently so: they occur as dreams of buildings like stage sets, future-oriented, a 'series of elaborate props for playing at living in the future'.[25] The buildings which did get built are incongruous now. They have occasionally 'a kind of sinister totalitarian dignity', the rest are 'relentlessly tacky, ephemeral stuff ... tending mostly to survive along depressing strips lined with dusty motels, mattress wholesalers and small used-car lots'.[26] The buildings themselves, old gas stations, movie houses, motels, have no potency, the dreams embedded in them long lost to mute decay and grime. Those dreams do circulate still, however, disembodied or demate-rialised, and after weeks of photographing these ruins of 'that lost future', Gibson's photographer starts to occupy a liminal space between dreaming and waking, one populated by impossible twelve-engine aeroplanes coated in dull silver and playing jazz, illuminated cityscapes out of *Metropolis* and *Things to Come*, all zeppelin docks and mad neon spires, and white, blond blue-eyed heirs of that once dreamt of future, 'wise and strong' and terrifying. The photographer can't bear these dreams: he seeks advice and uses porn and poor television to get 'these Art Deco futuroids' off his back, to 'exorcise semiotic ghosts'.[27] Porn and poor television are not inferior or more powerful forms of commercial culture, they are more current and hence more charged, dense with the meanings of the moment and thus capable of reconquering the mind of their consumers.

This concern with the waning of any interest in or hope for a future unifies Gibson's *Neuromancer* (1984) and Ballard's *Hello America* (1981). Both will be treated here as dystopias and in both there is a new dimension to what constitutes the dystopia: the future is here but has simultaneously ceased to be imaginable.[28] There is to be no more future in 1980s America: petroleum crises and nuclear hazards literalise the waning of any future-oriented thinking but something goes deeper. Gibson's dystopian novel *Neuromancer* will be read as a consequence of that deeper loss of faith in futurity, and of its refusal to go away, its return as phantoms, haunting the present with their own frail irreducibility. That novel, however, is so heavily enmeshed in its reputation as the launch model for cyberpunk that it is worth first discovering that absence of the future in a very different dystopia, in J.G. Ballard's slightly earlier *Hello America*.

Ballard's is a novel where the oil has run out, where the stalled present is the abortive progeny of a past unable to realise its own dreams of unlimited growth, of expeditions to the stars and other planets, of unending 'cold' and hot wars and a car for every human being to participate in an endless global traffic jam. The novel starts early in the twenty-second century. A 'world government' co-ordinates whatever is left of production, engineering alterations to the planet's climate so as to enable the continuation of Europe's candlelit stasis. By 2090, America is abandoned, the vast migration of Americans which took place in the 1990s having duplicated 'in reverse the original westward passage two hundred years earlier'. 'America' has, with Americans, dissipated back to its origins:

> White Americans emigrated back to Italy and Germany, Eastern Europe, Britain and Ireland, black Americans to Africa and the West Indies, Chicanos waded south across the Rio Grande.[29]

Millions did not make it, missing the last evacuation ships by days, finding when they arrived at city ports only nuclear-powered aircraft carriers scuttled by mutinous crews, as in New York when those crews refused to obey orders to 'fire on the thousands of small boats and makeshift rafts that jammed its harbour exit' (*HA*, p. 17). Over one hundred years after that 'great migration', whilst ethic divisions, articulated as unremarkable even as formative, persist, there are no conflicts, there is no energy for conflict any more, either materially in terms of resources or psychologically, there is no more quest for the new, for power or anything approximating 'progress'. The world is sustainable now, a planet consuming as much fuel in a month as one empty American city had once consumed in a day.

Out of this stable but exhausted world, an expedition sets off by boat for America, its task to investigate leaks of radioactivity which had started drifting across the North Atlantic fifty years earlier. Previous reconnaissance expeditions had reported back 'nothing of value', finding in the 'barren north American continent, a forgotten wilderness as distant as Patagonia' (*HA*, p. 26). One had not returned at all.

The expedition which is the protagonist of the story, giving it its temporal co-ordinates, is composed, however, of people little interested in the ostensible scientific purpose of their journey. Each of them carries like contraband

> their collective fantasy of America ... united by their shared dream of 'freedom' (the last great illusion of the twentieth century), the same conviction that they would make a new life and fulfil themselves that must have been felt by their distant forebears when they were herded through the immigration pens of Ellis Island. (*HA*, p. 27)

The 'freedom' they dream of has to remain illusory, was never meant to be anything but an illusion. Having never had illusions in the older or romantic sense, these new pioneers cannot be disillusioned but are condemned to wander on in the twilight of illusions generated from the time before, when the world still allowed of illusion. The first line of the novel runs '"There's gold, Wayne, gold dust everywhere! Wake up! The streets of America are paved with gold!"' (*HA*, p. 7). The 'gold' is sand, it rises up the ruined skyline of Manhattan as seen from the now derelict pier at the island's lower tip. The sand is the result of the sun's burning out of everything there ever was in the American East.

The expedition sails up the old East River bay, now crowded with the ruins of older vessels, and beaches itself on one of the radiating spikes from the crown of a drowned Statue of Liberty. It is not only the sun and excitement which turn the desertified city to a city of gold for the riverside spectators, however, it is memories which have been carried across the generations of refugees, surviving like toxins to create a vision of America as a place of and for projection.

There are no 'real' memories here, the 'collective fantasy of America' (*HA*, p. 27) is a creature of the entertainment industries of the mid-twentieth century, of images surviving in the hoarded brown copies of *Time* and *Look* magazines, illustrations of an older collective fantasy of America as the kindly, consumer-oriented superpower:

> illustrations of the Cape Kennedy Space Center, the Space Shuttle landing at Edwards Air Force Base after a test flight, and the recovery of an Apollo capsule from the Pacific ... a special bicentennial supplement celebrating every aspect of American life in the long-ago 1970s – the crowded streets of Washington on Carter's Inauguration Day, long queues of holiday jets on the runways of Kennedy Airport, happy vacationers lying by the swimming-pools of Miami, raking the ski-slopes of Aspen, Colorado, fitting out their yachts in a huge marina at San Diego, all the enormous vitality of this once extraordinary nation preserved in these sepia photographs. (*HA*, p. 11)

The expedition leaves the desert the Eastern seaboard has become behind them, striking out on horseback to the West. In New York, the ship's crew remain to fix the ship amidst the sand-choked hotels and high-rises of Manhattan. As the expedition presses on inland, the 'sight of the failed continent', abandoned supermarkets, deserted shopping malls and sand-covered parking lots, serves to spur them on. Each of the small number is possessed by different images of America, each image is composed of a series of media clichés. For Wayne, the young stowaway who becomes a leader, it is 'that vision of the United States enshrined in the pages of *Time* and *Look*, and which still existed somewhere', a world of Cadillacs and

Continentals, huge cars and small domesticities, honourable Presidents and quiet patriotisms (*HA*, p. 49); the Captain, Steiner, becomes in stature and approach 'some plainsman of the Old West', taciturn, enigmatic and enormously self-sufficient; Anne Summers,[30] a Professor of Physics and the expedition's radiologist, discovers decayed cosmetics and old copies of *Cosmopolitan* and loses herself in 'a dream of glamorous Hollywood villas' (*HA*, p. 73); the Italian nuclear physicist, Dr Ricci, turns gangster; and Orlowski, the Russian 'political leader', goes full-on colonial bureaucrat.

Scattered throughout America, and throughout the novel, are the 'tribes', the differentiated remnants, of '*real* Americans, direct descendants of the few thousands who had stayed behind' (*HA*, p. 63). These sun-wizened 'simple souls' skip the mediations of popular culture entirely to inhabit that realm instead. Though it is long gone, they survive: they call themselves by the brand-names of the long-defunct rusting products which still litter their 'failed continent': 'Heinz, Pepsodent, GM and Xerox were among the last remnants of one of the dozen tribes that roved the continent' (*HA*, p. 63):

> All of them had been illiterate for generations, and the only words they could read were the brand names on neon signs – their friends and relatives were called Big Mac, U-drive, Texaco and 7 Up. (*HA*, p. 64)

> 'Xerox' is a generic name for women as 'they make good copies'. (*HA*, p. 64)

These 'tribes'[31] are dying out, terrified of the holographic star-ships projected on to the ruined cities of the East by the political regime forming in Las Vegas, and poisoned when exposed to the nuclear fallout of that city's bombing of the cities of the East.

As they penetrate deeper, the dreams of the expedition crew get stronger: rather than being diluted by the cracked, decayed ruins of a real America lying abandoned and dissolving, the dreams themselves seem to strengthen, isolating them from each other, any collective purpose diminishing to an afterthought. By the time they reach the arid and silent Washington, embalmed in a desert haze, now a scene of sand dunes and cacti, mesquite and burrow-weed, they are silent themselves, withdrawn into some interior space of longing and satisfaction: '[u]nder the guise of crossing America ... they were about to begin that far longer safari across that diameter of their own skulls' (*HA*, p. 73).

Washington and New York are truly dead cities: composed of politics and government, of business and commerce respectively, the dreams they once generated disintegrate at the force of the fantasies emanating from the West. First signalled by the sight of enormous holographs of cowboys, John Wayne, Alan Ladd, Gary Cooper and Henry Fonda from the classic Westerns of the 1940s and 1950s, projected striding across the sky, these are the images which augur the new regime struggling to be born in the West. As the images flare up across the sky, they are seen by the survivors of the expedition, now dying, isolated from each other, of dehydration and the bankruptcy of their dreams:

> Two huge spurred boots, each the height of a ten-storey building, rested on the hills above the town, while the immense legs, clad in worn leather chaps and as tall as skyscrapers, reached up to the gunbelt a thousand feet in the air. The silver-tipped bullets pointed down ... like a row of aircraft fuselages. Beyond them rose the cliff wall of the cowboy's check shirt, and then the towering shoulders that seem to carry the sky. (*HA*, p. 97)

The holograms are projections from the West, from the base of President Manson, the forty-fifth President of the United States. Manson is a dictator, a deranged tyrant, a mutation of several fictions of power as pure and effective. He operates out of a base on the top floor of the Desert Inn in Las Vegas, mimicking in his nakedness and germphobia the symbolic energies of Howard Hughes as 'the last of the Great Americans'. Manson had escaped from Spandau in Germany, once the prison where Speer and Hess were held but which was given to the refugee Americans who turned it into a 'mental hospital' after their 'great migration' (*HA*, p. 174). In America, he had reclaimed Las Vegas from swamp, serving seven terms as President. Whilst he has 'taken over [Hughes's] empire, what those pigmies left of it' (129), and Hughes's reclusiveness, his corruption and his obsessions with disease, Manson had yet 'established the only base of organised power that had existed in north America for a hundred years':[32]

> The reclamation of this jungle city, the millions of coloured lights that shone through the tangled ferns and palms, the elaborate television and communications gear, the renovation of at least part of the old Hughes empire, together rekindled something of the power of the United States, and hinted at what could be done in the future. (*HA*, p. 131)

That this is a dystopian rekindling and a dystopian future is made clear in Manson's launching of reclaimed cruise and Titan nuclear missiles against the cities of the East. Manson chooses which city to target with a spin of a roulette wheel in the casinos of 'the strip', in a scene in which the 'ghosts of Charles Manson and IBM meet in Caesar's Palace, playing with cruise missiles in place of gold chips' (*HA*, p. 174). Manson visualises a 'Fortress USA', one which will be achieved via a scorched-earth policy, destroying the cities of the East to defeat 'the dangers of germs', and the imagined 'hordes of bacterially infected European immigrants clambering up the beaches of the Eastern seaboard, bearing rabies, polio, cancer and meningitis towards the Rockies at a steady three kilometres per day' (*HA*, p. 153).

Manson has as much a mimetic relation to Nixon as he has to Hughes. With Hughes, there is the life of a recluse to be followed, perched in the penthouse of The Desert Inn motel, working his empire from behind banks of sterilising units, air conditioners and television screens. Naked, 'an aerosol inhaler in one hand, a remote-control TV unit in another', when first introduced to the expedition's few survivors, this is a man as an image of another man's image: 'his eyes were fixed on the tier of screens, as if his real existence resided in this ionised flow of flickering images rather than in his own restless musculature' (*HA*, p. 127). Manson's 'resemblance' to Nixon is described as 'uncanny' and it is a relationship of similitude rather than of identity, its learnt apparatus meant to be noticed rather than elided. In his guise as Nixon, Manson appears as if

> the man in front of the television screens was a skilful actor who had made a career out of impersonating Presidents, and found that he could imitate Nixon more convincingly than any other. He had caught the long stares and suddenly lowered eyes, the mixture of idealism and corruption, the deep melancholy and lack of confidence coupled at the same time with a powerful inner conviction. (*HA*, p. 128)

Here in a reclaimed and lushly tropical Las Vegas, almost 150 years after the American city's own evacuation and extinction, Manson dreams of a 1970s America. He populates his casino with an army of life-sized electronic dolls of late-period Dean Martin and Frank Sinatra, the entertainers celebrated 'when America had clung to its last great icons, its emblems of self-confidence, forcing them to return again and again to the stage' (*HA*, p. 118). The most notable incarnation of his 'vision' for a renewed America, however, is Las Vegas itself. The last reports from the drowned city had described it as sitting abandoned, 'half-submerged in a lake of rain-lashed water, its wheels stilled, the dying lights of its hotels reflected in the meadows of the drowned desert, a violent mirror reflecting all the failure and humiliation of America' (*HA*, p. 48). Under Manson it has come to neon life again, a grotesque source and site of nuclear energy raining holographic cowboys and cruise missiles down on the deserted cities of America.

Manson's regime collapses of course, self-obliterated in the dual grotesques of neon entertainments and nuclear missiles, the city falling apart as the laser-image of Manson spread out across the sky also implodes. That 'of course' is important. Manson's was never destined to be more than his own feverish vision less of a 'new' regime than a fantasy of resurrecting older fantasies of crude individualism, self-reliance and all the supposedly untrammelled power of the free-market fundamentalism that had once destroyed America. This is a fantasy built out of past fantasies, their referents long dead, a built fantasy of an America that never was, a fantasy built up out of the phantom remnants of that America found in the old discourses of popular culture.

This is the collapse of history or its liquidation warned against by Horkheimer and Adorno in *Dialectic of Enlightenment*. In *Negative Dialectics*, Adorno describes it also as bourgeois society becoming conscious of itself once it can no longer overcome its own limits. One of the central antinomies of bourgeois society is that

> To preserve itself, to remain the same, to 'be,' that society too must constantly expand, progress, advance its frontiers, not respect any limit, not remain the same. It has been demonstrated to bourgeois society that it would no sooner reach a ceiling, would no sooner cease to have noncapitalist areas available outside itself, than its own concept would force its self-liquidation.[33]

Ballard seems to revel in the sheer weightlessness of history's absence. There is no sadness, no anger and no pain here. Each of the characters in the text obeys the logic of a reality they experience as one of consumption only: they consume images of themselves as they do faded images of the America that never was. In *Hello America*, we can glimpse two mutilated totalities, neither whole nor coherent. The world of the spectacle, still vivid in the minds of those it inhabits but belonging to a reality long dead, is now divorced from its task, left to blindly gesture at a real long illegible; the world outside of it, the parched and ruined world of an abandoned America, is a world without names as it is a world without meaning as it has no spectacle, and cannot itself have even the misery of a spectacular reality.

Neuromancer

If it was technology, science, and loosely the new cultural industries, which rendered the state a newly visible or newly potent agent of oppression in the classic dystopias of the first half of the twentieth century,[34] that oppression then has a historical form. What stands outside of oppression, necessarily antagonistic to it, then must also have a contemporaneously historical form. When that structural antagonism disappears from dystopian fiction, as, this chapter contends, it did in the 1980s, we need to read its absence historically to comprehend the forces governing its passing.

In Atwood, the 'I' or individual is no longer the antagonistic second term: the state remains but it has lost its antagonistic partner. This loss of faith in even the form of the liberal individualism which had been so integral an element of the early and classic tradition of fictional dystopia marks out the limits of Atwood's reworking of the older tradition.

In *Hello America* too, the older opposition between state and individual is dispersed. There we have a 'World Government', and the dreams of total power of the quasi-presidential figure Manson in Las Vegas. But these are ultimately irrelevant to the energies unleashed by the expedition which makes up the bulk of the novel. No individual sets themselves against either the world government or even against Manson's plans. Rather mutated forms of subjectivity, built out of the detritus, the cultural carcass of the old, emerge, collide, are destroyed or move on. Nothing is fought for, nothing is lost and nothing is gained.

Those new modes of subjectivity dance to old forms, forms foully superseded in climatic catastrophe, desertification and a return to an earlier episode in prehistory. The novel's insistence that this is all there is, reworkings of old disasters, is its own contribution to the dystopias of the 1980s. The opening line of Gibson's *Neuromancer* (1984) – 'The sky above the port was the colour of television, tuned to a dead channel' – can be read as if it were an epilogue to Ballard's President Manson's dreams having succeeded but failed. Manson wanted to outlaw nature, to remake the natural world as much as the social world in the fevered cast of old American dreams of supremacy. In *Neuromancer*, there is no more 'nature' but now its absence is not registered in any neon simulacra or engineered replacements but is registered in some 'dead channel' indistinction.

This indistinction, a technologically mediated greyness, saturates the world of *Neuromancer*: that this is a future world is clear, that, in its inequalities, insecurities, powerlessness and alienation, it is also the world of the 1980s is equally clear. Gibson's grey future is at once an indication and a critique of the failures of past imagined futures: there may be chrome-plated orbital living here but the violence on which it is built is so naked and so grimly unremarkable, that the contours of the world appear more feudal than futuristic. This dystopia in its very greyness acts less as a futuristic novel than it does one saturated with a futuristic melancholy that sings a dirge for the very idea of a future different from the present: the future is no longer possible.

The state continues to exist, even if only in the apparatus of police, intelligence agencies, identity numbers, but any sense of subjective belonging is long gone: nation-ness and with it patriotism are felt only once and then in the register of their betrayal. The individual too continues to exist but, perhaps because no longer defined in opposition to the state (or relatedly to any compliant 'masses') is a skeletal thing, existentially a nullity, each a homeless, history-less hunter or piece of prey. The only thickening of the subjects of the novel comes when they encounter each other; that will not last as their encounters do not last but, without them, they are hollow.

Neuromancer, from its position in the mid-1980s, turns us towards an airless or captured future but not wholly. For whilst the grim insistence of the novel that this is just the way things are marks it out as standing in opposition to the Reaganite truism, that people of his era inhabited 'the best of all possible worlds', that insistence is not quite relentless. The insistence, to be compelling as a fiction which is dystopian, had to have something to act as a narrative edge, some edge of difference to indicate that this dystopia is dystopian. Within this dystopian novum, history has been evacuated from everything: nothing there has roots or origins or a sense of home, everyone appears alienated but there is nothing to be alienated from. Yet the absence of history is given two exceptions, one personal and one corporate.

These two exceptions do not themselves belong to the present of the novel so cannot be treated as in any way redemptive of history or as opening any sort of breach for a new future out of the present. They are rather illustrations of the pastness of the past, of a certain type of social being ending, surviving as a relic not of any particular past but of the disappearance of the past; for an unchanging present not only has no need of the past but must abolish the concept as such.

The character of Corto opens a space in the novel for a buried past: his is the past of a man who persists only mutely and unknown to himself in the biochemically engineered figure of Armitage.[35] That he is present in the novel only at the moment of his psychic dissolution and death is less important than that his very existence opens a hinterland for the present, a shadow of its past.

Tessier-Ashpool SA, the corporation which will end the novel overcome by the binding together of Wintermute with Neuromancer, two Artificial Intelligences Tessier-Ashpool owns, provides the other eruption of the past. Where Corto was once a military man, a figure of patriotism and hence, by the 1980s, a figure of an almost inevitable betrayal by his country, Tessier-Ashpool is a historical hybrid, a fantastically wealthy twenty-first- or twenty-second-century corporation which is, however, still owned by a family or a merger of families, and one which turns its face to the eccentric dynasties of a much older age, burying into an ersatz Victoriana it erects for itself in orbit.

Before looking in more detail at why and how Gibson wanted these odd relics of historicity in his novel, I want to assess the novel's meaning in terms of its overcoming or undoing of the opposition between the state and the individual, once the signature of a dystopian novel. From the first, Gibson utilised the generic conventions less of science fiction than of hard-boiled or noir detective stories: his characters are deliberately thin, their meanings come from the actions a cruel world throws them into and not from any determinate personality or character. There is not here the interiority which still shaped Ballard's characters even as these lived mostly in their own imaginations, and which still shapes Atwood's use of a first-person narrator in *The Handmaid's Tale*, even as that novel used the first person to draw forward and make tangible what an alternative mode of being collective, an alternative 'we', would feel like. In *Neuromancer*, the individual is back as an individual but is stripped of everything, including an opponent. Trouble when it comes

> was like a run in the matrix … some desperate but strangely arbitrary kind of trouble … totally engaged but set apart from it all, and all around you the dance of biz, information marching, data made flesh in the mazes of the black market.[36]

Likewise, the state still exists but is diminished: it does not set or even frame the regime, any regime or system. What does rather is information, the gathering and holding of it, the protecting of it and the use of the power it gives. That power has become lethally consolidated, held by the few corporations, and their black-market predators, that exist. Power as data, however, is also flesh and the movements of flesh made data, and power is hence vulnerable to puncturing, to invasion and to appropriation. The conflict which drives the narrative happens here.

Alongside the opposition between state and the individual, a whole host of structurally homologous oppositions have disappeared. There is no longer a city to be distinguished from 'the country': in America, there is 'the Sprawl' of the Eastern Seaboard, 'the Boston-Atlanta Metropolitan Axis' or BAMA, and its equivalents elsewhere; the opposition between art and popular culture likewise has gone, there is now only product, ornaments to lives lived without recourse to any needs of the 'soul' or the sublime.

Colour, borders, distinctions, oppositions, overcoming these latter: all exist only in the new narrative space of cyberspace, and all exist there only as a totality for those who can access them. For Case, the novel's paid or blackmailed 'hacker', cyberspace is release from some unnamed suffering to some unnamed 'home': it

> flowed, flowered for him, fluid neon origami trick, the unfolding of his distanceless home, his country, transparent 3D chessboard extending to infinity. Inner eye opening to the stepped scarlet pyramid of the Eastern Seaboard Fission Authority burning beyond the green cubes of Mitsubishi Bank of America, and high and very far away he saw the spiral arms of military systems, forever beyond his reach.
>
> And somewhere he was laughing, in a white-painted loft, distant fingers caressing the deck, tears of release streaking his face. (*N*, p. 60)

Case's access to cyberspace is that of a 'cowboy', an illicit border-crosser, a traveller whose function is to penetrate those layers of data designed to keep such travellers out, and to liberate such quantities of data as he is paid to liberate. The description of cyberspace, which is canonical in the scholarly literature on *Neuromancer*, indicates the more quotidian, cartographic, storage and disciplinarian functions of the virtual space shared but inhabited differently by the hackers, cartels and security firms Gibson is primarily interested in. That description is given by the text as a mock encyclopaedia entry, a piece of public relations rhetoric:

> Cyberspace. A consensual hallucination experienced daily by billions of legitimate operators, in every nation, by children being taught mathematical concepts … A graphic representation of data abstracted from the banks of every computer in the human system. Unthinkable complexity. Lines of light ranged in the nonspace of the mind, clusters and constellations of data. Like city lights, receding …' (*N*, p. 59, original ellipsis)

Here rendered by the figure of the receding city whose lights it both moves from and recalls, cyberspace is a totality of data rendered as abstractions: it is the sum and the parts, mapping those abstractions into those new spaces which define globalisation's reliance on abstraction, even as they also map the multiplicity of 'real' sites and their 'real' activities and the now only abstract relationships between them. Cyberspace fulfils the function performed in the earlier or classic dystopias by the state: it provides a totality which is mappable, which is knowable because it is mappable. The narrative space of the story as it unfolds outside of cyberspace has no such frame. In 'meat space' (the term used by the hackers to signal their disdain for life outside of cyberspace), everything is multitudinous yet oddly the same.

Regardless of the physical site of a scene (typically a street, a vendor's stall, a hotel room or clinic foyer, each impersonal, a space of transit between other spaces), only momentary encounters, casual or not-so-casual violences, glimpsed crowds and deteriorated wastelands or glossy high-end hotels, occur. And nothing frames these spaces where only movement occurs. Cyberspace provides a displaced articulation for totality, for the text to posit this world as a totality, one rendered via the abstractions or visual images of data owned and stored and protected. As Jameson puts it in the 2015 essay 'A Global Neuromancer',

> What cyberspace promises then are the paths that lead from one moment in the system to another one, and finally to the various nodes and centers which command the operation as a whole; and in our caper story, these paths also promise access, how most easily to break in, and to find the object of the question which is, of course, like everything else in cyberspace, information as such.[37]

In giving access to a totality, cyberspace enables the system to have a ghostly
or immaterial presence. It is not the system but only a representation of it:
you cannot beat or defeat a representation but you can negotiate it and, in
negotiating it, moments of conflict and moments of change can happen.

Before going on to identify the importance of that possibility of conflict,
an importance which resides in the text's opening up a moment of change,
a shift in the order of things and hence a possibility of history re-entering
the world of the narrative, it is necessary to ground that importance historically. In its refusal of history, Gibson's novum, or cognitive world, closely
articulates that sense of an ending that Jameson associated with the 1980s,
with the transmutation of late capitalism to an order in which future-
thinking, 'catastrophic or redemptive, gives way to a sense of the airless
domination of the present'. Within the nexus of commodification, subsumption and simulation peculiar to late capitalism, the capacity to think
historically is alienated, and 'spectacular society' may be understood as a
form of 'historical arrest, or rather a separation from one's own history',
providing a way to interpret Gibson's otherwise oddly static future.[38] In
the worlds of *Neuromancer*, whether that of Chiba City, the Sprawl or the
hotels and clinics of the wealthy areas of Tokyo or Istanbul, every item fits
the general system: nothing is out of sync. Things are commercial down to
the last neon detail, scavenged down to the vat-grown pieces of flesh and
organs bought and sold in the clinics of the wealthy or on the black markets
of the various underworlds.

'Freeside', an orbital spindle, is a destination few get to but once there it
is a scene identical to those on Earth: under its artificial sky, there are only
more brothels, banks, restaurants, hotels, fur shops, branches of 'the
Beautiful Girl Coffee franchise' (N, p. 141), the wealthy and those who
service them. Freeside 'is Las Vegas and the hanging gardens of Babylon,
an orbital Geneva' (117), as well-engineered and designed as the system on
the Earth it is a break from, and just as lacking in depth, difference or any
chance of change.

In the text, the only things which register the passing of time are discarded things, junk, the no-longer useful and now incongruous lumps of
metal, plastic, electronics and other products now recategorised as waste
products. Perhaps in homage to Philip K. Dick's 'kibble',[39] Gibson draws
attention to the seeping of time through, and in, this matter-out-of-time. In
the Sprawl, the Finn protects his business (high-tech and illicit scanning for
implants, providing spaces which can not be infiltrated by bugs, fencing)[40]
by burrowing it inside a dense tangle of 'junk':

> The junk looked like something that had grown there, a fungus of twisted
> metal and plastic. [Case] could pick out individual objects, but then they

seemed to blur back into the mass: the guts of a television so old it was studded with the glass studs of vacuum tubes, a crumpled dish antenna, a brown fiber canister stuffed with corroded lengths of alloy tubing. An enormous pile of old magazines ... flesh of lost summers staring blindly up. (*N*, p. 55)

There is no utopian charge to junk, if anything it is saturated even more intensely with the sadness which inhabits the whole novel: these fragments are 'blind' to the present and the present is blind to them. They just are there. But in their mute and unseeing presence, they rebuke that present. On Case's second encounter with the dusty interior of the Finn's den, he feels whilst moving

> along the tunnel of refuse ... [that] the stuff had grown somehow during their absence. Or else that it was changing subtly, cooking itself down under the pressure of time, silent invisible flakes settling to form mulch, a crystal-line essence of discarded technology, flowering secretly in the Sprawl's waste places. (*N*, p. 83)

Elsewhere time is not registered but is overcome and forgotten. Surgical implants of organs bio-engineered in vats, cryogenics and cloning, defeat the body's biological time; simstim and the cyberspace matrix itself, all refuse time to experience. The system itself has no need of time any more. 'Power' in this world 'meant corporate power' but the

> zaibatsus, the multinationals that shaped the course of human history, had transcended old barriers. Viewed as organisms, they had attained a kind of immortality. You couldn't kill a zaibatsu by assassinating a dozen key executives; there were others waiting to stop up the ladder, assume the vacated position, access the vast banks of corporate memory. (*N*, p. 235)

In a world without time, there can be no politics. The only agents of change allowed in the novel are the AIs, one called Neuromancer, one Wintermute, and the change they seek – to unify their two halves – is of a different order from human temporality. The state polices the existence of AIs strictly: they are for limited purposes only: security, toy, status.[41]

In a novel which deprives its totality of history, any intimation of historical depths becomes extra-charged. This is the case in two instances. The first is the figure of Corto. Introduced into the text in the third person, he is a missing person, an assemblage of sketchy facts and speculation, 'a precis ... full of gaps' (*N*, p. 94). Once a real person, he had been emptied out of himself when betrayed by his superiors in a past operation over Siberia. Betrayed, then lied to by the state whose army he served as a colonel, 'Corto was shipped to a military facility in Utah, blind, legless and missing most of his jaw' (*N*, p. 95). Once '[r]epaired, refurnished and extensively rehearsed', this figure had provided manufactured testimony to serve the interests of a

'Congressional cabal with certain vested interests in saving particular portions of the Pentagon infrastructure' (*N*, p. 97). Abandoned then, he had slowly lost his mind and ended up in a Paris mental health unit where he was located by the AI, Wintermute, and rebuilt as 'a personality substitute called Armitage' (*N*, p. 139). Armitage has no past, Wintermute built him out of the wreckage of Corto.

When Corto does appear briefly in the text, when he erupts out of Armitage, it is only to die. In that moment, he knows not where he has been or what he has done as he is still mired in the torturous present of his betrayal over Siberia, in the military operation called Screaming Fist. This present is now decades in the past. Yet when Corto appears, this present defines him: he appears on a screen, a 'white lozenge snapped into position, filled with a close-up of mad blue eyes … Colonel Willie Corto, Special Forces, strikeforce Screaming Fist, had found his way back' (*N*, p. 225). The only witness to this man's emergence or re-emergence from the personality of an assembled man, is the hacker, Case. He is appalled less by the transmutation or its cessation than by the absence from time of Corto whilst locked into Armitage:

> *But where have you been, man?* he silently asked the anguished eyes. Wintermute had built something called Armitage into a catatonic fortress named Corto. Had convinced Corto that Armitage was the real thing, and Armitage had walked, talked, schemed, bartered data for capital, fronted for Wintermute in that room in the Chiba Hilton … And now Armitage was gone, blown away by the winds of Corto's madness. But where had Corto *been*, those years? (*N*, p. 225 – original ellipsis and italics)

Where he had been is not a question answered by the novel or even a question it returns to. Corto had been invaded, occupied and put to use by a power he knew nothing of, Wintermute the sister AI to Neuromancer. No character has a vocabulary capable of parsing Corto any further than that and the third-person narrative remains distanced and distancing throughout.

It is a question that has an echo later in the text, however, when the second and last site of history in the text is breached, the Villa Straylight, home to the owners of Tessier-Ashpool, a '[f]amily organisation. Corporate Structure' (*N*, p. 87). TA are an anomaly in this present: 'a very quiet, very eccentric first-generation high-orbit family run like a corporation' (*N*, p. 87). Whilst nominally a public company, there has not been a 'share of Tessier-Ashpool traded on the open market in over a hundred years' (*N*, p. 87). This is an 'industrial clan', a throwback and a throwforward equally, a 'family inbred and most carefully refined' (*N*, p. 118), composed individually of multiple clones of the original mother and father, some of whom take others out of cryogenic storage infrequently to have sex and run the corporation.

The Villa Straylight occupies one end of the orbital spindle, Freeside. It is broken into by the team assembled by Armitage. Once inside they find not 'some clean hive of disciplined activity' (*N*, p. 207) typical of earlier dystopian heartlands but 'a body grown in upon itself, a Gothic folly' (*N*, p. 200). The art- and artefact-ornamented winding ways of the Villa are without reason and without logic: nothing but fancy and inwardness, whim and wealth, organises this disorder, nothing fits or tries to fit. A once-beautiful door has been sawn down to fit a particular entrance but is all wrong:

> Even the shape was wrong, a rectangle amid smooth curves of polished concrete. They'd imported these things ... and then forced it all to fit. But none of it fit ... the fittings had been hauled up the [gravity] well to flesh out some master plan, a dream long lost in the compulsive effort to fill space, to replicate some family image of self. (*N*, p. 208)

The family are an entity out of time yet they have surrounded themselves with historical artefacts which too are plunged out of time: 'Straylight was all wrong' (*N*, p. 207). The Villa is hermetic, an inward-looking maze of collected fragments, the 'tons of knick knacks, all the bizarre impedimenta they'd shipped up the well to line their winding nest' (*N*, p. 234), all of which sits there without context, meaning or purpose now. When the character Case differentiates the Tessier-Ashpool corporation from the multinationals and the zaibatsus, he thinks of them as being of a different order: they were human,

> he sensed the difference in the death of its founder. T-A was an atavism, a clan. He remembered the litter of the old man's chamber, the soiled humanity of it, the ragged spines of the old audio disks in their paper sleeves. One foot bare, the other in a velvet slipper. (*N*, p. 235)

Corporate power elsewhere, everywhere else, has left the realm of 'human history', shapes that history rather than being subject to it. In the final confrontation between the inhabitants of Straylight and the motley assemblage of hackers commissioned to steal the code which will enable the unification of the two AIs, it is this humanness Case presses on, and he calls it 'change':

> 'Give us the fucking code,' he said. 'If you don't, what'll change? What'll ever fucking change for you? You'll wind up like the old man. You'll tear it all down and start building again! You'll build the walls back, tighter and tighter ... I got no idea at all what'll happen if Wintermute wins, but it'll *change* something!' He was shaking, his teeth chattering. (*N*, p. 301, original ellipses)

The code, just a word, not data, is given. The two AIs merge and become the unhuman agent, in full possession of all history and all autonomy there is left in the world, of the two novels which will follow *Neuromancer*. The Villa Straylight continues its decay, it will not change as much as just finish. And our characters, as the world they inhabit, likewise do not change but just continue.

Conclusion

In 2000, Susan Buck-Morss wrote of the passing of mass utopia out of the political horizon of both East and West as the cessation of the Cold War rendered 'competition for the loyalty of the masses' redundant. In a grim description of the consequent reconfiguring of late capitalism's centres of promise, Buck-Morss asks what happens when 'the working classes' are no longer 'wooed by the carrot of commodity consumerism':

> Production for export is the blueprint for the success of capitalist firms, threatening to make obsolete the Fordist principle of putting dollars into the workers' pockets in order to increase domestic demand. Under the new order of global capitalism, workers in the first world are dispensable. And so are the homes and cities in which they dwell.[42]

It is not necessary to cite Theodor Adorno on the violence done to utopia by the 'consumerist dreams' Buck-Morss traces, or Debord on the theft of temporal agency by the 'spectacle', to note the impossibility of a utopia premised on the 'Fordist principle of putting dollars' in pockets. But we can suggest that the waning of those older, postwar and Cold War-inflected utopian promises is tangible also in the utopia's negative image, the dystopia. The question Buck-Morss poses is a question which could also form the epilogue to the reading of *Hello America* and *Neuromancer*: 'Benjamin insisted: "We must wake up from the world of our parents." But what can be demanded of a new generation, if its parents never dream at all?'[43] Dystopias too are a type of dream.

Notes

1 Theodor Adorno, 'The Meaning of Working through the Past' (1959 – radio lecture), trans. Henry W. Pickford, in Theodor Adorno, *Can One Live after Auschwitz? A Philosophical Reader*, ed. Rolf Tiedemann (Stanford: Stanford University Press, 2003), p. 4.
2 That the project of critical theory as a (no matter how fractured) whole, and in particular within the work of the first generation of the Frankfurt School, can be conceptualised as finding ways to think the past, to blast it open, and to understand why this is important, is one reason why Adorno is a useful thinker with whom to approach the paradoxically forgetful genre of dystopia. On the centrality of the task of finding ways to redeem the hopes of the past in that first

generation, see the Introduction to Michael Löwy's *Fire Alarm: Reading Walter Benjamin's 'On the Concept of History'* (2001), trans. Chris Turner (London; New York: Verso, 2016), pp. 1–16.

3 Adorno, 'The Meaning of Working through the Past', p. 4.

4 Orwell, *Nineteen Eighty-Four*, p. 324.

5 George Orwell, *Burmese Days* (1934) (London: Penguin, 2014), p. 37.

6 On the relationships opened up by the critical utopia between itself and history, see Tom Moylan, 'Beyond Negation: the Critical Utopias of Ursula K. Le Guin and Samuel R. Delany', *Extrapolation*, 21: 3 (Fall 1980), 236–51; Bill Ashcroft, 'Critical Utopias', *Textual Practice*, 21:3 (2007), 411–31; Joe P.L. Davidson, 'Retrotopian Feminism: the Feminist 1970s, the Literary Utopia and Sarah Hall's *The Carhullan Army*', *Feminist Theory*, 0:0 (2021), 1–19. For a different reading of how history and genre intertwine in *The Handmaid's Tale*, see Raffaella Baccolini, 'Gender and Genre in the Feminist Critical Dystopias of Katharine Burdekin, Margaret Atwood, and Octavia Butler', in Marleen S. Barr (ed.), *Future Females, the Next Generation: New Voices and Velocities in Feminist Science Fiction Criticism* (London; New York: Rowman and Littlefield, 2000).

7 Atwood, *The Handmaid's Tale* (1985) (London: Virago Press, 1987), p. 13. All further references are indicated in the text in parentheses.

8 Hannah Arendt: '[t]he supreme goal of all totalitarian governments is not only the freely admitted, long-ranged ambition to global rule but also the never-admitted and immediately realised attempt at the total domination of man', in Arendt, 'Social Science Techniques and the Study of Concentration Camps', in *Essays in Understanding, 1930–1954*, ed. Jerome Kohn (New York; London: Harcourt, Brace & Co., 1994), p. 240 (essay originally published in *Jewish Social Studies*, 12:1 (1950)). See also Arendt, *The Origins of Totalitarianism* (1951), rev. ed. (London: Penguin, 1979).

9 Yevgeny Zamyatin's *We* (1924) is a first-person narrative but it seems likely that these were less frequent than some version of a omniscient narrator until at least the 1960s. Notable examples of first-person forms after that point are Anthony Burgess's *A Clockwork Orange* (1962), J.M. Coetzee's *Waiting for the Barbarians* (1980), Kazuo Ishiguro's *Never Let Me Go* (2005) and Suzanne Collins's *Hunger Games* quartet (2008–20).

10 For a discussion specifically of the treatment of race and of racialised forms of erasure in the novel, a discussion triggered by the 'colour-blind' casting of the television serialisation of the novel (2017 – ongoing), see Christabelle Sethna, '"Not an Instruction Manual": Environmental Degradation, Racial Erasure and the Politics of Abortion in *The Handmaid's Tale*', *Women's Studies International Forum*, 80 (May/June 2020) https://doi.org/10.1016/j.wsif.2020.102362 (accessed 22 January 2022); for an exploration which pre-dates the novel's translation into a televisual phenomenon, see Maria Varsam, 'Concrete Dystopia: Slavery and Its Others', in Tom Moylan and Raffaella Baccolini (eds), *Dark Horizons: Science Fiction and the Dystopian Imagination* (London; New York: Routledge, 2003), pp. 203–24.

11 Fredric Jameson, *Archaeologies of the Future: The Desire Called Utopia and Other Science Fictions* (London, New York: Verso, 2005), p. 200. I would disentangle 'the uncertainty of memory' from the wider 'elegiac sense of the loss of the past' in Orwell's novel. Roughly put, memory privatises so that even smells – perfume as well as less attractive odours (the cabbage for example) – become inevitably drawn into the sensuous specificity of one's past, one subject's own untouchable even if absent past. The past which relies on language, the one which is threatened by language's usurpation would be a collective or a social past, one which would transcend – even as it allowed or enabled the figuring of – those private memories.

12 Ernst Bloch's analysis of a secret or sedimented utopian charge at work in anything from daydreams, art, images, games, 'the little word if', has long been important resource for Utopian Studies. See Ernst Bloch, *The Principle of Hope*, vols 1–3 (1954–59) On the use of Bloch's approach to utopia, see Darko Suvin on Bloch as 'the great dialectical utopologist', in Suvin, *Metamorphoses of Science Fiction*, p. 377.

13 The women in the group of Japanese tourists who visit Gilead wear skirts that are short, lipstick, heels, their hair uncovered. The narrator refers to them thus: 'That was freedom. Westernized, they used to call it' (38). The 'freedom' here is used ironically, the women can barely walk and look disfigured. But the shift of 'Western' to Japan will be a feature in other dystopias of the 1980s, especially in the work of William Gibson where Tokyo as much as New York or Washington (and much more so than the faded elegant irrelevance of European cities) becomes one of the interchangeable cities of globalisation.

14 This woman, alone and eccentric and possibly unhappy, is emblematic of the novel's treatment of the liberation movements of the 1960s and 1970s. As they will be portrayed later in the dystopian fictions of Michel Houellebecq, these were the movements which not only failed but which failed irresponsibly, threw the whole social order up into the air and failed to make order of the pieces which survived this tumult. Too pathetic to be culpable, however, the mother figure in Atwood's novel is yet a figure forbidden political agency – not by Gilead but by her daughter's indifference.

15 Yevgeny Zamyatin, *We* (1924) (London: Penguin, 1993), p. 165. For 'collectivism' as the common object of fear in dystopias before the 1960s, see Gregory Claeys, 'Part III: the Literary Revolt against Collectivism', in Claeys, *Dystopia: A Natural History*.

16 Frederik Pohl and Cyril M. Kornbluth's *The Space Merchants* (1952) is an iconic and early example of a novel in which commerce with advertising, rather than the state with the police, forms the network of norms from which the individual must disentangle herself before those norms generalise themselves to become all there is. See Chapter 2's brief discussion of this novel.

17 On the subgenre of the critical utopias, see Tom Moylan, *Demand the Impossible: Science Fiction and the Utopian Imagination* (1986) and the responses to Moylan's exploration of works by Joanna Russ, Ursula K. Le Guin, Marge Piercy and Samuel R. Delany, collected in the Ralahine Classics edition

of *Demand the Impossible* (Bern: Peter Lang, 2014), pp. 227–86. See also Bill Ashcroft, 'Critical Utopias', *Textual Practice*, 21:3 (2007), 411–31.

18 William Gibson, 'The Gernsback Continuum' (1981), in William Gibson, *Burning Chrome* (1988), new ed. (London: HarperCollins, 1995), p. 47. Gibson's short story (as all of his fiction) is ripe with allusions to his own genealogy: here the Gernsback of the title is a nod to Hugo Gernsback (1884–1967), a legendary figure in commercial science fiction from the 1920s to the 1950s.

19 Adorno and Horkheimer, 'Introduction', *Dialectic of Enlightenment*, p. xv.

20 Because such personal autonomy – over bodies, in the nuclear family, in the workplace and as more generally social subjects rather than objects – was historically novel for American women, it would be wrong to characterise *The Handmaid's Tale* as merely continuing the classical dystopia's fetishisation of private life as the only sphere of autonomy possible. It does not however figure or prefigure any other way of imagining human freedom. A more significant critique of the private sphere as itself a key affective and institutional aspect of the apparatus of non-freedom is articulated by Marge Piercy's *Woman on the Edge of Time* (New York: Knopf, 1976). There the melodrama of everyday life is cast as one more scene of violence.

21 Gibson, 'The Gernsback Continuum', p. 44.

22 In the Gernsback story the future memories are fragments of a 'mass dream'. The masses themselves have disappeared from these postwar articulations of mass culture.

23 Ballard, in a 1979 interview with Christopher Evans, titled 'The Space Age Is Over': see also the details in the interview from 1984, 'Against Entropy', in Simon Sellers and Daniel F.J. O' Hara (eds), *Extreme Metaphors: Interviews with J.G. Ballard, 1967–2008* (London: Fourth Estate, 2012), pp. 90–1.

24 Gibson, 'The Gernsback Continuum', pp. 39–40.

25 Ibid., p. 39.

26 Ibid., pp. 40–1.

27 Ibid., p. 48.

28 The classic text here is *Blade Runner* (1982) directed by Ridley Scott.

29 J.G. Ballard, *Hello America* (1981) (London: Fourth Estate/HarperCollins, 2014), p. 47. Hereafter references to the novel are included in the text in parentheses.

30 Ballard never has much time for female characters. The character of Professor Summers, less her fantasy than the fantasy she serves, is given in her name: Anne Summers, the name of a well-known multinational (British-owned) chain of shops for women specialising in lingerie and sex-toys, founded in 1970.

31 The 'tribes' also take the nominalism of middle-class professionalism as the vocabulary of their identity and rituals of identity: one tribe is called 'the Executives', members of which wear 'old grey suits of pin-striped worsted taken from the Trenton and Newark department stories ... [Their] ancestral foraging grounds were New Jersey, Long Island, and the one-time commuter areas around New York City' (*HA*, p. 63). Others are 'the Professors of Boston', the 'Bureaucrats around Washington ... the Astronauts down in Florida ... the

Gangsters ... around Chicago and Detroit .... The Gays from San Francisco ... the Divorcees ... an all-woman tribe from Reno' (*HA*, pp. 64–5). These 'tribes' too live – as much as they do live – on the carcasses of old cultural forms, relentlessly backwards facing, unable to generate any new forms of their own.

32 The notorious recluse and eccentric Howard Hughes (1905–76) is less an individual for Ballard than a byword for the peculiar shapes American power and wealth achieved in the era after the Second World War, shapes solidly anchored by extraction and exploitation but legible socially only in the gloss and gossip of Hollywood and 'obsession'. For Ballard's use of Hughes, see Umberto Rossi, 'Images from the Disaster Area: An Apocalyptic Reading of Urban Landscapes in Ballard's *The Drowned World* and *Hello America*', *Science Fiction Studies*, 21:1 (March, 1994), 81–97. Richard Nixon (1913–94), elected President of the United States in 1968 and re-elected in 1972, resigned in 1974 to avoid being impeached as part of the fallout from the Watergate scandal. Nixon, with the Kennedys and Ronald Reagan, was for Ballard one of the 'sacred monsters' of postwar American political life. See Ralph Rugoff's interview with Ballard in *Frieze* (6 May 1997) – accessible at www.frieze.com/article/dangerous-driving (accessed 22 January 2022).

33 Adorno, *Negative Dialectics* (1966), trans. E.B. Ashton (London; New York: Routledge, 2004), p. 26. See also Peter E. Gordon, *Adorno and Existence* (Cambridge, MA; London: Harvard University Press, 2016), especially pp. 37–83.

34 The adjective 'new' is important there as the imperial states of nineteenth-century Europe were already militarised and administratively totalising machines of oppression in in the name of an exploitation deemed to be in the national interest but were so at one remove from the 'night watchman' state of the 'civilised' imperial centre.

35 Corto's 'war' receives only a sketchy explanation in the novel, as if there have been many, none particularly important. See *Neuromancer*, p. 41.

36 William Gibson, *Neuromancer* (1984) (London: HarperVoyager, 2013), p. 10. Hereafter quotations from the novel are referenced in the text in parentheses.

37 Fredric Jameson, 'A Global Neuromancer', in Jameson, *The Ancients and the Postmoderns: On the Historicity of Forms* (London; New York: Verso, 2015), pp. 221–38. Jameson sees the plot of *Neuromancer* operating at two levels, one utilising the generic conventions of the 'heist or caper story', and one involving the new task of finding ways to represent what becomes 'cyberspace'.

38 Tom Bunyard, *Debord, Time and Spectacle: Hegelian Marxism and Situationist Theory* (Boston; Leiden: Brill, 2018), p. 144.

39 On 'kibble' as used by Dick to articulate an odd inversion of 'authenticity' (which I would read as history itself), see Timothy H. Evans, 'Authenticity, Ethnography, and Colonialism in Philip K. Dick's *The Man in the High Castle*', *Journal of the Fantastic in the Arts*, 21:3 (Nov. 2010), 366–83.

40 The Finn's work as a fence is described thus: he deals 'a lot with the Memory Lane crowd, and that's where you go for a quiet go-to that'll never be traced' (*N*. p. 87).

41 The Turing Registry operates the agents who police these purposes. It operates under a number of treaties worked out between different governments. There may be no politics left in the world but there is still the official philosophy of the bureaucrat though transplanted now to the lethal Turning Agents. Regardless of the catastrophe the system has made of the world, it is still the best of all possible worlds. To plan to augment an AI is not to commit a crime as much as it is to sin against the established order. When one such agent speaks, she does so in the horrified tones of one who beholds blasphemy: "you have no care for your species. For thousands of years men dreamed of pacts with demons. Only now are such things possible" (*N*, p. 187).
42 Susan Buck-Morss, *Dreamworld and Catastrophe: The Passing of Mass Utopia in East and West* (Cambridge, MA: MIT Press, 2000), p. 209.
43 Ibid., p. 209.

4

Michel Houellebecq and the end of dystopia?

Introduction: France as the capital of 'Eurabia'

'Eurabia' is the name of a fantastic plot which unifies a layer of the twenty-first-century radical right across Europe, America, New Zealand and Australia with a layer of the conservative right in the same countries. It has been fattened online but also has its existence in institutions (think-tanks, newspapers, publishing houses) and their funding, and in nodes of scholarship. It has been codified by authors like Bat Ye'or, Robert Spencer, Oriana Fallaci and Peder Are Nøstvold Jensen or 'Fjordman', one of the sources of inspiration for the Norwegian mass-murderer Anders Behring Breivik.[1] In the manifesto released by Breivik, *2083: A European Declaration of Independence*, the term 'Eurabia' is used 171 times.[2]

One of the key texts articulating this plot is Bat Ye'or's *Eurabia: The Euro-Arab Axis* (2005). Continuing the revisionist historical work on Islam she had begun in the 1980s and 1990s, Bat Ye'or's *Eurabia* argues that a covert agreement between liberal European 'elites' and 'Arab' governments has as its objective the 'Islamicisation' of Europe. Greed for oil for the former, and for conquest for the latter, had led to the creation of the sinister potential of the Euro-Arab Dialogue, which had, led by France, begun the move towards the creation of a 'Kafkaesque world functioning as a totalitarian anonymous system', utilising 'political correctness and censorship' so as to conceal the pursuit of 'Islamic domination'.[3]

This text is mentioned in Michel Houellebecq's 2015 dystopian novel, *Submission*. A member of the 'secret police' in the Ministry of the Interior notes with some satisfaction that political events in the novel's imagined present of 2022 have proved that 'old Bat Ye'or wasn't wrong with her fantasy of a Eurabian plot'.[4] This intelligence specialist, Alain Tanneur, had already outlined the plausibility of the creation of a 'broad republican front' to see off the threat of a Front National Presidency in 2022. The first round of the Presidential elections has just been held and has resulted in Marine Le Pen taking first place. To defeat the Front National in the second round or run-offs would require a political coalition, one composed of the Socialists, the Centre-Right UMP and the new Muslim Brotherhood whose leader, Mohammed Ben Abbes, would take the Presidency. For Tanneur, Ben Abbes is plausible as a unifying figure: he is charming, 'educated', ambitious and has the European Union in his sights. He does not want to dismantle it but to enlarge it, and to alter its internal composition. To shift its centre of gravity to the south, Turkey and Morocco, later Tunisia, Egypt and Algeria, would join. The sovereignty of nation states would weaken and disperse as the European institutions – 'which right now are anything but democratic' (S, p. 128) – move towards 'direct democracy', with the logical outcome being a directly elected President of Europe elected by a people of Europe which will, by then, include 'populous countries with high birth rates, such as Turkey and Egypt' (S, p. 129).

Ben Abbes, a 'moderate' Muslim intellectual, will put not France but a new Roman Empire, one with an Islamic France at its heart, on the map: Bat Ye'or's great mistake, muses Tanneur,

> was in thinking the Euro-Mediterranean countries would be weak compared with the Gulf states. We'll be one of the world's great economic powers. The Gulf will have to deal with us as equals … In a sense, all [Ben Abbes] wants is to realise de Gaulle's dream, of France as a great Arab power, and just you watch, he'll find plenty of allies. (S, p. 129)

By the point in the novel when Tanneur is forecasting the realisation of 'Eurabia', France – as the rest of Europe – has been in a state of incipient 'civil war' for years: riots are frequent, the desecration of mosques common, the streets of Paris burn, other cities are sites of frequent clashes between 'nativists' and groups of 'young Africans of no declared political affiliation'. Speaking in the year 2022, a character notes:

> Two years before, when the riots started, the media had a field day, but now people discussed them less and less. They'd become old news. For years now, probably decades, *Le Monde* and all the other centre-left newspapers, which is to say every newspaper, had been denouncing the 'Cassandras' who predicted civil war between Muslim immigrants and the indigenous populations of Western Europe. (S, p. 43)

In the run-up to the Presidential elections of 2022, elections contested by the candidate of the five-year-old Muslim Brotherhood, Ben Abbes, and by the candidate of the Front National, Marine Le Pen, as well as the centre-right Union for a Popular Movement (UMP) and the Socialists, violence flares. The fighting reaches the centre of Paris. At the Museum of the Romantics, scene of a cocktail reception for scholars of nineteenth-century literature, gunfire and the smoke of fires and of tear gas cloud the soirée.

In the election's first round, the NF receives 34.1 per cent of the vote, the Socialists 21.8 per cent, the Muslim Brotherhood 21.7 per cent and the UMP 12.1 per cent (*S*, p. 61). The scene is set for an almighty outbreak of political conflict and, in the two weeks leading up to the run-off vote, negotiations on a deal between the Socialists and the Muslim Brotherhood ignite the rage of the National Front constituency who assemble and march for insurrection. Le Pen warns that her march will take place 'by any means necessary' and quotes the 1793 Declaration of the Rights of Man and of the Citizen:

> When the government violates the rights of the people, insurrection is for the people, and for each portion of the people, the most sacred of rights and the most indispensable of duties. (*S*, p. 93)

The march itself, made up of people bearing placards that read 'This Is Our Home', proceeds down the Champs-Élysées towards the Arc de Triomphe where it explodes in violence. Masked men roam the night with assault rifles and automatic weapons, cars burn, windows smash and people die (*S*, pp. 97–9, 106). On the day of the second poll, twenty polling stations across France are attacked by groups of armed men, and the ballots stolen. The elections are suspended and rescheduled to be held with military protection for all polling stations (*S*, p. 113).

It is at this point that the centre-right and the Socialists form a 'coalition, a "broad republican front" ... backing the Muslim Brotherhood' (*S*, p. 123), and it is in the context of this republican front's formal announcement that Tanneur speculates on the plausibility of a new 'Islamo-European' empire. From this point in the novel, there is no more (visible) violence: the political violence is halted and then erased by a programme to 'Islamicise' France. The election is won by Ben Abbes 'by a landslide' (*S*, p. 134), the Front National disappears, and the streets are quiet. The programme of the new coalition is put into place seamlessly and without any serious opposition. At its core is the 'restoration' of the family to the centre of social life. Women 'leave' the workforce, start dressing 'modestly', in trousers and 'a kind of long cotton smock, ending at mid-thigh' (*S*, p. 146–7); some shops close, some new ones open. The streets are cleared of 'riff-raff' (*S*, p. 146) and there is a 'dramatic drop in crime: in the most troubled neighbourhoods it was down 90 per cent' (*S*, p. 164).

A dual system of education is formalised country-wide: religious education, privately funded, can be attended and taught only by those who belong to or who convert to the creed of the institution – Jewish, Catholic or Islamic. Public education, drastically defunded, finishes at the age of twelve: 'from then on [for most children] vocational training was encouraged. Secondary and higher education had been completely privatised' (*S*, p. 165). Women no longer teach in either. Any man who does must convert. A majority of university lecturers convert to Islam, taking three or four wives as part of their conversion. The departure of women from the workforce means that unemployment plummets. There is a 'brief surge of hope'

> during the most optimistic moment that France had known since the Thirty Glorious Years half a century before. The first days of Ben Abbes's national unity coalition had been a unanimous success … All of these reforms were meant to 'restore the centrality, the dignity, of the family as the building block of society': so the new president and his prime minister [François Bayrou] declared … (*S*, pp. 164–5)

Saudi money, or, variously, 'petro-dollars', pour into the country to achieve this restructuration of a 'civilisation' along purportedly 'Islamic' lines. There is a large new subsidy 'for families', the 'highly symbolic first measure passed by the new government' who reserve the subsidy for 'women who gave up working' (*S*, p. 165). Without apparent coercion, women do give up working. By the time this initiative is passed and put into practice, the novel has created a figure of modern 'Western' woman as harried, desexualised and miserable. The key figure is present only in an anecdotal form, a memory conjured up by a man to illustrate his observation that such women, 'who spent their days dressed up and looking sexy to maintain their social status', unlike their 'rich Saudi' counterparts (who hide all day in 'impenetrable black burkas'), collapse after work, abandoning all femininity once they arrive home, and with it 'all hope of seduction in favour of clothes that were loose and shapeless' (*S*, p. 74). Conversely, the 'rich Saudi women' use the night to transform themselves into 'birds of paradise with their corsets, their see-through bras, their G-strings with multi-coloured lace and rhinestones' (*S*, p. 74).

This loose 'observation' is then made concrete by the recollection of a dinner party hosted by a professional couple at their family home. The wife, Annelise, earns more than her husband at her job in the marketing department of a telecoms network. The evening of the dinner, 'she'd been working all day and was exhausted'. The food is a disaster, the children scream, her partner is drunk. In a sequence of narrative moves which are the signature of Houellebecq's writing style, the outrageously general is given a nod in the direction of a specific example or illustration before settling down to the status of a given, now a premise for a new narrative move. Here the exhaustion of a professional woman on a Friday evening morphs into the determinate dilemma of 'the Western' de-domesticated and de-feminised family: such women get home

> around nine, exhausted … collapse, get into a sweatshirt and tracksuit trousers, and that's how she'd greet her lord and master, and some part of him

must have known – had to have known – that he was fucked, and some part of her must have known that she was fucked, and that things wouldn't get better over the years. The children would get bigger, the demands at work would increase, as if automatically, not to mention the sagging of the flesh. (*S*, p. 76)

A little later I will explore in more detail both the novel's reliance on this narrative style, and the anti-feminist and more widely anti-left politics which arguably underpin it, but for now I wish to stay with this sketch of the regime the novel inaugurates, the regime which posits this aggressive assimilation to a unified yet 'moderate' Islam as a 'solution' to the unhappiness and exhaustion of the contemporary 'Western' family. The figure to set beside Annelise, her contrary parallel, is a double figure, the two wives of a 'middle-aged Arab businessman, dressed in a long white djellaba and a white keffiyeh', travelling first class on the Poitiers to Paris train. The 'two young girls facing him, barely out of their teens – his wives, clearly – ... were excited and giggly. They wore long robes and multi-coloured veils' (*S*, pp. 187–8). These laughing 'Arab girls' are here the platform for a militant rejection of an autonomy whose function in the 'West' was only to erode happiness in women and men. 'Islam' gets gender right:

> Under an Islamic regime, women – at least the ones pretty enough to attract a rich husband – were able to remain children nearly their entire lives. No sooner had they put childhood behind them than they became mothers and were plunged back into a world of childish things ... There were just a few years where they bought sexy underwear, exchanging the games of the nursery for those of the bedroom – which turned out to be much the same thing. Obviously they had no autonomy, but as they say in English, *fuck autonomy*. (*S*, pp. 188–9, original italics)

The availability of such wives to the professional men who convert ('according to sharia law you could have up to four' (*S*, p. 189)) succeeds in securing the continuity of the institutions of France. With women no longer working, unemployment radically decreased, and professional men happy, the regime looks set to succeed. In this the most depopulated of dystopian fictions, the unhappiness of contemporary France is a matter of unhappy bourgeois couples or unhappy single professionals exiled from coupledom by age or bodily stigma. The regime 'answers' the unhappiness openly and proudly. In 'moderate' language, reassuring in terms of a familiar cosmopolitan and charismatic veneer, Ben Abbes enjoys a 'state of grace' (*S*, p. 164).

In keeping with the novel's prolific and knowing usage of Islamophobic tropes, Ben Abbes – who looks like the 'neighbourhood grocer' his Tunisian father was (*S*, p. 88) – is cunning, manoeuvring to realise his international ambitions while pacifying his domestic population. Turkey and Morocco are already in negotiations to join the EU: the 'rebuilding of the Roman

Empire was well under way' (S, p. 164). Finally, our narrator imagines his own conversion, imagines accepting his old job back at the now Islamic University of the Sorbonne, looking forward to 'choosing' his wives from amongst his 'new students – pretty, veiled, shy' (S, p. 249).

His last words, the words which finish the novel, speak of his conversion as that which would open for his life another chance at life, a future which would allow the cancellation of an unwanted past –

> it would be the chance at a second life, with very little connection to the old one.
>   I would have nothing to mourn. (S, p. 250)[5]

Where is dystopia?

The question 'where is dystopia?' is not one to put to the novel's geography. Its own sense of Europe's 'suicide', its 'putrid decomposition' in the multiculturalism and the 'soft humanism' of social democracies corroding from the inside, is clear: there is the West and there is the rest. This novum is not spatial as much as it is 'civilisational' – two spaces interact, the space of a hypostatised Islamic civilisation encounters an exhausted and enfeebled 'Western' civilisation which has nurtured this usurper within itself. The former 'wins'. The rest of the world enters into the novum only to illustrate the abstractness of the non-'Western' rest-of-the-world: India and China have made the mistake of not preserving 'their traditional civilisations'. They have been 'contaminated by Western values, they, too, were doomed' (S, p. 227). Only Islam is vigorous: its patriarchal model of family life the key mechanism securing its fertility and consequently its own civilisational health, and its capacity to become the chosen vehicle of 'world domination':

> liberal individualism triumphed as long as it undermined intermediate structures such as nations, corporations, castes, but when it attacked that ultimate social structure, the family, and thus the birth rate, it signed its own death warrant; Muslim dominance was a foregone conclusion.[6] (S, p. 226)

There is no such thing as a French Muslim as France was made out of medieval Christendom, a civilisation made over a millennium, one undone in just over two hundred years. For the temporal politics of this novum to work, much must be rendered invisible by the novel, not least the history of France's colonies and the work of counter-decolonisation movements, but also the 'war on terror', a war which arguably prepared the novel's context, and the context of its successful reception. The question is one rather of what the novum is itself, how does it manifest as a dystopia?

For Nouriel Roubini, in a 2015 *Guardian* article headed 'Europe's Politics of Dystopia', there was no question but that Houellebecq's novel was part of the genre of dystopia. Castigating the 'recent trend in Europe' for the supporters of an 'illiberal state capitalism' to attain political power, Roubini's ire is directed at how these political movements, 'led by populist right-wing authoritarians', target the EU or other institutions of supra-national governance. He adds to the recent electoral success of the right-wing Polish Law and Justice Party

> *Putinomics* in Russia, *Órbanomics* in Hungary, *Erdoğanomics* in Turkey, or a decade of *Berlusconomics* from which Italy is still recovering. Soon we will no doubt be seeing *Kaczyńskiomics* in Poland.[7]

Roubini uses his short essay to note a 're-emergence of nationalist, nativist populism' and to outline what is needed to 'halt Europe's slide toward secular stagnation and nationalist populism. He finishes with a passage that situates *Submission* in the tradition of dystopias as warnings:

> Failure to act decisively now will lead to the eventual failure of the peaceful, integrated, globalised, supra-national state that is the EU, and the rise of dystopian nationalist regimes. The contours of such places have been reflected in literary works such as George Orwell's *1984* [*sic*], Aldous Huxley's *Brave New World* and Michel Houellebecq's latest novel *Submission*. Let us hope that they remain confined to the printed page.[8]

This passage is useful in reminding us of the presence of the genre of dystopia as an interpretative force, a tradition shaping interpretation of any one novel which participates in that genre. *Submission* relies on the pre-existence of this interpretative force, relies on it and triggers it in its attention to the structural features necessary to establish a dystopia. In Houellebecq's novel, such features are present but are – like writing itself and the novel in particular – laughed at, so many formal features trying to hold back decay. In *Submission*, the dystopian novum is present formally but is turned inside out. This dystopia tempts, and individuals submit. There can be no counter-narrative in such a novum. Likewise, it is not the present which forms the object of any commitment, negative or otherwise, but a past which long precedes that present, one this dystopia knows is gone. This leaves the novel empty of commitment – as it is empty of much of the present – unless we count as committed the interpretation of modernity as a wholly negative force the novel asks its reader to abide by.

In putting *Submission* beside *Brave New World* and *Nineteen Eighty-Four*, Roubini mistakes Houellebecq's novel for one that cares. It is the classic dystopia's negative commitment to the present which organises Roubini's sketch of the world that we would lose if the dystopia of

Submission came off the page: an unarticulated but determined attachment to the 'peaceful, integrated, globalised, supra-national state that is the EU'. To come to such a conclusion, Roubini did not read *Submission*: he read it as the genre demanded, not noticing that the novel both despises that present and recreates it formally for a future where Islam is its content. In the remainder of this chapter, I will explore each of the two ways the novel shrugs off or turns away from, while relying on, the conventions of the genre.

The novel has the form of a first-person narration divided into five parts, with each part broken up into approximately seven unmarked chapters. The narrator is an academic, a single man in early middle age, unhappy, lonely, dissatisfied, an inhabitant of the relatively one-dimensional Houellebecqian repertoire of such male characters. His is the account of a dispassionate witness to events, an observer of a France, and a Europe, on the verge of 'civil war', and also of the swerve away from that implosion inaugurated by the Muslim Brotherhood. Although he ends the text on the threshold of his seduction by the new order, this in itself does not invalidate his structural position as one on the outside of the regime, one who can 'see' it. What renders his position odd, and innovative, is the relationship it has with the present, a present thereby given a substantial rather than an absent existence in the text. This narrator does not rage: Houellebecq's fictional universe is not one in which either characters or style rages. The final section of this chapter will consider that style specifically, what it does to the form of the dystopia, and what the latter does to it. For now, however, it is the novel's use of the genre's narrative conventions we need to explore.

Submission as it opens its novum seems to confirm the narrative schema of a classic dystopia: here is a future which is thrown into relief by an individual who watches it, judges it and eventually moves – though instead of moving against the regime, here our 'individual' moves towards it, seeking assimilation to it. The narrator, François, initially retires from his university position rather than convert to Islam to save that position. From the moment of Ben Abbes's government taking power and beginning its reformation of the world of France, he hovers on the edges, drinking, musing and noticing both the 'surface agitations' and the 'deep and rapid change' (*S*, p. 166) that France was undergoing beneath that surface turbulence. He is the reader's only guide and he is not of, but only a witness of, the new regime as it assembles itself by reassembling all else. His is not a narrative of counter-resistance or of rebellion, however. It is a narrative, by and large, of indifference pockmarked with moments of curiosity. One such moment is energised by a conversation with the figure of Robert Rediger, the new President of the Islamic University of the Sorbonne, a proselytiser for the Islam he converted to once he gave up his dalliance with a 'nativist movement' as he saw that Christian Europe had 'already committed suicide' (*S*, p. 213).

At the moment of speaking here, François is taking tea in Rediger's house at 5 Rue des Arenes, once the house of Jean Paulhan, the lover of Dominique Aury when she wrote *Story of O*.[9] The house's relationship to the novelist is invoked by Rediger moments before he launches into a description of the 'connection' between the erotic dynamics of *Story of O* and Islam's call to human beings left bereft by France's earlier embrace of an atheist humanism. As this comparison or 'connection' is key to understanding this dystopia's re-articulation of the counter-narrative of 'resistance' as a flattened and de-temporalised place of rejection, I want to reproduce it here.

Rediger admires Aury's novel: 'it is a constant source of happiness to think that I live in the house where Dominique Aury wrote *Story of O* – or, at least, in the house of the lover she wrote it for. It's a fascinating book, don't you think?' (*S*, p. 216). François agrees – 'the book had a passion, a vitality that swept everything before it' – and Rediger carries on:

> 'It's submission,' Rediger murmured. 'The shocking and simple idea, which had never been so forcefully expressed, that the summit of human happiness resides in the most absolute submission. I hesitate to discuss the idea with my fellow Muslims, who might consider it sacrilegious, but for me there's a connection between woman's submission to man, as it's described in *Story of O*, and the Islamic idea of man's submission to God.' (*S*, p. 217)

The submission to Rediger's God of Islam is a submission to the world as it is in its perfection. Before this creation, 'man' can only submit:

> Islam accepts the world, and accepts it whole. It accepts the world *as such*, Nietzsche might say. For Buddhism, the world is *dukkha* – unsatisfactoriness, suffering. Christianity has serious reservations of its own. Isn't Satan called 'the prince of the world'? For Islam, though, the divine creation is perfect. It's an absolute masterpiece. (*S*, p. 217, original italics)

The reduction of the sexual politics of *Story of O* to the simple misogyny of Houellebecq's novel's own understanding of women is not what is important here, nor is the novel's transmutation of Islam into a parodic vehicle of its own misogyny. This is not a novel that has any interest in women's sexual desires. It has even less of an interest in the life of any Muslim who might practise her religion in France. There is little point staying with the novel's pointed obnoxiousness except to note its moments and then to explore what purpose they serve in the narrative itself. What is important, at this moment in our exploration of that narrative, is the linking together of submission and a sexual charge, and the naming of this link as 'happiness': 'the summit of human happiness resides in the most absolute submission' (*S*, p. 217).

This link and its name are a recurring feature in the classical dystopias of the first half of the twentieth century, and arguably survive in the dystopias of our own day though in forms altered and minimised by an erosion of the novelty and shock of 'mass culture' as an everyday facet of life.[10] For the first generation of dystopian fictions, up to and into the 1950s, 'mass culture' was understood, from the perspective of a formally extant 'high culture', as a force of seduction or of addiction, a force designed to appeal to the 'instinct' in humans, to passion and to emotion, to that yearning for self-dissolution in another life – even if a fictional life. Study of this linkage is worthwhile as both the link itself and the frequency of its recurrence suggest that the narrative/counter-narrative schema of Raffaella Baccolini and Tom Moylan explored in Chapter 2 needs a third term. Their stress on language in dystopia as Janus-faced, as something the regime needs and the resistance takes, needs to be refined a little. Baccolini and Moylan note how certain things have to be done to language to generate a self-image for the regime adequate to its pretensions to be universal and eternal, to be necessary. It is this attempted control of language which provides a weak spot where the counter-narrative lodges and starts to build.

Baccolini and Moylan point out this reliance on language in a manner which is useful here:

> Throughout the history of dystopian fiction, the conflict of the text turns on the control of language ... discursive power, exercised in the reproduction of meaning and the interpellation of subjects, is a complementary and necessary force [to material ownership and material violence]. Language is a key weapon for the reigning dystopian power structure ... [T]he process of taking control over the means of language, representation, memory, and interpellation is a crucial weapon and strategy in moving dystopian resistance from an initial consciousness to an action that leads to a climactic event that attempts to change the society.[11]

The language pulled back from the regime is not neutral, however, though it is normative. This is a definite type of language-use, a peculiar type of literacy – a literacy for which Shakespeare is a cue, a literacy which can cope with truth, beauty and even with nature. This literacy is a key moment in the novum's relationship to the present, that negative commitment which cannot be figured but is pervasive. No matter how energetic its estrangement from that present is, no matter how energetic its own estranging work is, the novum has to find some way to articulate the moment Baccolini and Moylan call 'counter-resistance', and, in the classic dystopia, that moment is one reliant on thematising as valuable the language-use that the dystopian fiction itself relies on.

The articulation of submission as an eroticised surrender of autonomy is itself a narrative feature of the classic dystopia. In that model, the rituals of submission vary but the presence of an eroticism in those rituals across their many iterations suggests something structural, an understanding not of the dystopian regime or its narrative but of those that narrative incorporates as 'the people'. It suggests that, for dystopia, there is a sexual hunger in the need for domination, and this hunger can be instrumentalised by any political order with the correct knowledge and access to technologies to put that knowledge into practice, especially through the technologies and practices of what has become of culture, that complex Adorno theorised as the culture industry.

That it is an understanding of the political vulnerability of 'the people' to mass seduction confined, in that form, largely to the earlier moment of the genre's history is suggested by the transmutation of that surrender into a de-eroticised, sometimes almost dutiful acquiescence, in later iterations.[12] By the novels of the 1970s and 1980s, a significant minority of dystopian fictions use inequality rather than hegemony as any dystopian regime's premise and base.[13] This altered the narrative/counter narrative schema as theorised by Baccolini and Moylan and generated the analytic and periodising categories of the 'critical utopia' and, a little later, the 'critical dystopia'. In the work of Philip K. Dick or Joanna Russ, in Ursula K. Le Guin, Samuel R. Delany, Thomas Disch, Octavia Butler and Marge Piercy, 'the personal and the political are interrelated but not conflated' as Moylan argues in *Demand the Impossible*: in

> linking the process of personal experience and self-actualisation with the process of politicization and social change, the critical utopias reflect the experience of activism in the 1960s and 1970s and add to an understanding of revolutionary psychology that can continue to inform ongoing oppositional work.[14]

In the critical dystopias of the 1980s and 1990s, also in those novels written with a sensibility which would be called cyberpunk, there are 'winners and losers' only, the state has withered in its scope or reach, and in its need to demand or to otherwise secure submission: indeed it is not capable of generating or co-ordinating or even of needing any narrative of its own order. Rather the desperate, the 'losers', the 'have-nots' live lives of such desperation and deprivation that survival becomes an all-encompassing taker of time. Hardship interpellates the demands of everyday survival, leaving no room for a regime narrative to work, let alone to flourish.

To take just one example, *The Running Man*, the important but neglected dystopian novella published by Stephen King as Richard Bachman in 1982. Ben Richards is the televised prey, the running man of the programme of that name: '*The Running Man*, ... the biggest thing going on FreeVee ... filled with chances for viewer participation, both vicarious and actual.'[15] His job is to keep alive as long as he can while being hunted, earning one hundred 'new dollars' for each hour he remains 'free'.[16] Richards has to tape himself twice a day each day he is on the run. He then sends the tapes to the Games Authority who broadcast them each evening alongside commentary on the hunters' chase, and on Richards, his progress, place and potential victims. The broadcasts have a live studio audience and a viewing audience of two hundred million. While the studio audience bays for his blood with a rage and a fear which is 'half-sexual … blood hate in their eyes',[17] the viewing audience is made up of the 'technicos', the middle-class and prosperous well, *and* the working-class or unemployed Americans Richards himself comes from. His address to them splits in two the myth of 'the people' that inequality founds itself on:

> 'All of you watching this,' Richards's image said slowly. 'Not the technicos, not the people in the penthouses – I don't mean you shits. You people in the Developments and the ghettos and the cheap highrises. You people in the cycle gangs. You people without jobs. You kids getting busted for dope you don't have and crimes you didn't commit because the Network wants to make sure you aren't meeting together and talking together. I want to tell you about a monstrous conspiracy to deprive you of the very breath in y -'[18]

The Games Authority, an arm of the Network, interrupts the broadcast and dubs his words so that they become an undifferentiated expression of obscenity and objectless rage. The programme needs Richards to be a unifying object of hatred: Richards himself addresses no unity but two constituencies, his own and those he deems to be so comfortable they are oblivious to where comfort comes from, that it comes from anywhere at all except the magical realm of individual effort or luck. When he kidnaps a middle-class woman, she cannot understand his desperation as anything other than an expression of his own moral degeneracy. She hears his words as the expression of that degeneracy, he uses words which are as 'dirty' as he is. These words do not refer to anything but Richard's corrupt self. As Richards rebukes her, he realises there 'was no base of communication with these beautiful chosen ones. They existed up where the air was rare':

> 'When this is over … you can go back to your nice split-level duplex and light up a Doke and get stoned and love the way your new silverware sparkles in the highboy. No one fighting rats with broom handles in your neighbourhood or shitting by the back stoop because the toilet doesn't work. I met a little girl five years old with lung cancer. How's that for disgusting? What do -'
> 'Stop!' she screamed at him. '*You talk dirty!*'[19]

All dystopian fictions split 'the people' as they organise their counter-narratives. To be counter or to be against the 'narrative' of the regime does not always require an appropriation and reconstruction of the regime's understanding of 'the people', however. If in the early decades of the modern dystopia's existence, a counter-narrative of resistance is central to the genre's operations, it is one which cannot capture or align with itself the majority of the population – either as 'the masses', 'the proles', or a more socially neutral 'majority'. The classic dystopia, that is, is so wedded to or reliant on a concept of dystopian power as reciprocally imbricated with a historically shaped but fundamentally ontological human need or desire to submit, to be governed absolutely, that it typically gives the regime 'the people', leaving opposition to be the property or function of the one or the few, and the reader, still a member of a public, a reading public now banned from the world of the novel, to be the interlocutor, the addressee of the counter-narrative's understanding of what it is to be human.

Houellebecq's *Submission* returns to and re-energises the older narrative schema of the classic dystopia, but so deep and wide is this novel's indifference to people – an indifference which is not a political indifference but one mandated by Houellebecq's style even as the classic form of the dystopia demands some notion of 'the people' – and to what they do that there are no people here to act the surrender, to *be* submissive. Rather the submission becomes an abstract or cerebral event, on the one hand a description of what the text has no interest in dramatising, and on the other a 'civilisational' submission, the sigh and sign of an exhausted, a hollowed-out France (and by lazy extension, Europe, and by lazier extension, 'the West') which has already surrendered all the good of itself to that mixture of capitalism and hypocrisy Houellebecq sees as modernity. The novel's Islam seduces not France or Europe but these hollow remains, modernity's leftovers.

The vehicle of the non-submission, François, the place formally of our counter-narrative in the novel, is also the site or filter where the 'values' of civilisation become tangible and tangible as gone, lost to a past which is long gone, knowledge of it increasingly inaccessible or accessible only in glimpses, flashes of a beauty which moves one, or a homeliness which answers a wordless yearning.

In place of commitment

With a turn to François, however, we enter the moment where the second of the novel's two breaches of the dystopian form must take centre-stage. The first was the invocation and emptying out of a narrative of resistance: that narrative, the genre's *counter-narrative*, should be there, and is not there. The second is the use of a negative commitment *in* the novel itself, a scorn for a (long) present which present thus becomes vividly visible and objectified as to blame for the dystopia it brings into being. Islam is the future's punishment for France's – and more widely for Europe's – modernity in a dance of temporal levels which breaks the rules of dystopia even as confirming their potency. The novel has no quarrel with the regime of 'minority sharia' that the Muslim Brotherhood initiate (*S*, p. 67). It does not need one, as that will be provided by the reception the novel knowingly nods to. Where other dystopias leave the reader to provide the context in which the present becomes valuable, and vulnerable because threatened, Houellebecq's dystopia tosses the present aside in favour of a past so distant that few can hear its echoes.

The official publication date of *Submission* in France was the day of the attack on the *Charlie Hebdo* offices, 7 January 2015. In that attack, only the most lethal of several related attacks in that month, twelve people were shot dead and eleven were injured. The edition of the magazine published that day had a cover caricaturing Houellebecq as a 'masturbating drunkard'.[20] The novel or rather its reception was caught up in the narrative which congealed the bloody events of January 2015 into a defining episode of where France stood in the 'war on terror', and of what 'Islam' was capable of doing. *Submission* was hailed for its 'prophetic' nature and became a bestseller in France, then in Italy and Germany, and, later in 2015, in English-speaking countries. It is necessary to draw attention to the immediate context of its publication as it is necessary to resist the lure of critiquing the novel in the light of that immediate context. The situating of 'Islam' as not *of* France is centuries old. The role of the French children and grandchildren of postwar immigrants from the Maghreb in contributing to the 'decline' of France, the corrosion of what then becomes an essentialising *laïcité* or secularism, is a more recent phenomenon and is one tributary within the transnational flow of Islamophobia quickened and enriched by the 'war on terror' mounted after the events of 11 September 2001.

Indeed, the narrative which articulated the attacks on the offices of *Charlie Hebdo* and a Jewish grocery on the eve of 7 January interweaved itself sufficiently with those earlier American attacks to create its own temporal pattern, a pattern which served to 'institute a traumatic rupture in time that severed the events from any prior history and ensnared the nation as unwitting witnesses in a spectacular present'.[21] As Nicholas De Genova elaborates in his examination of the prehistory of the narrative of *Charlie Hebdo* versus 'barbarbism', this articulatory move was made if not easier, then at least made possible, by the previous decades' practice of a 'classical act of postcolonial historical amnesia', an amnesia made difficult by the presence in France of the descendants of immigrants from the former French colonies. That present had been subjected to a militant form of *laïcité* for decades as part of a narrative of Frenchness which demanded that French Muslims should practise visible forms of de-solidarisation, a de-ethnicisation of their own way of being French so as to properly be French:

> France's desire to retreat into a sanitized narrative of national greatness, miraculously cleansed of the filth of its colonial legacy, ha[d] been met with the postcolonial boomerang effect that presents itself in the form of mass migration, above all from the countries formerly subjugated by France.[22]

When *Submission* depicts women wearing the burka walking confidently in public, Houellebecq plugs his dystopia into the twisted skein of that decades-old 'sanitized narrative' and its complicated inability to see French Muslims as French. On the morning after the first round of elections, François notes that, in the university, 'the girls in burkas' were carrying themselves differently: 'They moved slowly and with new confidence, walking down the very middle of the hallway, three by three, as if they were already in charge' (*S*, p. 63). The confidence of these women the morning after the first round of elections, the absence of their need for protection by their 'brothers', bodes ill for France. The 'submission' hymned later by Rediger is one they have already undergone, submission to their God, and to the patriarchal cycle of life mandated by that God, and they flourish in it, they thrive. Veiled, they move down 'the very middle of the hallway, three by three, as if they were already in charge' (*S*, p. 63). This identification of public space as vulnerable to such appropriation provides an analytic moment which can link us back to the question of genre and from there to what Houellebecq's novel does to give the present in *Submission* a shape.

The dystopian fictions of the first half of the twentieth century used a classically liberal model of civil society, one in which there is a clearly defined sphere of privacy, the bourgeois family, and a model subjectivity capable of operating outside that sphere once the subject achieves maturity. The intimate domain of the family and more widely the household embody an autonomy which is not given to the child but which he achieves as a contingency requiring much practice once he reaches his manhood (the model of autonomy assumes masculinity). That autonomy then, as much as reason itself, is constitutive of individuality, of the subject's being legally, economically and socially visible, the signature of what it is to be human in the world. As an autonomous being, the individual may then experience the world with some agency, may experience the private spheres of others, but above all that agency will enable experience of the exhilarating, frightening, uncertain world of a civil society speeded up, expanded and rendered both unknowable in its scope and intensely knowable in its profusion of technologies and processes of knowledge. All outside the subject may threaten his autonomy, his personally possessed privacy, or may extend and enrich it. Dystopian fictions involve models of domination which have as their premise not that such autonomy is alienable but that *it should be inalienable*: the taking of it, the reduction of autonomous beings to the status of 'children' or of 'slaves', is what is dystopian about these illegitimate forms of domination, these 'unnatural' excesses of order.

In Houellebecq's work, however, privacy, as the habitus of autonomy, does not work as it should: there is no 'home life' to be at home in, and autonomy is not so much a fiction, an illusion kept alive in bad faith by those unwilling to surrender the shallow freedoms of the generation of 1968, as a joke: the body's materiality, its steady and inevitable degradation, sees to it that failure, decay, loneliness and a chronic low-level depression are what happens when time, as it must, meets autonomy.[23] For autonomy to be thus present as something so bleakly ontologically futile, a wisp to be cancelled out not by a political force but by the metonymic work of a bout of erectile dysfunction, for example, or of dyshidrosis, or of haemorrhoids (each of which afflicts François in *Submission*), then autonomy has to be already assumed as present. Worthless it may be but only because it is possessed and yet does not secure happiness. In other words, autonomy is, in the *monde houellebecquien*, treated as a bourgeois male property, the property of those who have no material cares (saving the weight of ageing), who want for nothing and are hence 'free' to want what they cannot have – be that a health, vigour, strength or beauty possible only in the very young, or a happiness possible only in moments of sexual *extremis*, moments which cannot last.

In her 2013 study of Houellebecq's writing, Carole Sweeney notes the shaping or contouring force of consumption in this fictional world; a world of 'an overwhelming feeling of acedia', a world inhabited by 'protagonists who can neither understand nor enjoy the alienating "sex and shopping" world of consumption around them'.[24] It is that world, a world of spectacle, in which everything meaningful is on show, and is in competition with everything else on show; a world in which everything visible is available, and that availability is tedious or painful; this is the world in which 'autonomy' does not take on meaning as much as have meaning sucked out of it, leaving it one more relic of a bygone age. It exists, it was fought for, and in the realm of economic transactions, it was won but in the world that triumph generated, autonomy is just another name for atomisation. For Houellebecq, autonomy exists at its most powerful in the form of money, the capacity to buy, a capacity never not present in Houellebecq's world, but one which never succeeds, a capacity which fails to issue forth the happiness promised by the marketing campaigns which dress commodities.

For Sweeney,

With few kinship ties and working long hours, Houellebecquian characters (if they can even be properly called that) live alone in a quotidian round of ready meals, sexual disappointment, and mail order catalogues. Economically affluent, they are often erotic paupers ... [who] live insignificantly and move indifferently within an environment so systematically reified that the quintessence of freedom is now defined as the ability to order a 'guaranteed delivery of hot food at a given hour.'[25]

These are the 'failed subjects' of capitalism only if capitalism becomes consumption, however, and if subjectivity becomes only affect. These are indeed subjects who cannot feel pleasure in the food, bodies or places they encounter or purchase access to, but they are fully functioning subjects in their relationship to the means of such consumption. Houellebecq's protagonists have in common their professional status. Starting with the thirty-year-old narrator of *Whatever* (1994), an analyst programmer in a computer software company – 'I'm in middle management ... my salary is two and a half times the minimum wage; a tidy purchasing power, by any standards'[26] – Houellebecq's central figures get older and richer, move higher up the managerial ladder or become more successful in the arts, as Houellebecq's fame progresses.

In *Atomised* (1999/2000), Michel Djerzinski is a scientist, the head of his department with fifteen researchers in the team he leads. His 'half-brother', Bruno, is a teacher of literature who, after a breakdown when he sexually abuses one of his students, is 'found' a job by the Education Nationale with the Commission des Programmes des Français: 'I couldn't teach any more, and I didn't get the school holidays, but I was on the same salary.'[27] Michel in *Platform* (2001/2003) is an accountant in the Ministry of Culture before he inherits money from his father and fades into becoming an adviser on the entrepreneurial potential of sex tourism. By *Possibility of an Island* (2005/2005), the protagonist, here a comedian who makes films and music as well as doing stand-up, all in the 'vein of right-wing anarchy, along the lines of "one dead combatant means one less cunt able to fight"',[28] earns millions. This escalates again in *The Map and the Territory* (2010/2011) where the art of Jed Martin moves from obscurity to multi-million Euro auctions, before de-escalating in *Submission*. As a senior academic, François earns the salary of a 'full professor' in a literature department (*S*, p. 16) before retiring, in his mid-forties, on a full pension of €3,472 a month, 'to be adjusted for inflation' (*S*, p. 148).

The specificity of the milieux needs to be pointed out to rebut the argument that Houellebecq's novels are somehow 'about' the contemporary world as a historical place, a realm of a generalised acedia or hopelessness. Their internal rendering of that world is paradoxically too specific even as the rhetoric of the inhabitants of that world is glibly generalising.

Houellebecq's world needs affect to be everything, to be the layer which covers and mediates all, if the absence of affect is going to be registered as the symptom of modernity's failure. He achieves that by radically shrinking the purview of that world to those whose jobs bore them but give them the means to peer out onto the world of consumption, of exchange beyond their labour, and see it as one which is debased, which always falls short of the promise commodities in a mass-market must operate within. Money must be assumed for this perspective to be possible as without money despair takes on a different, a more energetic, character.

When Sweeney writes that 'each of the characters in Houellebecq's novels is representative of workers in the age of post-industrialism', it is possible to agree and to disagree with her.[29] Representative of a 'post-industrialism' as posited by these novels but not of a post-industrialism defined by non-salaried and non-pensionable service work – work which appears in the novels only faintly as the invisible hands which get the goods into the supermarkets, service the restaurants, bars, cafés and hotels which make up so much of the social space of Houellebecq's novels, or much more immediately as the work of the women who sell sexual services so that the legions of Houellebecquian men can be disappointed all over again that sex does not save them from their ennui.

It is necessary to be clear about this as the depiction of the present in *Submission*'s novum must not be read without an understanding of the interpretative work it is there to do. If it is read representationally – as a portrait of contemporary France – then the novel becomes a chastisement of contemporary France. This is what happened in many reviews of the novel. In *The New Yorker*, Adam Gopnik wrote that the 'charge that Houellebecq is Islamophobic seems misplaced', that the target of his satire is the cosmopolitan, literary and intellectual France of the 'collaborators':

> He's not Islamophobic. He's Francophobic. The portrait of the Islamic regime is quite fond; he likes the fundamentalists' suavity and sureness. Ben Abbes's reform of the educational system is wholesome, and his ambitions to rebuild France are almost a form of neo-Gaullism.[30]

Writing in the *New York Times Review of Books*, Mark Lilla rebuked those critics who had met the publication of the novel with 'hysteria', giving as an example the call of 'the reliably dogmatic Edwy Plenel', editor of *Mediapart*, to journalists to stop writing articles on Houellebecq. For Lilla, this 'Soviet style' behaviour betrayed an irony which was 'beyond anyone's imagination'. The novel was not

> the story some expected of a *coup d'état*, and no one in it expresses hatred or even contempt of Muslims. It is about a man and a country who through

indifference and exhaustion find themselves slouching toward Mecca. There is not even drama here – no clash of spiritual armies, no martyrdom, no final conflagration. Stuff just happens, as in all Houellebecq's fiction.[31]

In Adam Shatz's more careful review in the *London Review of Books*, *Submission* is not 'saying that France has sunk so low that even Islam would be preferable to the state religion of *laïcité* ... *Soumission* is too ambiguous to be read as satire.' For Shatz,

> There are strong indications, both in the novel and in interviews, that Houellebecq sees Islam as a solution, if not the solution, to the crisis of French civilization. Yes, civilization, that word evocative of the *longue durée*, religion, tradition, shared values and, not least, clashes with civilizational rivals. But the word is unavoidable.[32]

The word is unavoidable but in a peculiar guise. What is invoked is the familiarity of the 'clash of civilisations' thesis but it is invoked in a way that dissolves the clash: one 'civilisation' is a corpse and one is a fear. They cannot clash. The complete disappearance of the Front National from the novel once Ben Abbes assumes the Presidency, and of the 'nativist', Lempereur, whose predictions of civil war gave political shape to Books I and II, belong to that dissolution of any antagonistic relationship. A civilisation is not so much mourned as its passing is marked. The 'civilisation' whose passing is marked is not *of the present*, however, but rather visible only as faint ruins or rubble in this present. The present of France, France pre-'Islamicisation', is visible from one perspective as not a present at all but the long drawn-out civilisational death that is modernity, that was modernity once 'Islam' appears to cast that present back into being the prehistory of itself. The 'civilisation' at stake is itself long gone. In this – the reaching out to a past which *has to be* gone – *Submission* betrays a difference from the rest of Houellebecq's oeuvre, and suggests something of the seriousness of this novel's endeavour.[33]

When the retired François pays a visit to the Sorbonne-Paris III, as he is pondering a return to his job there, a return which will necessitate his conversion, he notes the ugliness of the buildings. As a whole, 'the place really was extremely ugly' with 'hideous buildings ... constructed during the worst period of modernism'. But

> nostalgia has nothing to do with aesthetics, it's not even connected to happy memories. We feel nostalgia for a place simply because we've lived there, whether we lived well or badly scarcely matters. The past is always beautiful. So, for that matter, is the future. Only the present hurts, and we carry it around like an abscess of suffering, our companion between two infinities of happiness and peace. (*S*, p. 222)

By this point in the novel, neither the pronouns here, the collective 'we', nor the declarative nature of the sentences are expected. As with previous first-person narrators in Houellebecq's world, the 'I' or perspective of François has throughout the novel been narcissistic, capable of revolving in the mind aspects of this or that momentarily but only ever in the context of a swiftly returned-to inertia, the style of which is, for the novel, indifference. The moment quoted above is different, and in its difference it works retrospectively to knit together a web of relations and of meanings that François as narrator is incapable of knitting together on his own.

That web lies under the novum's present; it is not accessible directly, has no immediate presence in the narrative but must be glimpsed through the movements of François's thoughts on the past, and that one moment above where some need bursts out of or exceeds the thin or deprived subjectivity of François. These reflections glimmer as the past of a France which had once had a 'civilisation', the civilization the novel locates outside the fallen modernity of Paris; in Rocamadour, the site of 'one of the most famous shrines in the Christian world' (S, p. 131); and at the monastery where Huysmans took his own vows when he returned to Catholicism, the Ligugé Abbey; and at Martel, the village fifteen kilometres from where François sees the dead bodies of a service station cashier and of 'two young North Africans' (S, p. 107). Martel is described in the novel as taking its name from Charles Martel – 'Charles the Hammer – fought the Arabs at Poitiers in 732, ending Muslim expansion to the north. That was a decisive battle, it marks the real beginning of the Christian Middle Ages' (S, p. 121). Knitting together these sites is the presence of Joris-Karl Huysmans, and in particular the progression of his movement back to Catholicism. Catholicism is itself disallowed any present in the novel: Huysmans may have found succour there eventually but that possibility is gone. Equally, there is no possibility of achieving any synthesis of these flickers or residues of a long-gone past. Houellebecq's style disallows any use of any symbolic order which could function to knit these glimpses into an order of significance greater than the text's own irony.[34]

Houellebecq's style is too relentless to allow of any such gathering place for value, any synthesising point for history and meaning, to be articulated through his novel. There are infrequent moments when a character voices a thesis about value, ventriloquises some understanding of 'civilisation' – always placed in the past tense for Europe – but these are only moments, formally set apart from the narrative of François by both their content and style, and subject to that narrative's monotone of indifference. They scaffold the historical understanding of the novel, an interpretative frame which is nowhere challenged or rejected even if it is equally nowhere accepted but they cannot address the reader directly: they are addressed to François, our ineffectual mediator. When Rediger describes for François his youthful dalliance with the 'nativist movement' (*S*, p. 212), he does so in some detail, moving from the epochal to the personal and back again:

> we weren't racists or fascists – though, to be completely honest, some of us were pretty close. But not me. Fascism always struck me as a ghastly, nightmarish, false attempt to breathe life into dead nations. Without Christianity, the European nations had become bodies without souls – zombies. The question was, could Christianity be revived? I thought so … And then one day everything changed for me. It was 30 March, 2013, I'll never forget – Easter weekend. At the time I was living in Brussels, and every once in a while I'd go and have a drink at the bar of the Métropole. I'd always loved art nouveau … [but] the bar of the Métropole was closing for good, that very night. I was stunned … Yes, that was the moment I understood: Europe had already committed suicide. (*S*, p. 213)

When Rediger draws attention to the historical context of Huysmans's pessimism, a moment when the 'European nations were at their apogee, when they commanded vast colonial empires and dominated the world!' (*S*, p. 214), François notes that 'he was right, of course. In the "art of living" alone, there had been a serious falling-off.' He thinks of a book on the history of brothels, and of his shock when he had realised that some sexual practices available during the *belle époque* were now

> completely unknown … had vanished from human memory, in one century – not unlike certain forms of skilled labour, such as cobbling or bell-ringing. How could anyone argue that Europe wasn't in decline? (*S*, p. 214)

François's response – that he had no idea of what 'a "voyage through the yellow land" or a "Russian imperial soap" could possibly mean' as sexual acts (*S*, p. 214) – may puncture some of the grandiosity of Rediger's claims but it does not rebut them. Just as Rediger's own lament over the disappeared glories of the bar of the Métropole, the now gone 'sandwiches and beer, Viennese chocolates, and cakes with cream in that absolute masterpiece of decorative art' (p. 213), puts something pathetic into the bathos of his account of his conversion to Islam but not enough to undermine the thrust of his account of the 'suicide of Europe' – or that Europe had been 'the summit of human civilisation' before destroying itself (*S*, p. 215).

The work of a previous civilisation, that which the text calls 'Christian Europe', is not subjected to any ventriloquism, however. It needs no propositions or claims made on its behalf. It just is, barely there, mute in ruins or traceable in faint and frequently incomprehensible outlines in the conclusion of Huysmans's life. What the above does, acting as a palimpsest underneath the novel's present, is to stretch that present to include the First Republic, the whole of modernity; it is not 1968 which functions here as the threshold of the downfall of France but 1789. The failed experiment of a secular republicanism is pulled away like a veil at moments to reveal the civilisation it buried:

> The French Revolution, the republic, the motherland ... yes, all that paved the way for something, something that lasted a little more than a century. The Christian Middle Ages lasted a millennium and more. (*S*, p. 132)

Patriotism, born in 1792 at the 'Battle of Valmy', began to die in 1917, 'in the trenches of Verdun': it yielded too much self-consuming violence to survive. That gives republicanism just over a century before it was to undo itself, its self-destructive momentum visible to Huysmans even at the height of Europe's Imperial glories: the 'War of 1870 had been fairly absurd too, at least according to Huysmans' description, and had already seriously eroded patriotic feeling of all kinds. Nations were a murderous absurdity, and after 1870 anyone paying attention had probably figured this out' (*S*, p. 215). The short moment of the novel's immediate present – the first three decades of the twenty-first century – are but one final episode in this narration of the self-undoing of a wrong turn taken, one finished as France turns into the heartland of a new civilisation:

> [patriotism lasted] hardly more than a century – not long, if you think about it. Today, who believes in French patriotism? The National Front claims to, but their belief is so insecure, so desperate. The other parties have already decided that France should be dissolved into Europe. Ben Abbes believes in Europe, too, more than anyone, but in his case it's different. For him Europe is truly a project of civilisation. (*S*, p. 130)

We cannot give the premodern 'Christian' past a theological or even a social meaning. It works structurally rather, to fuse the present into a longer history, the history of modernity. The 'values' of the premodern civilisation are gone. That loss is what is monumentalised at Rocamadour when François goes to see the Black Madonna.

If we reserve the term 'the past' for the civilisation which modernity undid, and reserve 'history' for the long present of the novel, then François's sense, when at Rocamadour, that he has 'somehow stepped out of historical time', makes sense: outside of historical time, he 'barely noticed when, on the evening of the second electoral Sunday, Mohammed Ben Abbes won by a landslide' (*S*, p. 134). He visits the Chapel of Our Lady daily and sits before the 'Black Virgin', the tenth-century statue which 'for a thousand years inspired so many pilgrimages, before whom so many saints and kings had knelt. It was a strange statue. It bore witness to a vanished universe' (*S*, p. 135). François is there to experience not an epiphany but precisely its opposite: he needs to experience his own failure to achieve belief. He cannot access even that residue of belief which lent to Huysmans the necessary bridge to conversion in the late nineteenth century.[35] But he does not need an epiphany: the unseeing statue, 'calm and timeless', has no need of him:

> What this severe statue expressed was not attachment to a homeland, to a country; not some celebration of the soldier's manly courage; not even a child's desire for his mother. It was something mysterious, priestly and royal that surpassed Péguy's understanding, to say nothing of Huysmans' ... The Virgin waited in the shadows, calm and timeless. (*S*, p. 139)

The present then is a historical present: what lies before it is the Christian past, and what lies beyond it is the civilisation being designed by the Muslim Brotherhood. When François notes that 'Only the present hurts' (*S*, p. 222), it is that long present of the French Republic which is at stake. The inclusion of a past beyond that long present acts as the touchstone to render that present negatively, it has lost something: that is how it gets its meaning. The arid dryness of the life of one middle-aged and disappointed male misogynist pales whilst still acting as the narrative frame for the world thus given temporal limits.

Through the form of the narration, the conventions of the dystopian genre are ironised, the rebellion or resistance of the counter-narrative is flattened into rejection. What is rejected is the present, however. This leaves the purported dystopia, the future to come, with no internal critique – that will be provided by its readership.

Conclusion

François is someone to whom history happens. It comes at him from outside, as impact or effect. He holds no political beliefs with the exception of his misogyny and that is presented not so much as a positive belief as an opinion, a suspicion that female emancipation may not have been a 'good idea'.[36] He has no interest in history, or in politics. The

> idea that political history could play any part in my own life was still disconcerting, and slightly repellent. All the same, I realized – I'd known for years – that the widening gap, now a chasm, between the people and those who claimed to speak for them, the politicians and journalists, would necessarily lead to something chaotic, violent and unpredictable. For a long time France, like all the other countries of Western Europe, had been drifting towards civil war. That much was obvious. (*S*, p. 94)

In this description of the 'gap' between the people and those who would speak for them, there is no mention of novelists or of art. This is an important absence as, arguably, Houellebecq's odd style, flattened and neutral, repetitive and toneless, can be understood only in terms of either a rejection of the reading public, or as a register of its disappearance into that 'widening gap, now a chasm'.

For François, novels are important but they are so as a medium rather than in or for themselves. Novels open up the past, giving 'access' to the spirits lost to that past. The first paragraph of the novel runs:

> Through all the years of my sad youth, Huysmans remained a companion, a faithful friend; never once did I doubt him, never once was I tempted to drop him or take up another subject; then, one afternoon in June 2007, after waiting and putting it off as long as I could, even slightly longer than was allowed, I defended my dissertation, 'Joris-Karl Huysmans: Out of the Tunnel', before the jury of the University of Paris IV-Sorbonne. The next morning (or maybe that evening, I don't remember: I spent the night of my defence alone and very drunk) I realised that part of my life, probably the best part, was behind me. (*S*, p. 5)

As the paragraph above intimates, the relationship with literature is here peculiar. Inside the professional relationship is a personal one. In that relationship, literature is not a 'value' or cannot carry 'values'. An author may be a companion, a friend, but that companionship will be made as much by the reader as by the book. And what the reader relates to is not the book but its author. The

> beauty of an author's style, the music of his sentences have their importance in literature, of course … but an author is above all a human being, present in his books, and whether he writes very well or very badly hardly matters – as long as he gets the books written and is, indeed, present in them. (*S*, p. 7)

What to make of this? I have argued that the narrative style of *Submission* is one of indifference, an indifference against which objections to or rebukes of the novel's meaning bounce off as they are irrelevant to what this novel thinks of itself. That indifference has a social layer of meaning within its own materiality: to have gained that status of onlooker-only, permanent bystander, a narrator must have reached a level of prosperity which can shut out basic needs, the narrator must, in a sense, want-for-nothing. Once that is secured, the materiality of social life can be silenced: it too does not matter. Wants now are pared down to existential relations (company, love) or to the bodily ones of health even if no longer of vigour. But if this gives our dystopian narrative a social premise, and even gestures at how to historicise it in the ennui of French professional life, an ennui as old as the generation of Huysmans, who was a clerk in the Ministry of the Interior 'writing reports for the Sûreté Générale' for thirty-two years,[37] it still does not go far enough in helping us understand why the book takes the shape it does. How does this narrative maintain meaning when its unity is its indifference?

Adorno's essay on the position of the narrator in the novel as a form can help us here. First given as a radio talk, 'The Position of the Narrator in the Contemporary Novel' was published in *Akzente* in 1954. In the Introduction above, we looked at the dilemma for the novel generated by Adorno's understanding of the painful redundancy of a model of individuality – a model which was never more than a scar on being but which may have held out a promise of something more – brought about by a world grown abstract and an agency grown thin. The dilemma for the novel, the 'literary form specific to the bourgeois age', is that it 'is no longer possible to tell a story, but the form of the novel requires narration'.[38] The narrator can no longer tell of the world with confidence or with love: the world is not 'there' any longer, neither is the narration's own premise in the coherence of an individual's capacity to catch and to tell the world:

> Apart from any message with ideological content, the narrator's implicit claim that the course of the world is still essentially one of individuation, that the individual with his impulses and his feelings is still the equal of fate, that the inner person is still directly capable of something, is ideological in itself.[39]

A subjectivism in which not the subject but the world is given refuge is one way to manage this dilemma and was the way taken, for example, by Marcel Proust. Proust's narrator

> establishes an interior space, as it were, which spares him the false step into the alien world, a faux pas that would be revealed in the false tone of one who acted as though he were familiar with that world. The world is imperceptibly drawn into this interior space – ... – and anything that takes place in the external world is presented the way the moment of falling asleep is presented on the first page: as a piece of the interior world.[40]

In the slip-stream of this widened and altered, this 'unleashed subjectivity', what would once have been thought of as 'reflection' or 'commentary' is so interwoven with action, with whatever movement the narrative can maintain, that the 'distinction between the two disappears'.[41]

Narratorial distance once enabled a reader to inhabit a position of 'contemplative security in the face of what he reads'; such a reader could be 'an uninvolved spectator'. Uninvolved was not indifferent however, it was *disinterested* – that mode of deep and sympathetic involvement which was all the more precious because it was disinterested, the mode of public intimacy the novel used to found itself as the model of bourgeois narrative. In *Submission*, François's reflections on Huysmans, his dependence on him for companionship, makes a promise which is broken even as it is made:

that in this novel, too, in *Submission*, there will be a presence, the 'being' of the author; that we as readers will have a deep engagement with an individuality, a 'human being, present in his books' (*S*, p. 7). There is no such presence in these pages, however. François is a puppet made quite skeletally out of words which cannot summon up the energy to hide this. He is a figure pointedly familiar from Houellebecq's previous novels. There is no interiority for the reader to befriend, to be addressed by. The conventions of first-person narration are used mechanically, they are nakedly conventions, utterly indifferent to their own incapacity to render subjectivity. There will be in its place clipped detail, much of it empirical, in the right order. Once François successfully defends his dissertation, he dreads the life of work. A dread which is expected from a student and which lasts but a sentence: the life of a student 'was all over now. My entire youth was over. Soon (very soon), I would have to see about entering the workforce. The prospect left me cold' (*S*, p. 9). A page later, he is offered a 'tenured position as a senior lecturer', and working life begins: the job means that 'that my boring, predictable life continued to resemble Huysmans' a century and a half before' (*S*, p. 11). There is something of the dispassionate tone of the report in the narrative, almost as if François were a third-person narrator of his own life, a narrator charged with reporting rather than narrating that life. The 'futile omniscience' noted by Martin Crowley in his anatomy of the stand-off between social diagnosis and provocation in Houellebecq's fiction, comes from his narrators.[42] There is nothing they do not know or could not know but there is no point in knowing anything. This 'futile omniscience' is as much a cage for the reader as it is for the narrative. *Submission* – as with the other novels – articulates an injunction which is non-negotiable, it demands indifference. The mode of address is one designed to interpellate the reader as a callous figure, one who can only recognise, nod and move on. This is the reader as bystander, the reading public as corroded as modernity itself. For such a public, the novum can only be ornamental: there is no estrangement possible as no subjectivity exists which is capable of it.

Notes

1 As the blogger 'Fjordman', Peder Are Nøstvold Jensen introduced the work of Bat Ye'or to Norwegian mainstream media in 2003 with an editorial in the tabloid daily *Verdens Gang*. He later went on to meet Bat Ye'or at a 'counter-jihadist' conference in The Hague in 2006 to commemorate the Dutch Islamophobe Pim Fortuyn who had been assassinated by an animal rights activist. The American white supremacist Richard Spencer also attended that conference. On the circulation and elaboration of Bat Ye'or's ideas, see Matt Carr,

'You Are Now Entering Eurabia', *Race and Class*, 48:1 (2006), 1–22. Anders Behring Breivik is a Norwegian far-right extremist who killed seventy-seven people on 22 July 2011. He used as targets those he thought most culpable for the 'dilution' of European culture by 'multiculturalism' and immigration – members and youth activists of the Norwegian Social Democratic Labour Party. For Breivik, see Lars Erik Berntzen and Sveinung Sandberg, 'The Collective Nature of Lone Wolf Terrorism: Anders Behring Breivik and the Anti-Islamic Social Movement', *Terrorism and Political Violence*, 26:5 (Feb. 2014), 759–79.

2 Liz Fekete, 'The Muslim Conspiracy Theory and the Oslo Massacre', *Race and Class*, 53:3 (2011), 30–47.

3 Bat Ye'or, *Eurabia: The Euro-Arab Axis* (Madison: Fairleigh Dickinson University Press, 2005), p. 148. For a closer account of the foundational ideas of 'Eurabia', see Sindre Bangstad, 'Bat Ye'or and Eurabia', in Mark Sedgwick (ed.), *Key Thinkers of the Radical Right: Behind the New Threat to Liberal Democracy* (Oxford: Oxford University Press, 2019). It should be stressed that 'mainstream' conservative and liberal opinion also plays host to the 'alienness' of Muslim cultures in a way which both feeds from and feeds into the more radicalised understanding of 'Eurabia'. See Fekete, 'The Muslim Conspiracy Theory and the Oslo Massacre', and Carr, 'You Aare Nnow Entering Eurabia', for the latter.

4 Michel Houellebecq, *Submission*, trans. Lorin Stein (London: William Heinemann, 2015), p. 129. All further quotations from the novel are referenced in the text.

5 The switch to a future conditional in the last fragmentary quasi-chapter of the last of the five books of the novel is a pointed part of its caricature of the dystopia as such. It could be compared with the formal finality of the last sentence of *Nineteen Eighty-Four* (a novel much in the mind of *Submission*): 'He loved Big Brother.'

6 Passages such as the above should be taken as signalling the indifference Houellebecq has to being a critic of neoliberalism. He ostentatiously does not care about capitalism. The extension of the domain of the struggle to a loosely understood late-late bourgeois culture is as far as he goes. Liberal individualism – self-preservation let loose – is the source of the violent exclusion of the male 'unfit' from the pleasures of heterosexuality. This is neoliberalism only if we take neoliberalism as it sees itself, all competition, no regulation, all luck, no state.

7 Nouriel Roubini, 'Europe's Politics of Dystopia', *The Guardian*, 29 Oct. 2015. www.theguardian.com/business/2015/oct/29/europes-politics-of-dystopia (accessed 22 January 2022).

8 Ibid. It might need to be pointed out that 2015 was a year when the borders of 'fortress Europe' were themselves in the headlines as a 'refugee crisis' interrupted the scenario Roubini describes of a peaceful Europe. See www.unhcr.org/uk/news/stories/2015/12/56ec1ebde/2015-year-europes-refugee-crisis.html (accessed 22 January 2022).

9 Aury was one of the pseudonyms used by Anne Cécile Desclos when she wrote *Story of O* (1954).

10 For an exploration of the politics of submission in one such contemporary novel – Dave Eggers's *The Circle* (2013) – see Patricia McManus, 'Happy Dystopians', *New Left Review*, 105 (May/June 2017), 81–105.

11 Raffaella Baccolini and Tom Moylan, 'Introduction. Dystopia and Histories', in Moylan and Baccolini (eds), *Dark Horizons*, pp. 5–6.

12 A useful example here is the figure of Anita Proteus in Kurt Vonnegut's *Player Piano* (1952). When put beside the absorption or total belonging of Mildred Montag – a character wholly surrendered to the regime in Bradbury's *Fahrenheit 451* (1953) – Anita Proteus's sense of propriety is starkly visible as too personal, too saturated in her own need to be noticed, to be taken care of, for it to be legible as the designed working out of things as they should be: it is less the realisation of the order of things than one more symptom of how unhappy that order makes people. Such a system cannot either compel obedience or elicit what Houellebecq would call submission.

13 That submission may still be a matter of seduction, that oppression can work without force, is still a recognisable part of the repertoire of dystopias in the twenty-first century, though it has been largely degendered, or disarticulated from the 'feminisation' of what was once 'mass culture'. The first series of *Black Mirror* (2011), in particular the episode 'The National Anthem', relies on the act of looking – elicited rather than demanded from a passive population – at mass-mediated spectacles to lock the norm into being the norm, unnoticed and unquestioned. See also the dystopian novel by Nicola Barker, *H(A)PPY* (London: William Heinemann, 2017).

14 Tom Moylan, *Demand the Impossible: Science Fiction and the Utopian Imagination*, ed. Raffaella Baccolini (Oxford; Bern: Peter Lang, 2014), p. 196.

15 Stephen King, *The Running Man* (1982), in Stephen King, *The Bachman Books* (London: Hodder and Stoughton, 2012), p. 750.

16 Ibid., p. 751.

17 Ibid., p. 768.

18 Ibid., p. 823.

19 Ibid., p. 883, original italics.

20 Mark Lilla, 'Slouching Toward Mecca', *New York Review of Books*, 2 Apr. 2015. https://bit.ly/3zGNc89 (accessed 1 December 2020). The English translation of *Submission* was published in October 2015.

21 Nicholas De Genova, 'The Whiteness of Innocence: Charlie Hebdo and the Metaphysics of Anti-Terrorism in Europe', in Gavan Titley et al. (eds), *After Charlie Hebdo: Terror, Racism and Free Speech* (London: Zed Books, 2017), pp. 98–9.

22 Ibid., p. 99.

23 For discussions of Houellebecq's reliance on a vision of the 'West' as ruins, specifically ruined by the selfishness which was emancipated from the purely 'economic' realm of competition, into the realms of sexual competition by the liberation movements of the 1960s, see Martin Crowley, 'Houellebecq – the Wreckage of Liberation', *Romance Studies*, 20:1 (2002), 17–28; Nancy Huston, 'Michel Houellebecq: the Ecstasy of Disgust', *Salmagundi*, 152 (Fall 2006),

20–37; Wendy Michallat, 'Modern Life Is Still Rubbish: Houellebecq and the Refiguring of the "Reactionary" Retro', *Journal of European Studies*, 37:3 (Sept. 2007), 313–31.

24 Carole Sweeney, *Michel Houellebecq and the Literature of Despair* (London; New York: Bloomsbury, 2013), p. xiii.

25 Ibid., pp. xiii–xiv. The quotation inside the passage from Sweeney is from Houellebecq's first novel, *Extension du domaine de la lutte*, translated into English as *Whatever* (1994/1998).

26 Houellebecq, *Whatever* (1994), trans. Paul Hammond (London: Serpent's Tail, 1998), p. 13.

27 Houellebecq, *Les Particules élémentaires*, translated into English as *Atomised*, trans. Frank Wynne (London: Vintage, 2001), pp. 238/239.

28 Houellebecq, *La Possibilité d'une Île*, translated into English as *The Possibility of an Island*, trans. Gavin Bowd (London: Phoenix, 2006), p. 45.

29 Sweeney, *Michel Houellebecq and the Literature of Despair*, p. 82.

30 Adam Gopnik, 'The Next Thing', *The New Yorker*. 26 Jan. 2015. www.newyorker.com/magazine/2015/01/26/next-thing (accessed 30 July 2021). Gopnik also reads the novel in the tradition of dystopia, linking it to Jonathan Swift's *Modest Proposal*, to Orwell's *Nineteen Eighty-Four* and to Huxley's *Brave New World*.

31 Lilla, 'Slouching Toward Mecca'.

32 Adam Shatz, 'Colombey-les-Deux-Mosquées', *London Review of Books*, 37:7 (9 Apr. 2015). www.lrb.co.uk/the-paper/v37/n07/adam-shatz/colombey-les-deux-mosquees (accessed 22 January 2022). The title of Shatz's essay comes from a report of a conversation between de Gaulle and Alain Peyrefitte in 1959, three years before the end of France in Algeria. According to Peyrefitte, de Gaulle said that France could not 'give' full citizenship rights for the *indigènes* as to do so would Islamicise France: 'Do you believe that the French nation can absorb 10 million Muslims, who tomorrow will be 20 million and the day after 40 million? ... My village would no longer be called Colombey-les-Deux-Eglises, but Colombey-les-Deux-Mosquées!' (Shatz, ibid.).

33 It should be noted that something of the same strain, a yearning for something which should be protected, which is not to be subject to any derisive irony, appears in *Serotonin* in the figure of the farms of rural France, and their beleaguered farmers, victims of the incomprehension of those in Brussels and Paris charged with implementing EU agricultural policy. Houellebecq, *Sérotonine*, translated into English as *Serotonin*, trans. Shaun Whiteside (London: William Heinemann, 2019), see especially pp. 123–31, and the suicide of Aymeric, last of the line of owners of the Chăteau d'Olonde.

34 Joris-Karl Huysmans (1848–1907), a key figure in *Submission* (the subject of François's scholarship) and more widely in Houellebecq's work, was a French novelist and art-critic, and as such a formative force in what became known as the Decadent movement.

35 The epigraph used for *Submission* is from Huysmans, *En Route* (1895). The passage used seems chosen to tease out the enticements that Catholicism offered

Huysmans beyond belief: 'I should have tried to pray ... but pray? I have no desire to pray. I am haunted by Catholicism, intoxicated by its atmosphere of incense and wax. I hover on its outskirts, moved to tears by its prayers, touched to the very marrow by its psalms and chants. I am thoroughly disgusted with my life, I am sick of myself but so far from changing my ways! And yet ... and yet ...' (*Submission*, Epilogue, second ellipsis original).

36 When he expresses these doubts about equal rights for women to his ex-girlfriend, Myrian, she asks him if he is 'for a return to patriarchy?' The response is that '[y]ou know I'm not *for* anything, but at least patriarchy existed. I mean, as a social system it was able to perpetuate itself. There were families with children, and most of them had children. In other words, it worked, whereas now there aren't enough children, so we're finished' (p. 31, original italics).

37 Robert Baldick, 'Introduction', J.-K. Huysmans, *Against Nature* (1884), trans. Robert Baldick (London; Baltimore: Penguin, 1959), p. 13.

38 Adorno, 'The Position of the Narrator in the Contemporary Novel', *Notes to Literature*, vol. 1, p. 30.

39 Ibid., p. 31.

40 Ibid., p. 33.

41 Ibid., p. 34.

42 Martin Crowley, 'Houellebecq – the Wreckage of Liberation', p. 24.

5

American dystopia

Introduction

In his introduction to *Capitalist Realism* (2009), Mark Fisher discusses how carefully Alfonso Cuarón's cinematic translation of *Children of Men* (2006) differentiated itself from the novel by P.D. James (1992). Whereas James follows the older model of a classic dystopia, an anti-democratic regime ruling over a bewildered and fearful populace confronted, finally, with a resistance which crystallises in some realisation of the responsibilities of individuality, Cuarón mutes the estrangement involved in casting England as a dictatorship. Indeed, in Cuarón's text, 'England' could be anywhere, just another Northern hemisphere wet and dilapidated country in whose social order the intolerable and the familiar or unremarkable have become indistinguishable. In the world of the film, Fisher writes, 'as in ours',

> ultra-authoritarianism and Capital are by no means incompatible: internment camps and franchise coffee bars co-exist … The catastrophe in *Children of Men* is neither waiting down the road, nor has it already happened. Rather it is being lived through.[1]

To achieve this eclipse of the future, the folding of dread into a world recognisably of the present, the film made many changes but one key generator of the flattening out of time was the switch in occupation and habitat of the novel's focalising individual, Theodore Faron. A disenchanted and dishevelled metropolitan office-worker in the film, he is an Oxford historian in the novel. In keeping with the novel's much more localised sense of itself, Faron's specialism is the 'Victorian age'[2] and it is the solidity of that specialised knowledge which provides the novel with the poignancy and power of its own polemic against modernity and against knowledge itself. The novel does not dwell on history in any thematic way. It does not need to as the quiet longevity of Oxford itself and the quasi-pastoral villages the novel wends its way through do the work of both summoning up and dismissing the centuries of science and technology, of calculation and reason now utterly unable to understand or to reverse the global cessation of fertility and the disappearance of children from the world. Faron's stoic academic knowledge is worn lightly but thoroughly and provides the authority with which the novel allegorises the need for knowledge to be both dispersed or moved out of certainty, and to be supplemented with that return to faith which can move humanity out of the sterility of self-sufficiency.

> We are outraged and demoralised less by the impending end of our species, less even by our inability to prevent it, than by our failure to discover the cause. Western science and Western medicine haven't prepared us for the magnitude and humiliation of this ultimate failure ... Like a lecherous stud suddenly stricken with impotence, we are humiliated at the very heart of our faith in ourselves. For all our knowledge, our intelligence, our power, we can no longer do what the animals do without thought.[3]

With the film's removal of this site of antipathy to a doubly reified science (at once all-causal and futile), and the recasting of Theo as a Ministry of Energy employee, jaded and hopeless, the film can move the present into the background, the place which the novel gives to the ambivalences of the past. The novel opens with the future entering Faron's household (that private realm existing outside of the future's temporality even as physically sited in it) via a radio announcement – all the regularity and yet strangeness of the 'nine o'clock programme of the State Radio Service' – which describes the death of 'the last human being to be born on earth', his dying in a 'pub brawl' adding familiarity to something which remains far away and fearful.[4]

In the film, Faron does not have a home or his home does not figure. England dissolves as an experiential locus even as it remains the geopolitical space the film takes as its own. Filmic Faron is an outside figure, moving through streets and roads which are, as Fisher puts it, recognisably of the present, presenting an alienation pervasive and profound with a world in which nothing more can ever happen. In this way the film participates in what Fisher diagnoses as 'capitalist realism': the film of *Children of Men* 'connects with the suspicion that the end has already come, the thought that it could well be the case that the future harbours only reiteration and re-permutation'.[5] This suspicion is a suspicion which haunts twenty-first-century dystopias but it is one which arguably runs against – whilst running with – Fisher's diagnosis by re-localising that present, the same present which prevents escape to any new future. The early forms of the classical dystopia had a relationship to their present which saw it threatened by epochal-altering shifts in technology or discoveries in psychology, the present promise of utopian possibility being taken by the dystopia as ground for its own existence, as the ground for its own commitment to protecting that present from itself. The present in contemporary dystopias is subject to no such splitting; it is surrendered to itself, replete only with the energies of its own undoing. It will destroy itself and it will be unmourned when it does. Unlike either the early forms of the classical dystopia with their negative commitment to their own present, or the sadness of the unwanted present in the 1980s dystopia, the contemporary dystopias explored in this chapter are able to imagine the present's relationship to the past: it is a curtailed past, one which is causal but also localised, frequently most powerful when familial, but it is there, inert yet responsible, unilinear yet not unloved. Space as much as, if not more than, time is a dynamic feature of these dystopias, the localisation of space a constitutive moment in the shrinking of the novum, a moment providing the opportunity for this chapter to explore two explicitly if not doggedly 'American' dystopias. The absence of any commitment to the present is a remarkable feature of dystopias in the twenty-first century. The novum these novels make appears to substitute for estrangement a type of paralysis or panic, the genre flailing as it unfolds a present which is threatened by nothing outside itself or germinating within itself but just by its own systemic energies, its productivity and inchoate forward momentum. The present is what is at stake and the present is what is at fault. Estrangement's dialectical partner, familiarity, is also subject to a transformation as it ceases to be something which the reader must be shocked out of not noticing and instead becomes something desired, a safe place within the maelstrom which is the present.

The two novels this chapter will read, Gary Shteyngart's *Super Sad True Love Story* (2010) and Lionel Shriver's *The Mandibles* (2016), take place in worlds presented as familiar, and do so through casting their near futures firstly as recognisably episodes of an American present, and secondly as moments in a catastrophe which can never end but only take mildly varying forms (Shteyngart), or one which, though likewise unlimited and elastic, can be seceded from only by a return to a more openly or nakedly violent past (Shriver). Brought into such intimate proximity with what the texts cast as the present, the nova of each novel are deflated, barely there things. No narrative device – not a technological innovation nor a political form, not linguistic variation nor bodily enhancement – is different enough from anything which exists to gather up the strangeness necessary to generate a distance from that present. That proximity, arguably the twenty-first-century form of what was once the dystopian novum, produces the future as unthinkable except in terms of the present. A future will happen but it will be very much like this, it will have the inequalities, the violence, the predictable unpredictability of economic and climate disaster, the crises without change, which give the present whatever shape it has.

Now this is interesting as the job of the dystopian novum – that carefully delineated future in all its terrifying detail – was to gesture towards some unwanted possibility, towards the unwanted future. The novum in the classical dystopia was an instrument of critical negativity powered by a commitment to the present it could not speak of. Remove any future that looks and feels like a future – that feels and looks different from the reader's now – and what is left? One conclusion has to be that the present is no longer defensible even as the content of a textual unconscious. It repels any commitment to it even as that same present withdraws the possibility of any future different to it.

It is possible that, by the turn of the twenty-first century, the projects of utopian thinking (where utopia is nowhere rather than anywhere in particular), which includes the genre of science fiction, were themselves jaded, chastised by the triumph of a capitalism which had emerged from the Cold War in the form of the irresistibility of a liberal democracy positing capitalism as the best a world could get. This generic exhaustion could also be identified as stemming from within the genre itself, the articulation of the disappointments of a generation of writers and readers who

> have been plagued by the perpetual reversion of difference and otherness into the same, and the discovery that our most energetic imaginative leaps into radical alternatives were little more than the projections of our own social moment and historical or subjective situation.[6]

It is indeed possible that these two combined or converged to weary the genre itself, such that it could no longer identify any alternative which would shift the foundations of the social and political if not the ontological world, and which it needed to hurl itself against. And simultaneously, that it got fed up with the tools at its disposal for the realisation of any such energetically critical movement. But this explanation leaves too much out, not least the astounding commercial success and volume of dystopias which flooded the world in the first decades of the twenty-first century. Would a weary or defeated genre be simultaneously so productive?

Likewise, the explanation which uses capitalist realism as a periodising category cannot do much interpretative work for us when it comes to certain aspects of contemporary dystopian texts which recur – a backward-looking glance which enters into the novels as normative even as also unreachable; the shrinkage to particular countries or even cities and the associated assemblage of a depleted but still historical (and frequently 'ethnically' specific) nationalism or patriotism which accompanies that geographical specificity; the casting off of culture as a value which measures the loss of value, a move which should be existentially profound for the dystopian form but which is achieved without sadness or even formal quiver.

To explore an argument through two novels is to limit that exploration terribly but I hope in this last chapter that we can see what we can learn of the genre's situation in the twenty-first century if we treat capitalist realism – or the disappearance of the future as something which would limit the present – as the name for a shift we have yet to understand generically rather than as an affect. As a feature or assemblage of features afflicting and shaping important iterations of the genre in the twenty-first century, capitalist realism is another name for the disappearance of dystopia's negative form of commitment or the fragmentation of commitment so that it is no longer commitment to something universal and unifying – the present or the past, the promise of either – but is instead commitment in search of something, somewhere to lodge itself.

The novum of both Shteyngart's and Shriver's novels is localised and involves a play with local pasts. The availability of the past should be noted. These are novels for which the past is not threatened by the near futures they conjure up. Unlike the classic dystopia or the volatilisation of the past in the 1980s dystopia, these novels assume that the past remains the same. We do however also need to note how localised and familial the past becomes in both novels. The American past itself, or history, being something they refuse to grapple with, a refusal which ensures the catastrophe they picture does not have to pale beside the catastrophe they cannot bear to look at.

Both these novels prize familiarity in place of estrangement, and both rely on country and family in place of the demystification of these. The worlds portrayed are familiar but are familiarity condensed and speeded up. Both are parables of American decline, more or less pragmatic about the end of American exceptionalism, more or less opportunistic in the ease with which they create analogies between the decay of American imperial and domestic power and prowess, and the situation of other, poorer or 'third-world' countries, an ease arguably matched in the textual worlds of the novels' 'America' by the casualness of the despatch of large numbers of working-class poor people by the state in Shteyngart's novel or in the violent tumult of civil breakdown in Shriver's.

The near futures they create involve political forms, dramatising the terrors of a state in crisis, but these function largely as the landscape in which the real crises come in a private life which can no longer pose as just private. The jobs lost, homes taken, onset and generalisation of hunger and fear, risk in each case the opening up of the energies of nostalgia, the positing of a moment in the past when stability and certainty locked private life into the mode of the good and the right. Shriver's novel eschews this nostalgia for much of its course only to release it fully in the novel's concluding hymn to a resurrected frontier spirit, the libertarian 'free state' a walk away from old dependencies. Shteyngart's private life is so caught up with family, and family is so painful that he lets it go, cutting any nostalgia off at its knees.

These temporal and experiential shifts – the proximity or 'present-ness' of this future, and the removal of the private sphere's immunity from all that is rotten in this future – provide the interest of these novels. I will read them here in their own terms before going on to suggest that the failure of the private realm they articulate positions them against the more openly or conventionally political dystopias which have returned dystopian fiction to public attention. The private realm for both novels promises a sovereignty the state can no longer secure in property or in itself. Shteyngart's novel walks away from the promise in disgust, giving up on sovereignty itself; Shriver's novel repurposes the family as a sovereign site capable of overtaking the state, and the individual the latter was to have served. This repurposed family summons up a survivalist utopia with the family acting as protector, provider and locus of all the history that is needed.

Super Sad True Love Story: inescapable present or fallen form?

Moving into the final third of itself, Gary Shteyngart's novel, first published in 2010, creates a moment of urban warfare, and of panic. His group of New Yorkers, funny, university-educated, unhappy thirty-somethings with incomes which put them on the wrong side of the category of 'High Net Worth Individuals' or HNWI but safely beyond the majority of the population who are LNWIs, have been attending a party on Staten Island, now gentrified and pretty, to celebrate a pregnancy. In the midst of the speeches, America's credit-market debt exceeds a threshold and China pulls out of US treasuries. Simultaneously, the bipartisan regime, the 'American Restoration Authority' or ARA, launches an attack on camps of homeless people and unpaid military veterans scattered across the city. A message from the ARA sent to the digital devices that everyone but the very wealthy now wears tells citizens to get to their 'primary residence' as 'Insurgent attacks have been launched on the Borrower-Spender-Financial-Residential Complex'.[7]

The following passage will give some idea of how tightly, ineluctably knit together the 'disaster' and the everyday are, how the novel does not so much refuse an idea of normality as take it and caricature it to the point where it yields up its own internal violence, the hierarchy of bodies and ways of seeing necessary to keep the everyday on the road:

> Behind the old courthouse, a municipal area had become a National Guard staging ground, choppers taking off, armored personnel carriers, tanks, Browning guns in mid-swing, a small area cordoned off into a holding pen where some older black people were interred.

We ran. It meant nothing. It all meant nothing. All the signs. The street names. The landmarks. Even here, amidst the kingdom of my fear, all I could think about was Eunice not loving me, losing her respect for me, Noah the decisive leader in a time when she was supposed to need me. Staten Island Bank and Trust. Against Da' Grain Barber Shop. Child Evangelism Fellowship. Staten Island Mental Health Society. The Verrazano Bridge. A&M Beauty supplies. Planet Pleasure. Up and Growing Day Care. Feet, feet. Shards of data all around us, useless rankings, useless streams, useless communiques from a world that was no longer to a world that would never be. I smelled the garlic on Eunice's breath and on her body. I confused it with life. I felt the small heft of a thought that I could project at her back. The thought became a chanted mantra: 'I love you, I love you, I love you.'

   'Tompkins Park,' she said, her stubbornness clawing at me. 'My sister.' A surge of black humanity from the ungentrified neighborhood just beyond St George merged with ours, and I could feel the hipsterish component trying to separate themselves from the blacks, an American survival instinct that dated back to the arrival of the first slave ship. Distance from the condemned. Black, white, black, white. But it didn't matter either. We were finally one. We were all condemned. (*SSTLS*, p. 244)

What 'meant nothing' is everything, including the seismic injustices called attention to and dismissed in the black bodies which stream out of poor areas, and the movement of the white bodies as they surge away from the bodies more likely to be military targets. It is the streets which are a litter of brand names, and the digital streets of data 'useless' when you are being shot at by your 'own' National Guard. All this, everything known and unknown, becomes or is rendered meaningless because a middle-aged man is jealous that his girlfriend looked to his friend for decisiveness in an emergency before she looked to him, our narrator, Lenny Abramov. The novel knows the absurdity and insists on it. As the two couples run to the Staten Island Ferry Terminal, Abramov is gripped in a jealousy which does not so much outrank his fear as feed it, his love object so foundational to his masculinity, he confuses her with life itself.

   The couples separate and board two different ferries to get back to Manhattan. One of these ferries is blown up by the ARA, a military helicopter momentarily circling the skies overhead as Abramov inadvertently feeds information on his dissident friend's whereabouts to the authorities. The helicopter's 'armed golden beak' points 'in our direction' (*SSTLS*, p. 245) before the 'golden beak turns orange' and unleashes a rain of missiles directed at one of the ferries, the *John F. Kennedy*, which splits in two and disintegrates 'in the warm waters':

A moment of nonscreaming, of complete äppärät silence, overtook the *Guy V. Molinari*, older people holding tight to their children, the young people lost in the pain of suddenly understanding their own extinction, tears cold and stinging in the sea breeze. And then, as the flames bloomed across the ferry's upper decks, as the *John F. Kennedy* reared up, split in two, disintegrated into the warm waters, as the first part of our lives, the false part, came to an end, the question we had forgotten to ask for so many years was finally shouted by one husky voice, stage left: '*But why?*' (*SSTLS*, p. 246, original italics)

There are two layers of meaning in that ending to the 'first part of our lives, the false part', and it is not their interdependence but their dawning separation which means that the second part of 'our lives' or the second act will be as untrue as the first part. The level of the individual life is the level of the second-generation immigrant, a level which is less individual than familial as it has all the peculiarities of a structure which is still being made as the child is born, of parents who themselves had to 'fit in' even as their child was growing older. Lenny Abramov is his family even as he cannot bear to be his family's only son. His experience of America is as the only child of two Russian-Jewish emigrants, an experience of assimilation rather than one of ownership even as social mobility escalates him past his parents' working-class American income bracket. The other level is the America which the passage quoted above poses the question to: why turn your weapons on your own citizens? That the question is one 'we had forgotten to ask for so many years' is of a piece with the novel's self-consciousness about its own ability to understand the past. Whether the forgotten question remembered when the guns are turned on those 'at home' summons echoes of 9/11 or of Vietnam, or brings momentarily to the surface the everyday use of violence in the policing of racialised communities in the US, is less important than the 'forgetting' which covers a multitude.

American citizenship, American subjectivity and American sensibility, these are spread out in the novel's 'pre-Rupture' sections as co-existing if not painlessly then still plausibly for those subjects who can afford to do as they are told. The 'harm reduction' programme of the Restoration Authority operates as a 'noises-off' narrative device: terrible things are happening but they are happening elsewhere to others: some citizens are shot, others deported, others still disappear into 'some Secure Screening Facility In Troy' (*SSTLS*, p. 87), but these are background noises, scenes witnessed but not lived and not cared for. Even when politics breaks out of the sphere of headlines and information, as it does when a friend warns Lenny Abramov that another friend may be a collaborator – as 'People are being forced into all kinds of things now … Half of Staten Island is collaborating' (*SSTLS*, p. 93) – it makes no inroads into a private life which has become dependent on an identification with a country and with the past and future posited or promised by that country. In an earlier, pre-Rupture moment, when travelling back from Staten Island to Manhattan, Lenny Abramov reaffirms his commitment to New York, that icon of a hospitable harsh America, a city which is ripe with an aggressive historicity, a 'never forget' formula which is all about forgetting so that the future can be suitably warned to behave:

> We watched the silhouettes of oil tankers, guessing at the warmth of their holds. The city approached ... the bankrupt 'Freedom' Tower, empty and stern in profile, like an angry man risen and ready to punch, celebrated itself throughout the night.
> Every returning New Yorker asks the question: Is this still my city?
> I have a ready answer, cloaked in obstinate despair: It is.
> And if it's not, I will love it all the more. I will love it to the point where it becomes mine again. (*SSTLS*, p. 94)

The next time and the last time the novel brings us to that vision of Manhattan and its bridges seen from the Staten Island ferry, it is the moment of 'Rupture', one of the two ferries is about to be split asunder and 'my country' is, however momentarily, rejected:

> just as stray gunfire opened up behind us, thundering up and down Hamilton Avenue, the resulting screams sneaking into my earlobes and momentarily turning them off. Deafness. Complete silence ... The *Guy V. Molinari's* oblong snout cut into the warm summer water, and we displaced ourselves furiously in the direction of Manhattan, and now more than ever I hated the false spire of the 'Freedom' Tower, hated it for every single reason I could think of, but mostly for its promise of sovereignty and brute strength, and I wanted to cut my ties with my country and my scowling, angry girlfriend and everything else that bound me to this world. I longed for the 740 square feet that belonged to me by law, and I rejoiced in the humming of the engines as we sailed toward my concept of home. (*SSTLS*, p. 246)

'[S]overeignty and brute strength' or the twin aspects of the American Empire as cast into being by the 'Freedom Tower,' an echo of America's post-9/11 history which slices into the text only as a static symbol of a past which 'promised' but which did not deliver, are here recognised for what they are and are misrecognised as things which you could reject. The moment of clarity lasts but a moment and is petulant and fearful. The object turned to when 'my country' or its 'false spire' – a monument both to pain imagined as exceptional and to the revenge which will be exacted in the name of that pain – is turned away from, is a 'home' become abstract and yet concrete, all 740 square feet of an apartment known and loved but only his by way of the law of that same country: an idea of sovereignty shrunk to the personal, a 'concept of home', which is as fugitive as it is concrete, confined to those who can afford that which in post-financial crisis America is no longer familiar or normal, a family home.

Lenny Abramov is not a twenty-first-century equivalent of the individual of the classic dystopia, and there is no 'regime' for him to set himself against so as to license individuality as outside of the dystopian regime, counter to it, even as or especially as it is defeated. The hegemony/counter-hegemony narrative form for dystopias has survived into our century, arguably it is again even a dominant form if we take popular, and in particular young-adult, dystopian fictions into account. But in the subset of dystopian fictions most likely to be treated as 'literary fictions', neither the model of the classic dystopia nor that associated with the critical dystopia seems to have purchase. Arguably, this is to do with the new temporal relationships incurred by making the present the scene of the dystopian future: by making that future proximate rather than estranged.

In the classic dystopia, an individual needed a regime to define himself against – it was typically a male individual though female characters would provide room for the types of libidinal investments which would energise or plump up the masculinity necessary to rebel. This antagonistic structure lends these classic dystopias their narrative interest: they are effectively reverse *bildungsromans* as one character unlearns himself and in the process learns what it is to be an individual as what it is to be alone, to not be social, to refuse the social. Any model of individuality which cannot be social or cannot tolerate social relations is doomed to fail or not to flourish, however, and these novels end with the defeat of the individual which is the triumph of the social's claims to totality. In the critical dystopia, it is not one who rebels but a few, a collectivity even as they may not know each other as such. In either case, however, the regime – the social order which those who rebel stand against – requires definition, standardisation, all the simplification which comes with narrating the unimaginable complexity of a whole social world complete with its rules, resources and relations.

Super Sad True Love Story does not create such a world but leaves its characters half at home, half in love, half at ease with a world falling apart. It is a world recognisably 'ours' in Fisher's sense, and what is dystopian is not the threat of what will replace it but the world itself, one without a regime, without planning in the centralised sense of the old dystopias, but yet a regime saturated with and generative of pain. That pain or rather the experience of it is not, however, presented as something capable of providing a space for rendering capitalism or even 'America', non-normative, vulnerable to critique and to change, but is more local and more confused. If it would not be too reductive (and misleading if taken as something more generally or sociologically true of the contemporary dystopia itself, as a genre), it might be possible to think of this text (as of the novel by Lionel Shriver to be read in the next section) as a middle-class dystopia, as one of a number of dystopias which register the shock of hunger, fear, state violence and insecurity when incurred by those parts of a population not used to it. It is no longer possible to present hunger, fear, insecurity or the suffering which threads through them, as features of a threatened future when the world of the novel, the world it comes from rather than the world in it, is so ripe with those elements in the present.

The elements are not evenly distributed, however, either in the novel or outside it. Here, it is necessary to disagree with Fisher's reading of the telescoped temporality of *Children of Men*: the coffee shops and internment camps co-exist but those who inhabit the former are not those immured in the latter. The line dividing the population of England in the film's dystopia is that between 'citizens' of the ultra-authoritarian regime and those who are not citizens, the 'fugees' or refugees whose caged suffering lines the streets where the cafés are but which is of an order different to the undeniable misery of the disenchanted coffee drinkers.

As with *Children of Men*, Shteyngart wants to present his world, the world of twenty-first-century America, as unjust, as fuelled by injustice, but that injustice must be everywhere for the novel to keep its breezy, ironising approach. Two formal choices made by the novel lock its narrative into a position from which it can only register pain, can neither understand it nor analyse it, and has no hope of providing any critique of its non-necessary character. The first is the choice to have a first-person narrator for the bulk of the book's time, Lenny Abramov's diary, a space in which, erudite and witty and self-pitying, solipsism seems unable to be repelled. The second is a smaller but yet a significant choice, to divide people into High Net Worth Individuals and Low Net Worth Individuals (HNWIs and LNWIs), a choice which was made initially to satirise the business practices of Lenny's company, and the ways of seeing embedded in his job, but one which spills out over into the novel itself, and becomes inescapable for the reader who is given detail only about those HNWIs whose lives crash down around them, and nothing about lives which were always crashed, that chorus of 'ubiquitous singing beggars, break-dancers, and destitute families begging for a Healthcare voucher, the ragtag gaggle of Low Net Worth Individuals who had turned the regular [metro] cars into a soundstage for their talents and woes' (*SSTLS*, p. 101) who make regular appearances in street scenes but are only ever background.

As an example of both choices working to provide an insulating layer of comedy around the novel's reliance on a sense of injustice it must simultaneously treat as universal, cosmic even when clearly caused, consider the following excerpt from Abramov's diary in the first third of the novel.

Abramov's company, one where he holds a peculiar position as both old friend of the CEO and employee who is not performing well, sells 'life' or expensive treatments to prolong youth or to reverse ageing. He is a 'Life Lovers Outreach Coordinator (Grade G) of the Post-Human Services division of the Staatling – Wapachung Corporation' (*SSTLS*, p. 3), a company which also sells security services to the state, and property development packages to foreign investors. The company's 'life lovers' services are only accessible to HNWIs, to the novel's equivalent of a ruling class, one caricatured to the point where the caricature doubles back on itself and invites sympathy rather than scorn.

In a canny piece of marketing but also to ensure only the most driven or self-obsessed individuals get access to the 'treatments', prospective clients are assessed and only 'on average, 18 percent' are accepted. Abramov tells us about one such rejection, 'let's call him Barry [who] ran a small Retail Empire in the Southern States' (*SSTLS*, p. 121). The intake assessment lasts a day. The description entered in Abramov's diary runs as follows:

> The Intake lasted a while. Barry, trying to subdue any remaining trace of his Alabama drawl, wanted to sound knowledgeable about our work. He asked about cellular inspection, repair, and reconstruction. I painted him a three-dimensional picture of millions of autonomous nanobots inside his well-preserved squash-playing body …
>
> I gave Barry the willingness-to-live test. The H-scan test to measure the subject's biological age. The willingness-to-persevere-in-difficult-conditions test. The Infinite Sadness Endurance Test. The response-to-loss-of-child test. He must have sensed how much was at stake, his sharp WASP-y beak aquiver as the Images were projected against his pupils, the results streaming on my äppärät. He would do anything to persevere. He was saddened by life, by the endless progression from one source of pain to another, but not more than most. He had three children and would cling to them forever, even if his present-day bank account would not be able to preserve more than two *for eternity*. I entered 'Sophie's Choice' on my intake. (*SSTLS*, pp. 121–3, original italics)

The candidate, 'Barry', is rejected: as he cannot afford the treatment for all three of his children ('his problem of having too many children, whom he loved, and not enough money to save all of them' (*SSTLS*, p. 124)), he himself would be a poor candidate for 'life loving'. This 'perfectly reasonable, preternaturally kind fifty-two-year-old would not make the cut. He was doomed, like me' (*SSTLS*, p. 123). What to do with this moment, with 'Barry,' a HNWI seeking to prolong life or to synthesise youth, and what to do with the text's telling of him, with the easy reference to 'Sophie's choice,' or to the 'blazing funeral pyre of history' he is thrown on to when, with 'a tap of my finger' against a screen, Lenny Abramov rejects his application? (*SSTLS*, p. 123).

The product being sold – or not being sold – to 'Barry' is a nonsense, a thinly parodic play on the credulity of the wealthy and the powerful and those close to them, a parody which catches also the material limits of unimaginable wealth in ageing and in death, an unavoidable loss to come whose avoidance seems yet to lure imagination out of the normally hard-headed and risk-averse. When, at the end of the novel, the clients of the service start to drool or experience tremors and organ failure, or die, the text is brusque in its assertion of 'nature' over science: 'Our genocidal war on free radicals proved more damaging than helpful, hurting cellular metabolism, robbing the body of control. In the end, nature simply would not yield' (*SSTLS*, p. 327). The board of directors of the Staatling-Wapachung Company rework what had once been the 'Post-Human Services' division into 'an enormous lifestyle boutique doling out spa appointments and lip-enhancement surgery', the failure to develop post-human technologies or modes of life not a disappointment but just one more moment of transformation in an era of capital which thrives on just such innovative, flexible and deterritorialised procedures or services.

The speculative or invented client 'Barry' is an income bracket translated momentarily into flesh, family and love, the novel's only vectors for humanising people, and then forgotten about as Lenny Abramov, and the text, are filled with the 'sadness' of his own exclusion from the club of life-lovers: 'My sadness filled the room, took over its square, simple contours' (*SSTLS*, p. 124). The style of telling moves on, the incident an illustration, serving at one level to articulate Abramov's job, the mechanics of it, the demand for 'dechronification treatments', for 'soft-tissue maintenance' or the shaving off of a 'few bio years' (*SSTLS*, p. 124). It serves at the narrative level as one more miniature pocket of sadness, just specific enough to have some concrete presence (the fifty-two years, the three children, the 'Alabama drawl' (*SSTLS*, p. 122)) but not specific enough to enter into any relationship with any other element in the text. It does not need to, as what is needed is the dispersed sadness, the sadness of an America gone to seed, the sadness of wealth which cannot buy what it wants, the sadness of middle age and of unattainable beauty, of approaching death and the inevitable failure of the equally inevitable desire to stave off that mortality.

There is satire here, the novel is a satire but the satire is too gentle, too fond, to conclude that its object is the idiocy or credulity of those who can buy everything except more life. The echoes of the Holocaust – as gratuitous as they are determinate – do not darken the 'sadness' released into the text but thin it; it is not a sadness for the world or for history or even for the injustices visited on the very rich but a sadness which cannot not be the emanation of Lenny Abramov's own prolonged and lethally personal melancholy. Lethal for the novel that is, for its capacity to realise its function as a dystopia. It cannot generate conflict as it has privatised the present. The private sphere, that realm which was to have protected the self's inner core while expressing it in personal relations, 'home' or intimacy and the choices which comprise it, and which was the core realm under threat or experienced only as lost, in the tradition of the classic dystopia, is here given full sway, balloons or blossoms and swallows all that is not private.

If this novel were to be taken or understood only in terms of its themes, it would seem to fit quite seamlessly with that tradition of classic dystopian fiction. Indeed, Simon Willmett's work on Shteyngart's novel positions it as a worthy inheritor to Orwell's *Nineteen Eighty-Four*. The latter's understanding of surveillance technologies is of limited salience in the twenty-first century:

> *Nineteen Eighty-Four* was written before personal computing, before the internet, before social media and before big data. Doesn't every crystal ball have a shelf life, even the most prescient?[8]

Shteyngart's novel updates Orwell's warning and hence here joins a decade-long 'proliferation of dystopian visions …warn[ing] us of the potentially disastrous consequences of our increasing dependence on digital technologies that are rapidly eroding our privacy'.[9] The grid of external references organising the interest in contemporary technologies of surveillance includes Edward Snowden and the leaking of detail about the American state's mass-surveillance practices post 9/11; the racialised practises of corporate surveillance, including the ranking of credit histories; and the institutionalisation of permanent, pervasive self-surveillance through the 'voluntary' use of mobile computing and communication devices which collect and project 'torrents of personal data'.[10]

For this reading, Foucault's disciplinary model of surveillance could have been used to understand how Orwell's centralised state subdues by massing and moulding its citizens, then *Super Sad True Love Story* can be read as pushing hard in the direction of Deleuze's rejection of the model of disciplinary power in favour of notion of a 'control society':

> The control society … does not mould but 'modulates' our subjectivity via a set of constantly fluctuating metrics that reduce the social collective, and the individual to a state of 'perpetual metastability.' One consequence of this is that individuals feel threatened by a sense of permanent social precariousness. This is quite distinct from the surveillance societies imagined by Orwell and his literary contemporaries. Remember that in classical dystopian fiction, social status is permanently conferred … In SSTLS, however, rather than solidify class distinction and identity, surveillance is fundamentally destabilising,

subjecting the individual to continuous transformation. Rather than fixed and conferred, identity under conditions of surveillance capitalism is always an 'unfilled project' in which the individual is in a permanent state of becoming.[11]

A similar reading of *Super Sad True Love Story* as an updating of the classic dystopia is proffered by Aaron S. Rosenfield in his study *Character and Dystopia: The Last Men* (2021). For Rosenfield, it is Forster's 'dystopian humanism' in 'The Machine Stops' which informs the figure of Abramov as, like Kuno, another 'last man' – 'the bookish humanist, believing in the ineffable human spirit, stand[ing] as the last man to fall to globalising materialism'.[12] Here, Shteyngart's novel differs from the sensibility of Forster's story only in its greater pessimism: no longer a warning, this is dystopia as an act of mourning. *Super Sad True Love Story* is

> a self-conscious version of the 'last novel,' drawing our attention to the precarious fate of novelistic discourse. Lenny is a 'last man' clinging to an outmoded version of what it means to be human ... [T]his is the novel's project; not to quantify but to stage such a human. No longer celebrating the private individual or affirming such an individual by depicting incursions on its turf, Shteyngart looks back on a dying animal, remembering with a kind of affectionate horror. If it were merely politics, we might still make other choices. Shteyngart is less concerned with warning than with mourning.[13]

J. Paul Narkunas in his book *Reified Life* (2018) does interpret the novel in ways which take into account its existence in the second decade of the twenty-first century, and all that that means for 'the human' and the forces which both enable and damage that humanity. Here the 'modular control of existence' inaugurated by financialised capitalism ensures that the social contract has been 'reengineered' to 'follow the economic logic of a derivative, a structured debt' such that '[a]gency (human and otherwise) exists in relationship to economic calculations, in terms of its usefulness and ability to honor debt'.[14] The value of speculative fictions within this world of a 'semiocapitalism' or the capture of semiotics and subject production by capitalism, is speculation itself, the unmoored evental assemblage of enunciations which exist in 'inchoate form right now, but which remain marginal or latent within the consensual reality of financial and economic instrumentality'.[15] Here Shteyngart's Abramov is the 'quintessential antiquarian humanist out of place in an economic and technology-driven reality, where the market humans (HNWIs) call the shots, and actual beings are secondary to the programmed judgements of algorithms'.[16] Cut off even from alienation – as such a form of being requires a consciousness which can be the organ of alienation – the novel dramatises characters who cannot live as humans:

Shteyngart offers speculative models of indefinite reality emerging in the United States, and outlines how historical notions of human agency are captured by the intersections of financial capital and inchoate digital technologies. By tracing these new formations of human existence, he asks the reader to envision ahuman agency, even if negatively, as often unintelligible within our current political modes of Enlightenment agency.[17]

This is an interesting reading of the operations of a particular conceptualisation of language as disruptive and gestural, but, in order to apply it to the specific dystopian novel that is *Super Sad True Love Story*, Narkunas has to refuse genre altogether. Speculative fiction has to be as free from form as the 'figures of thought' it then becomes capable of generating. Speculative fiction is a category used by Narkunas to indicate 'liberation'

> from the straitjacket of genre ... Any act of thought can be a speculative fiction ... My focus on literature stems from its non-instrumental function as a medium for thinking in transit, for enfiguring worlds, that refers back to the Latin root of speculation, *specio* – to examine or look at ... Perhaps the act of noninstrumental looking through literature, of undirected attention and solitude, can provide strategies for political acts. Stop streaming and start speculating.[18]

This positioning of literature – liberated from genre – as providing access to a non-instrumentalised and non-instrumentalising sensibility, a 'clean' way of looking and of thinking, suggests that Narkunas has not yet liberated his own thinking from the genre of dystopia. It is that opposition between a language hopelessly lost to ideology and one still protected within the peculiar type of literacy which is art or culture, the classic dystopia maintained to figure its model of the 'last man' as the novum's bridge to the reader. It is the undoing of that bridge which is remarkable in *Super Sad True Love Story*, a novel in which our reader, Lenny Abramov, is not helped by his books regardless of how scorned those books are by those younger or richer than him. Books, as art more widely, are irrelevant even as they continue to exist. In the novel's closing pages, Lenny Abramov and Eunice Parks go to an art exhibition the launch of which occurs as a 'welcome' to visiting members of the 'Chinese People's Capitalist Party' (*SSTLS*, p. 314). A series of canvases hang 'like meat' from hooks that descend from the hundred-foot-tall ceilings of a wealthy man's triplex home. The novel's treatment of these canvases reproduces in miniature its own way of looking at pain – something it cannot resist doing and yet does not know why it is doing it. The purposelessness of art is still here but it is only part of art's irrelevance:

> Dead is dead, we know where to file another person's extinction, but the artist purposely zoomed in on the living, or, to be more accurate, the forced-to-be-living and the soon-to-be-dead ... All the works had these

disarming titles, like *St. Cloud, Minnesota, 7:00am.*, which made them worse, even scarier. There was one called *The Birthday Party, Phoenix*, with five adolescent girls, anyway, I don't want to talk about this anymore, but these works were amazing to see – real art with a documentary purpose. (*SSTLS*, p. 316)

The Mandibles: putting civilisation back to work

Early in Part One of Lionel Shriver's *The Mandibles: A Family, 2029–2047* (2016), the novel's longest section, a father talks to his daughter about the fears motivating fictions set in the future. Such fears are fears about the present, he claims, fears which are projected into the future: the future is the 'far away' which lends sufficient distance to make those fears tangible and thinkable – a forming which also usefully dodges the monstrous unknowability of the future itself. That the fears are without foundation is secondary. *Nineteen Eighty-Four* seemed

> '… far away when Orwell wrote it, but then the real 1984 came and went, and it wasn't nearly as horrible or alien or sad as he predicted. Plots set in the future are about what people fear in the present. They're not about the future at all. The future is just the ultimate monster in the closet, the great unknown. The truth is, throughout history things keep getting better. On average, the world's population has a higher and higher standard of living. Our species gets steadily less violent. But writers and filmmakers keep predicting that everything's going to fall apart. It's almost funny. So don't you worry. Your future's looking sunny, and it'll only get sunnier.'
>   She looked at him with curiosity. 'I wasn't worried.'
>   *Well, that makes you a colossal idiot* popped into his head before he could stop the thought.[19]

The novel is going to realise itself in a detailed recording of things falling apart, of American living standards moving 'backwards', and the violence which ensues once the infrastructure of private life becomes unaffordable and survival takes the place of lifestyle. That the novel so unspools does not contradict the words of Lowell Stackhouse to his seventeen-year-old daughter. But his own internal thoughts do. The father's unspoken response to the teenager's nonchalance – 'colossal' idiocy – is designed not so much to index his own worry as to underscore his role-playing as father. He thinks but does not say what he feels in a gesture at once humane and hypocritical.

It is this hiatus between speech and feeling, between appearance and thought, which is the signature of a Shriver novel in general. *The Mandibles* participates in this naturalist economy where the real is the internal, the unspoken but deeply felt interpretation of the way of the world: that the things of the world are like this, not that. The worldly conventions which forbid the articulation of certain feelings or thoughts blind as well as ease the way for relationships – familial, marital, sexual and intergenerational – but they cannot just be shrugged off as they cover for the cruelty which lies just underneath. 'Unsparing', 'brutally honest', 'unflinching' are adjectives frequently applied by reviewers to Shriver's prose and in truth hers is a prose which thrives on the creation of conjunctions in which the not-said or the merely thought provides most of the narrative interest. This stress on what's underneath politeness, what gets covered over by the social practices of a speech too saturated with civilisation, the layers of resentment, shame and envy which Shriver sees crawling underneath the surface of the most intimate *and* the most impersonal of interactions, creates the effect of a doubling in her narrative style. Her characters are always either struggling not to say what they think or regretting having said it, or regretting not having said it, but the gap between thinking and saying, a gap in which 'civilisation' has form and is both forceful and judged for it, is a stylistic constant. This is not anything as blunt as a critique of 'political correctness'. Shriver is too careful a novelist, and too militantly libertarian, to cast social life as something which is either homogenous or external. There is no separately social usurper of a then equally separate individual responsibility but a reading of the dialectic between the two which casts it as a struggle without end or clear issue. It is the very relentlessness of that struggle, its pervasive, sticky presence, which works against history in Shriver's novels. The more she injects historical specificity, the more elastic or timeless that struggle appears. In *We Need to Talk about Kevin* (2003), the 'backdrop' to the narrative of the child's murderous assault on his school peers and family is the tussle over the Presidential election of 2000 – Bush or Gore. The father is a Republican, the mother a Democrat and they argue about politics, pointedly argue. But this remains a chronological framework, the tail end of the twentieth century with none of the sense of either decay or renewal, decadence or triumphalism associated with the step into the twenty-first century.

The drama remains within interpersonal relations, those moments where intimacy fails to enable honesty, and honesty fails to garner sympathy or even support. The family – in an extended, intergenerational rather than as a nuclear formation – is the field of operations for the struggle over the self, its dimensions small enough for claustrophobia to add darkness to everyday interactions, and its dimensions deep enough in terms of social expectations, for either the breaking of unspoken rules or sullen adhering to them to generate layers and nodes to the network of tensions which constitute tangled relations between siblings or partners, or children and their parents.

Shriver's style is the embodiment of that privatisation and dehistori-cisation of struggle and its consequent tensions. It is a wordy scrutiny of the unsaid and the unspeakable. Her characters are frequently unhappy – dissatisfied in some very specific and some very contained way – and are frequently unpleasant but they are worthy focalisers of plot and narrative as they are honest with themselves, with that honesty being less a 'value' for Shriver's novels than their *sine qua non*. In *We Need to Talk about Kevin*, Eva Khatchadourian despises the compromises she feels forced to make as a pregnant woman not because she misses the wine she can no longer drink or the dancing she feels obliged to no longer do but because she is not allowed to *say* that she resents the self-sacrifice involved. The compromises with her own will or desires are *for* positive reasons – the health of herself or her baby – but having to feign positivity about making them is experienced as akin to coercion or censorship:

> Funny how you dig yourself into a hole by the teaspoon, the smallest of compromises, the little roundings off or slight recastings of one emotion as another that is a tad nicer or more flattering. I did not care so much about being deprived of a glass of wine per se. But like that legendary journey that begins with a single step, I had already embarked upon my first resentment.
>
> A petty one, but most resentments are. And one that for its smallness, I felt obliged to repress. For that matter, that is the nature of *resentment*, the objec-tion we cannot express. It is silence more than the complaint itself that makes the emotion so toxic.[20]

I wanted to stress the socialised situation of silence in Shriver's style, its meaningfulness as a measure of the spread of a politeness which alienates individuals not from their world but from their selves, as this style is not called upon to do its normal work in *The Mandibles*. As a dystopia which tracks the disintegration of one regime and the creation of another, *The Mandibles* is too busy with externals – with securing the wherewithal to survive – to indulge in a critique of politeness or a tracing of the existential damage done to those for whom what 'everyone thinks' is an irresistible guide to living.

Instead of a tussle within the self being the device which dramatises where 'the real' lies and what it means (it typically means nothing as important as the battle to let it out, to externalise it, finally, in speech), in *The Mandibles*, 'society' comes in – in the form of federal fiscal policy and federal forces – and wrecks private lives which have been spatialised rather than rendered in speech. Households – and *The Mandibles* multiplies them – are the figure with which the dystopian drama is emplotted and house invasions, literal and figural, propel the characters finally towards Nevada, the novel's resting place, a determinedly anti-utopian utopia.

The novel begins with the third generation of a once wealthy family, three siblings, all of whom have houses and hence have homes. Equilibrium is assaulted when a nefarious international alliance – led by Russia and propped up by an eagerly rising China – introduces a new international currency, the 'bancor',[21] and demands that all American debt now be repaid in bancors. America defaults on its national debt, hurting domestic and international bond holders. The federal government outlaws the possession of bancors, the dollar collapses, inflation rockets and the government conscripts all gold and refuses to let any wealth greater than $100 out of the country. The 'savings' of Americans disintegrate overnight as US treasury bonds – the *'safest investment in the world'* – return to being mere paper (*Mandibles*, p. 97, original italics).

Because America refuses to trade in bancors, shelves begin to empty, inflation reduces affordability where stoppages in trade have already shrunk availability. Ordinary groceries become scarce and mortgage rates rise. The different branches of the Mandible family, all rendered homeless by the American government's 'universal "reset"' (*Mandibles*, p. 57) converge on the one household left – a brownstone in Brooklyn. A house which used to hold one small family and a tenant swells with the return of a sibling's family (two adults, three children), then parents and grandparents, then aunt. A tense equilibrium, reached through reconciliation to hardship and overcrowding, is breached when neighbours, under the guise of having a sick child, enter the house and force the Mandibles out at gunpoint. Themselves evicted when their own house was put in foreclosure, the neighbours are not bad people but are desperate and are not willing to share. Hardship might force families together but it forces strangers into competition, even strangers who are neighbours and from the same class: 'Having moved in with the wave of moneyed homebuyers that hit the neighbourhood in the last decade, the desperadoes in this foyer were "gentry"' (*Mandibles*, p. 269).

The last chapter of Part One (titled 'A Complex System Enters Disequilibrium') does not shy away from calling attention to its job as preparatory material for the novel's denouement: the family or families are homeless.[22] The thirteen family members walk, painfully laden and at night, to Prospect Park, site of a homeless encampment, a

> sorry version of the promised land: edge to edge across what was once the site of picnics and games of ultimate frisbee, a patchwork of plastic tarpaulins, planks, pressboard, Sheetrock and corrugated iron, many of the materials for these improvised dwellings salvaged from the abandoned construction sites that hulked across all five boroughs. (*Mandibles*, p. 284)

Desperate, destitute and now homeless, the family decide to trek to Gloversville in upper New York State, where a brother has a farm, 'food, shelter and a well', each concrete item a castigation of the insubstantiality of debt, money, interest and credit (*Mandibles*, p. 288). To get there, they need to walk close to two hundred miles by the back roads, which are marginally safer than the highways. Knowing that his body could not handle the trek, the family patriarch shoots his partner and himself: 'it happened in a trice' (*Mandibles*, p. 292).

The novel's first part ends there, in 2032 on the brink of a journey. Neither the journey to the farm at Gloversville nor the time spent there is given any space. Paying no narrative attention to either the travails of the journey out of New York city or the decade of civil unrest, social breakdown and famine which follows may seem a strange decision. It fits, however, with this novel's need to spatialise its plot in terms of spaces no longer just domestic, households re-spatialised as citadels of a sociality which can work, which can – if left to itself – put conventions to one side and can work. Taking the whole mess of family life on the road would amount to a turn outwards the novel is not willing to risk.

Part Two, which begins over a decade later in 2047, circles not only back to Brooklyn but to the same house in Brooklyn as Willing Mandible, a thirteen-year-old child in Part One, returns to regain 'possession of his childhood home' (*Mandibles*, p. 296). He is now an adult and whilst '[r]eturning full circle to East Flatbush should have been gratifying', it involves evicting the current 'usurpers' and involving himself in the red tape of a restored state. Twenty-five when he leaves the farm to retake his mother's house, Willing is thirty-one by the time he overcomes the bureaucratic hurdles and regains possession. Every working-age citizen has now to be 'chipped', a procedure which presents the state as intent not on surveilling its citizens for the sake of knowledge and control but on surveilling their income for the sake of taxation. Local, state and federal taxes take 77 per cent of the pay packet of every working citizen and the chip communicates citizens' 'every purchase to the agency known until 2039 as the Internal Revenue Service', and known thereafter as the Bureau for Social Contribution Assistance or colloquially as the 'SCAB' (*Mandibles*, p. 304). Negative interest rates are used to prohibit savings: were the chip to 'accumulate an excess of fiscal reserves – an amount that surpassed what he required on average to cover his expenses for the month – it would dun the overage at an interest rate of –6 percent' (*Mandibles*, p. 305).

This is dystopia as bad fiscal policy, the state as an overweening welfare machine, taking money from those who work to distribute it to those who do not. The souls of the old, the disabled and the work-shy, the souls of the 'entitled' weigh on the lives of the industrious:

after a dip in the thirties, life expectancy had better than recovered. On average, Americans were living to ninety-two. The US sported an unprecedentedly large cohort of senior citizens. In contrast to Willing's passive generation, typified by low rates of electoral participation, nearly all the shrivs voted, making it political anathema to restrict entitlements. Together, Medicare and Social Security consumed 80 percent of the federal budget. The labour force had shrunk. Dependents – the superannuated, the disabled, the unemployed, the underage – outnumbered working stiffs like Willing by two to one ... Mind control? No one in DC gave a damn what you were *thinking*. They just wanted your money. (*Mandibles*, p. 309, original italics)[23]

A society which takes care of two-thirds of its population through general taxation makes for an odd dystopia but Shriver leaves no space for oddity or ambivalence. America in the 2040s is a miserable, oppressive and unhappy place. High levels of taxation on ordinary income may incense the narrative the most but much time is spent also on tracing America's external humiliation as it no longer is able to fund military operations overseas. Not 'doing anything' when 'China annexed Japan', sitting 'idly by, and making excuses for sitting idly by' disgraces and shames Americans of a certain age or generation. For the generation who came of age in the disastrous 2030s, it makes no difference. America for them is a place rather than an identity: Willing Mandible

> was American as an adjective. He was no longer an American as a noun. He saw no necessity in taking the US demurral from declaring war on China personally. If it meant that he himself hadn't been forced to become a paratrooper billowing onto the rooftops of skyscrapers in Chengdu, this was a good thing. Otherwise, if he were to feel powerless, the source of the sensation would be closer to home: he was obliged to have a cousin to dinner whom he did not like. That was impotence ... His country did not help because it could not help. It did not have the money. That was relaxing. This must have been what it had felt like to live in most countries, when the United States was sending bombers and ships and troops and airlifts whenever something went wrong. (*Mandibles*, p. 331)

Likewise, now that America has joined the 'bancor', and 'foreign' investment has overtaken any national form of capitalism (India and China have 'colonised American agriculture' for example (*Mandibles*, p. 364)), 'American' jobs are low-status, 'low-skilled' and only bring in low pay. Any American who can, any who are entitled by ancestry to 'go back', filter 'back to the land of their forefathers'. But no 'non-Lat whites' can move across a border which now has a fence built by Mexico to keep Americans out, a fence 'electrified, and computerised and 100 percent surveilled, from the Pacific to the Gulf ... they think we're lazy. And they definitely think we're stupid' (*Mandibles*, p. 330). When Hispanic Americans left, the

loss was greater than one of numbers. They'd been American with the zeal-
otry of converts. Emigration being at an all-time high, the US population was
contracting for the first time in its history. The remaining public felt trapped,
stranded, left behind ... Now that outsiders didn't risk their lives to reach
America anymore, the native-born felt abandoned. They missed their own
resentment. They felt unloved. (*Mandibles*, p. 329)

As with the passage above, one related by a third-person narrator who has
to work much harder in Part Two than in Part One where the job of exposition was given to dinner-table dialogue, arguments which concretised character simultaneously with ideological critique, *The Mandibles* here has little
to no interest in *narrating* the world of 2047, in making it a story. There are
some exceptions to this Part's reliance on description, however, and one of
them is key to the plot of Part Two as it motivates the departure from the
US and the entry into the determinedly anti-utopian space of Nevada and
the novel's final resting place on the veranda of a house in the family's
'Spanish Modern compound' (p. 400).

The Mandibles is a dystopia for which abstractions are intolerable –
when social they are unreliable and prone to disintegration (credit and debt,
for example, money itself when uncoupled from gold, patriotism, 'fair-
ness') and when they take the guise of individual properties, they are typically revealed to be overly reliant on the perception of others, a reliance
which increases illusion and decreases autonomy or the self's independence
(beauty, intelligence, goodness or generosity). The narrative pushes everything towards the concrete: what can be eaten needs to be grown with an
exertion of manual labour; what can be used for shelter has to be built
or paid for outright; for protection a gun is necessary. Given this allergic
relation to universals, however, it is difficult for the novel to give form to
freedom. It manages this by figuring the consequences of taking freedom
away: it is a bodily violation which snatches freedom and to regain freedom
it is necessary to regain the body. Willing Mandible spent his twenties on
the farm of his uncle, 'the Citadel', and so was not 'chipped'. When he
returns to Brooklyn to take ownership of the family home, he has to be
chipped. This is presented as a physical violation first and foremost. Not
the tracking the 'chip' enables or the capacity of the state to so track its
citizens but the insertion of a foreign body into his body. It is presented not
as analogous to a sexual assault but as a sexual assault: 'Willing was raped'
(*Mandibles*, p. 300).

That was the only word he had for it, a word he did not, therefore, use to
anyone else ... The very word, as it applied to the experience, in addition to
recollection of the experience itself, was stored in a 'private place.' The stasis
with which he was now afflicted six years later, that pessimism about whether

there was even anywhere to go were he to suddenly discover an ambition to get there, this heavy unmoving sameness – he couldn't help but wonder whether it was all related to having been raped. (*Mandibles*, p. 300)

The procedure itself, this 'most minor of medical indignities … less of an ordeal than getting your teeth cleaned' (*Mandibles*, p. 300) is treated by Americans in 2027 as routine:

> everyone said so. Like applying for a social security number. A bureaucratic matter, a relatively painless, pro forma protocol of the modern day. Thus Willing had not considered the inevitability of the procedure with sufficient seriousness. He had been lulled by what was regular, by what was expected and customary. (*Mandibles*, p. 298)

Inserted at the base of the skull, the 'foreign object' is tiny and the insertion painless. However the 'real trauma' – which has 'little to do with physical torment' – is the loss of ownership of a body which is the root of all ownership. And it is ownership which is at stake here rather than the body itself as a mortal and limited thing. The 'chip' inserted into Willing's skull tracks not him in terms of his location or movements, it has no interest in or care for his conversation or thoughts. It tracks his money – his income, his expenditure – and ensures that he does not dodge his taxes. The 'chip' is 'merely a means of accounting' (*Mandibles*, p. 345) and as such a means it catches everything: not only wages but any 'assets' an individual might have or inherit. With taxes on capital gains at 85 per cent and the possession of gold being illegal ('hoarding'), there is no way of owning any liquid wealth at all which the state does not know about and exact taxes from.

That this is a peculiar form of oppression the novel is aware of with an almost self-parodic awareness:

> 'I'm sick of this … America is not a police state. This is a free country, and you can say whatever you fucking well want. I've had it up to the gills with people like you, always mouthing off about 'oppression' and 'subjugation' and 'tyranny.' So you're expected to do your part, to help keep this economy's show on the road, and what's wrong with that? Nothing wrong with people over sixty-eight getting medical care, either, or drawing a modest stipend from a retirement system they've paid into their whole lives … [J]ust because you have to contribute to the same system … doesn't mean you live under the heel of goose-stepping Nazis …' (*Mandibles*, p. 324)[24]

But the loathing felt for the chip, its positing as a double violation – of the body and of the money that body should own outright – gives the novel its form for freedom. A chipless skull moving unencumbered through a low-tax state with others so unencumbered. The organic form of the relationship with such others is the family, the political form for the whole is a state where families are left alone. Freedom is a feeling for the characters of the novel, an affective disposition which is sufficient in itself:

> 'Isn't freedom a sensation? After all, you don't have to exercise a freedom to possess it. I don't have to get up for a drink of water. But knowing that I could get up, it changes the way it feels to sit, even if I stay sitting.' (*Mandibles*, p. 339)
>
> 'Freedom is a feeling. Not only a list of things you're allowed to do.' (*Mandibles*, p. 392)

For the novel as a whole, the apparatus which enables that disposition is gold, the most concrete form of 'wealth'. Like the chipless skull, the possession of gold provides the foundation and medium of a free (family) life. The externalisation of this fetish is Nevada, a state which has seceded from America precisely because of its inhabitants' desire to materialise their freedom in a state for which 'continentals' are the currency. Backed by gold, 'the continental', Nevada's resurrected currency – first 'currency of the original thirteen colonies'[25] – is limited ('if you can't make it, mine it, fix it, grow it, or invent it in Nevada, you can't get it' (*Mandibles*, p. 378)) and is pragmatic:

> Before we cut loose, the Free State produced the majority of American gold anyways. But supply of continentals is real restricted. Learned our lesson from the thirties. Everybody round here pretty much agree that on the face of it the gold standard's dumb. *Arbitrary* the governor calls it. Not much to do with the stuff but wear it around your neck. Can't eat it. But for currency, it works. Even if we don't quite know why. One continental buy you a whiskbroom today? One continental buy you a whiskbroom tomorrow. So it's not that dumb. (*Mandibles*, p. 378, original italics)

Cut off entirely from the other states of America, and from the world, the Free State is recognised only by Eritrea and trades with nobody but itself. Within its borders, guns are legal, hard work and family ties are the only way to survive:

> You bring in old people, you pay for old people. No Medicare here. No Social Security. No Part D prescription plans. No Medicaid-subsidized nursing homes. No so-called *safety net*. Every citizen in this rough-and-tumble republic gotta walk the high wire with *nada* underneath but the cold hard ground. Trip up? Somebody who care about you catch you, or you fall on your ass. (*Mandibles*, p. 379)

With gold owned by the novel's only artist – bought with the proceeds from her novel, *Better Late Than*, and illicitly smuggled into first the US, then into a welcoming Nevada – the Mandible family set up their own family household in Las Vegas. By the novel's end, not only are the surviving three generations ensconced within these walls but there is a new generation. Anyone who was chipped has had their chip removed, everyone works hard, and everyone keeps the fruit of their labours. This is how the novel ends. A form of closure which arguably breaks the form of the dystopia as a narrative form even as it confirms the ideological potency of the dystopia as a form of critique, here a critique of social democracy made from the right. The novel is very bad as a dystopian novel and yet is very successful as a piece of reaction – a politically committed fiction – aligned with the wider movement of the contemporaneous American right. It should be stressed here that *The Mandibles* is an expression not of a dystopia which switches its temporal allegiance to look backwards but of a politics which insists that, to find the future again, it is necessary to look backwards. The 'Free State is an experiment in going backwards' (*Mandibles*, p. 392), in going 'back' to that imagined point when the pioneer spirit could colonise energetically without interference, and where labour was respected and anyone who could not labour was unfortunate. But the thing of most value in that backwards move is not the past at all but the horizon to the future it opens. This is a form of militant nostalgia, a remembering of the past which is peculiarly oriented to using that past to carve out new futures. This is the temporality which positions Shriver's novel as itself part of the longings caught up in the 'alt right' in America. The widespread reception of *The Mandibles* as a dystopia which was 'chillingly plausible',[26] which has a 'sharp social eye' and nailed down 'economic nitty-gritty' in its plot,[27] a novel which lulled one reviewer into thinking more kindly of 'tinned goods and a gun',[28] positions that 'alt-right' temporality as something which exceeds the 'alt-right', however. Shriver's novel exists at the point where not Trump but his electoral base meets survivalists and the political logic of militias and insurrection.

In an interview with the *New York Times* in 2017, Peter Thiel, a figure who also pinpoints that border or overlap between the Republican right and the 'alt-right', noted the popularity of nostalgic forms of futurism in his own moment:

> There are reduced expectations for the younger generation, and this is the first time this has happened in American history. Even if there are aspects of Trump that are retro and that seem to be going back to the past, I think a lot of people want to go back to a past that was futuristic – *The Jetsons, Star Trek*. They're dated but futuristic.[29]

When Shriver said of *The Mandibles* in an interview she gave in 2017 that she 'wanted the reader to enter this story like walking into the next room', she pinpointed the reworking of the novum in some contemporary dystopias to focus on the present and on the intimate heart of the present,

the family and family life.[30] The novel itself gives the lie to any suggestion
that such a move is a way for dystopia as a genre to reckon more openly or
honestly with where we are. Even the family becomes for it a machine for
circulating wealth, for privatising utopia and for cleaning up a present fit
only for a future from the past. America is at the heart of *The Mandibles*. It
is a lost future which the novel struggles to incorporate in a sub-Thatcherite
secessionist Nevada with only the faintest presence of a state, the pioneering
journey to which takes up the second and final part of the novel. And it
is also the field of the novel's present, the dystopian present of the text in
which 'Latinos' are ascendant, the Chinese are gathering and the native
'elites' are too stupefied by the optimism of their own strained moralism to
see the writing on the wall.

Conclusion

'Good. There's our catastrophe. In the bag.'[31]

There is a return of history in *The Mandibles* as a dystopia also. Unlike *Red
Clocks*, however, *The Mandibles*'s use of history is unashamedly opportunistic. What can be used will be taken, what gets in the way will be shoved
aside, as the past of Luella, the novel's only African-American character, is
wholly surrendered to her dementia, and then her violent death. That the
death of Luella is part of what secures the success of the family's journey
is telling. As with the source of the Mandible wealth, a source indicated
only vaguely as 'old', as 'amassed' by 'Carter's great-grandfather Elliot, a
midwestern industrialist' (*Mandibles*, p. 42), the past is for *The Mandibles*
a resource, one to be looted but one which can also be ignored. It has no
agency or presence of its own. Where *Red Clocks* traced innumerable fine
threads holding the present to the past – with that past responsible in some
way for a present which cannot yet access that past – *The Mandibles*
invokes the past only to swerve it: the great project of beginning again in
Nevada a rejection not only of the United States of America but also of
Utopia. Adorno's essay on *Brave New World* provided the initial impetus
for this study of how critical theory can help us understand the cultural
phenomenon which is dystopian fiction. Adorno's critique was able to
sharply centre both the allure and the limits of Huxley's novel's shifting of
'guilt for the present to the generations of the future'.[32] The novels which
make up the classic dystopia are marked by their negative commitment
to the present, one they wish to hold to even as they can find no purchase
on it – no reason for that hold. As we move deeper into the twenty-first
century, it is not surprising that the present should become a more troubled

feature in dystopian fiction. The present for us can no longer be its own thing or can no longer be thought to be pregnant with futures which will be free of the past: it is too riddled with the past, with a historicity we can see now as not yet finished – whether that is in the deep currents of global warming or the seismic injustices of colonisation and the creation of whiteness.

For it is clear that the classic dystopia needed the late nineteenth and early twentieth century for what Adorno would have called its external meanings. Other societies in other times have imagined catastrophes in other ways: the societies that have dystopias imagine the catastrophe to be the unspeakable thing that endures, that becomes speakable or 'normal' and no longer a catastrophe. For this work of imagination to be possible, a machinery of power is needed which is not premised on the end-times, on apocalypse or on any final judgement. The state formation of late European imperialism, in particular the state formation of British imperialism, was needed, as was the self it posited, a self subject to total forms of control, forms long nurtured in the colonies but in the late nineteenth century beginning to be thinkable in relation to the 'domestic' populations as well.

It seemed to me that Adorno's reading of *Brave New World* was one more widely applicable – not just to other examples of the subgenre but to its underlying machinery in the classic dystopia, however. In the following passage, Adorno substitutes Huxley for the novel but if we reinsert the novel and treat it as belonging to a genre, we can catch sight of the logic of the early or classic form of dystopia:

> Huxley criticises the positivistic spirit. But because his criticism confines itself to shocks, while remaining immersed in the immediacy of experience and merely registering social illusions as facts, Huxley himself becomes a positivist ... Instead of antagonisms, Huxley envisages something like an intrinsically non-self-contradictory total subject of technological reason, and correspondingly, a simplistic total development ... Although he gives an incisive physiognomy of total unification, he fails to decipher its symptoms as expressions of an antagonistic essence, the pressure of domination, in which the tendency to totalization is inherent. Huxley expresses scorn for the phrase, 'Everybody's happy nowadays'. But the essence of his conception of history, which is better revealed by its form than by the events which make up its content, is profoundly harmonious.[33]

Adorno identifies both the squeezing out of historicity from the dystopia's urge to render the future as total and the splitting of the individual into the now struggling or beset ideal – which is where the reader is positioned – and the fallen or failed individuality of the masses or 'mass man' which provides raw material for the horrors to come:

the socially valid recognition of the nullity of the individual turns into an accusation levelled against the overburdened private individual. Huxley's book ... blames the hypostatized individual for his fungibility and his existence as a 'character mask' of society rather than a real self ... For Huxley, in the authentic bourgeois spirit, the individual is both everything – because once upon a time he was the basis of a system of property rights – and nothing, because as a mere property owner, he is absolutely replaceable. This is the price which the ideology of individualism must pay for its own untruth. The novel's *fabula docet* is more nihilistic than is acceptable to the humanity which it proclaims.[34]

This is no longer a reading which can help us with the temporal relationships or political commitments of contemporary dystopias but what it can do is help us think those relationships and commitments historically. Adorno, that is, can be put to work to understand the operations of a genre historically and formally.

Notes

1 Mark Fisher, *Capitalist Realism: Is There No Alternative?* (London: Zero Books, 2009), p. 2.
2 P.D. James, *Children of Men* (London: Faber and Faber, 1992), p. 4.
3 Ibid., p. 6.
4 Ibid., p. 3.
5 Fisher, *Capitalist Realism*, p. 3.
6 Jameson, *Archaeologies*, p. 211.
7 Gary Shteyngart, *Super Sad True Love Story* (London: Granta, 2010), p. 237. Hereafter quotations from Shteyngart's novel are included in the text in parentheses.
8 Simon Willmetts, 'Digital Dystopia: Surveillance, Autonomy, and Social Justice in Gary Shteyngart's *Super Sad True Love Story*', *American Quarterly*, 70:2 (June 2018), 267–89.
9 Willmetts names Dave Eggers's *The Circle* (2014), Shummet Baluja's *The Silicon Jungle* (2011), Cory Doctorow's *Little Brother* (2008) and *Homeland* (2013).
10 Willmetts, 'Digital Dystopia', p. 272.
11 Ibid., 'Digital Dystopia', p. 272. Willmetts refers to Zygmunt Bauman's thesis on 'liquid modernity' (Bauman, *Liquid Modernity* (Cambridge; Malden: Polity Press; Blackwell, 2000)), and Gilles Deleuze's work on the labour of control (Deleuze, 'Postscript on the Societies of Control', *October*, 59 (Winter 1992), 3–7) to differentiate the work Shteyngart's novel does from Orwell's. That the model of social order the novels relate to is historically different is not here in question: what is, is the mode of relation. Willmetts sees both novels as simultaneously reflecting and critiquing a world outside them which is transparent to

them. The interesting thing about Shteyngart's novel is just how unwilling it is to do this.

12 Aaron S. Rosenfeld, *Character and Dystopia: The Last Men* (London: Routledge, 2020), p. 101.

13 Ibid., p. 102.

14 J. Paul Narkunas, *Reified Life: Speculative Capital and the Ahuman Condition* (New York: Fordham University Press, 2018), p. 184.

15 Ibid., p. 183.

16 Ibid., p. 187.

17 Ibid., p. 192.

18 Ibid., pp. 185–6. Narkunas's notion of speculative fiction is indebted to Gilles Deleuze and Félix Guattari's argument for thinking the existence of language as a form of experimentation, of invention being allowed to happen when enunciation itself substitutes for the previous primacy of the enunciator (Deleuze and Guattari, *A Thousand Plateaus* (1980)., trans. Brian Massumi (Minneapolis: University of Minnesota Press, 1987)). This is an argument which can accommodate Beckett's '"drilling holes" in language in order to see or hear "what was lurking behind"' (Deleuze, *Essays Critical and Clinical*, trans. Daniel W. Smith and Michael A. Greco (London: Verso, 1998). cited Narkunas, *Reified Life*, p. 181) alongside a dystopian fiction and has therefore too little interest in the historicity of form to be of use here.

19 Lionel Shriver, *The Mandibles: A Family, 2029–2047* (New York: HarperCollins, 2016), p. 78, original italics. Hereafter quotations from the novel are reference in parentheses in the text.

20 Lionel Shriver, *We Need to Talk about Kevin* (2003) (London: Serpent's Tail, 2016), p. 64.

21 Calling the new international currency which destroys the dollar a 'bancor' is one of the curt ways Shriver attempts a critique of Keynesianism. That critique itself cannot get off the ground as the contemporary (post-2008/9) American scene the novel roots itself in is just too far removed from social democracy; levels of national indebtedness in the US likewise have little to do with spending on public goods. For a brief history of the proposal for the bancor as an international reserve currency at Bretton Woods by Keynes and Schumacher, see Nadia Piffaretti, 'Reshaping the International Monetary Architecture: Lessons from Keynes' Plan', World Bank Policy Research Working Paper No. 5034 (1 Aug. 2009), https://ssrn.com/abstract=1471132 (accessed 22 January 2022). For a discussion of why Keynes was interested in the bancor after 1940, see Radhika Desai's account of his worry that a 'national economy, no matter how large, without colonial surpluses to export, was bound to either fail to provide international liquidity or do so only in unstable and financially dangerous ways. That was why, at Bretton Woods, Keynes called for a world reserve currency multilaterally managed by nation-states, which he called "bancor".' Desai, *Geopolitical Economy: After US Hegemony, Globalization and Empire* (London: Pluto Press, 2013), p. 63.

22 The novel uses a very young character, Willing Mandible, to act as the voice of a pragmatic, modest but none the less rock-solid realism and measure of reason. His is the voice which uses the phrase the novel uses for the chapter title: 'We should have left earlier … I miscalculated. This city. It's a complex system, which has entered disequilibrium. It's unstable. That is why there's no reason to "plot." We have to leave anyway. The people downstairs [the 'home invaders'] won't end well' (*Mandibles*, p. 276).

23 A 'shriv' is a retired person; the term itself is only one of many the novel uses in an attempt to register social change at or in the level of lexical change. The attempt is so poor it deserves comment but I don't know what to say about it. It should be noted too that the form of 'entitlements' which so exercises the novel is to do with the elderly. Retirement age is sixty-eight in 2047 and benefits for the retired seem to be universal: 'People used to dread being put out to pasture. Desperate to qualify for entitlements, these days everyone couldn't wait to be old' (*Mandibles*, p. 322).

24 Chipping is voluntary for older people. Having to submit same-day tax returns on every purchase and deposit is an effective form of persuasion, however: 'Coercion is crude and invites tantrums … the *long-lived* are persuaded to embrace chipping as a welcome salvation from the paperwork equivalent of Abu Ghraib' (*Mandibles*, p. 337).

25 On the history of the continental as a form of paper currency issued in the 1770s, see Mary M. Schweitzer, 'State-Issued Currency and the Ratification of the US Constitution', *The Journal of Economic History*, 49:2 (June 1989), 311–22.

26 Stephanie Merrit, 'Review', *The Guardian*, 8 May 2016. www.theguardian.com/books/2016/may/08/the-mandibles-lionel-shriver-review-biting-near-future-satire (accessed 22 January 2022).

27 Alexandra Schwartz, 'Lionel Shriver Imagines America's Collapse', *The New Yorker*, 30 June 2016. www.newyorker.com/books/page-turner/lionel-shrivers-american-collapse (accessed 22 January 2022).

28 Rosamund Urwin, 'Review', *The Evening Standard*, 5 May 2016, www.standard.co.uk/culture/books/the-mandibles-a-family-by-lionel-shriver-review-a3240756.html (accessed 22 January 2022).

29 Maureen Dowd, 'Peter Thiel Explains Himself', *The New York Times*, 11 Jan. 2017. https://nyti.ms/3JSlxpr (accessed 22 January 2022). *The Jetsons* makes an appearance in *The Mandibles* precisely as an image of futurism disappointed: Because they are poor (and not because of climate change), Americans no longer buy cars: '[m]ajor American cities like New York bore more resemblance to mid-twentieth-century Shanghai than to the whizzing futuristic metropolis of *The Jetsons*. In eerie silence, multitudes of electric bicycles swarmed single public buses' (*Mandibles*, p. 348).

30 Lionel Shriver, 'Dystopia in the Next Room', *TLS*, 3 Feb. 2017. https://bit.ly/3qaqZw6 (accessed 22 January 2022).

31 Samuel Beckett, 'Catastrophe' (1982), in *Collected Shorter Plays* (London: Faber and Faber, 1984/2006), p. 300.
32 Adorno, 'Aldous Huxley and Utopia', in *Prisms*, p. 117.
33 Ibid., p. 114.
34 Ibid., p. 115.

Bibliography

Adorno, Theodor W., *The Adorno Reader*, ed. Brian O'Connor (Oxford: Blackwell, 2000).

———, *Aesthetic Theory* [1970], ed. Gretel Adorno and Rolf Tiedemann, trans. Robert Hullot-Kentor (London: Bloomsbury, 2013).

———, *Can One Live after Auschwitz?: A Philosophical Reader*, ed. Rolf Tiedemann (Stanford: Stanford University Press, 2003).

———, *Critical Models: Interventions and Catchwords*, European Perspectives: A Series in Social Thought and Cultural Criticism, trans. Henry W. Pickford (New York: Columbia University Press, 2005).

———, *The Culture Industry: Selected Essays on Mass Culture*, ed. J.M. Bernstein, Routledge Classics (London; New York: Routledge, 1991).

———, *Negative Dialectics* [1966], trans. E.B. Ashton (London; New York: Routledge, 2004).

———, *Notes to Literature*, ed. Rolf Tiedemann, trans. Shierry Weber Nicholsen, vol. I (New York: Columbia University Press, 1991).

———, *Notes to Literature*, ed. Rolf Tiedemann, trans. Shierry Weber Nicholsen, vol. II (New York: Columbia University Press, 1992).

———, *Prisms* [1967], trans. Samuel and Shierry Weber (Cambridge, MA: MIT Press, 1983).

Adorno, Theodor W., Walter Benjamin, Ernst Bloch, Bertolt Brecht, Georg Lukács and Fredric Jameson, *Aesthetics and Politics*, Radical Thinkers 13 (London; New York: Verso, 2007).

Adorno, Theodor W. and Max Horkheimer, *Dialectic of Enlightenment*, Verso Classics 15, trans. John Cumming (London: Verso, 1997).

Adorno, Theodor W. and Michael T. Jones, 'Trying to Understand Endgame', *New German Critique*, 26 (Spring–Summer 1982), 119–50.

Alderman, Naomi, *The Power* (London: Viking, 2016).

Alkon, Paul K., 'Gulliver and the Origins of Science Fiction', in Frederik N. Smith (ed.), *The Genres of Gulliver's Travels* (Newark: University of Delaware Press, 1990).

Amis, Kingsley, *New Maps of Hell: A Survey of Science Fiction* [1960] (London: Penguin, 2012).

Arendt, Hannah, *Essays in Understanding, 1930–1954*, ed. Jerome Kohn (New York; London: Harcourt, Brace & Co, 1994).

———, *The Origins of Totalitarianism* [1951], rev. ed. (London: Penguin, 1979).

Ashcroft, Bill, 'Critical Utopias', *Textual Practice*, 21:3 (2007), 411–31.

Atwood, Margaret, *The Handmaid's Tale* [1985] (London: Virago Press, 1987).
———, *The Testaments* (New York: Nan A. Talese/Doubleday, 2019).
Baccolini, Raffaella, 'Gender and Genre in the Feminist Critical Dystopias of Katharine Burdekin, Margaret Atwood, and Octavia Butler', in Marleen S. Barr (ed.), *Future Females, the Next Generation: New Voices and Velocities in Feminist Science Fiction Criticism* (London; New York: Rowman and Littlefield, 2000).
Baccolini, Raffaella and Tom Moylan (eds), *Dark Horizons: Science Fiction and the Dystopian Imagination* (London; New York: Routledge, 2003).
Barker, Nicola, *H(A)PPY* (London: William Heinemann, 2017).
Ballard, J.G., *Hello America* [1981] (London: Fourth Estate/HarperCollins, 2014).
Barr, Marleen S. (ed.), *Future Females, the Next Generation: New Voices and Velocities in Feminist Science Fiction Criticism* (London; New York: Rowman and Littlefield, 2000).
Bauman, Zygmunt, *Liquid Modernity* (Cambridge; Malden: Polity Press; Blackwell, 2000).
Beaumont, Matthew, *Utopia LTD. Ideologies of Social Dreaming in England, 1870–1900*, Historical Materialism Book Series 7 (Leiden; Boston: Brill, 2005).
Beckett, Samuel, 'Catastrophe' (1982), in *Collected Shorter Plays* (London: Faber and Faber, 1984/2006).
———, *Endgame* [1957] (London: Faber, 2009).
Bell, Daniel, *The Coming of Post-Industrial Society: A Venture in Social Forecasting* (London: Heinemann, 1974).
Bellamy, Edward, *Looking Backward, 2000–1887*, Oxford World's Classics (Oxford; New York: Oxford University Press, 2007).
Berlant, Lauren, *Cruel Optimism* (Durham, NC: Duke University Press, 2011).
Bernstein, J.M., *Adorno: Disenchantment and Ethics*, Modern European Philosophy (Cambridge: Cambridge University Press, 2001).
Beveridge, Sir William, *Social Insurance and Allied Services*, Command papers Cmd. 6404, Cmd. 6405 (London: HMSO, 1942).
Bloch, Ernst, *The Principle of Hope* [1954–59], trans. Neville Plaice, Stephen Plaice and Paul Knight, 3 vols (Cambridge, MA: MIT Press, 1986).
———, *The Utopian Function of Art and Literature: Selected Essays*, Studies in Contemporary German Social Thought, trans. Jack Zipes and Frank Mecklenburg (Cambridge, MA; London: The MIT Press, 1988).
Bould, Mark, 'Dulltopia: On the Dystopian Impulses of Slow Cinema', *The Boston Review / Global Dystopia*, 22 Jan. 2018. http://bostonreview.net/literature-culture-arts-society/mark-bould-dulltopia (accessed 30 July 2021).
Bradbury, Ray, *Fahrenheit 451* [1953] (London: HarperVoyager, 2008).
Bradshaw, David, *Hidden Huxley: Contempt and Compassion for the Masses* (London; Boston: Faber & Faber, 1994).
Brecht, Bertolt, *The Resistible Rise of Arturo Ui* [1941] (London: Methuen Drama, 2007).
Brooker, Charlie, *Black Mirror*, Television Series (Channel 4; Netflix, 2011–19).
Buck-Morss, Susan, *Dreamworld and Catastrophe: The Passing of Mass Utopia in East and West* (Cambridge, MA: MIT Press, 2000).
Budakov, V.M., 'Dystopia: An Earlier Eighteenth-Century Use', *Notes and Queries*, 57:1 (Mar. 2010), 86–8.

Bumiller, Kristin, *In an Abusive State: How Neoliberalism Appropriated the Feminist Movement against Sexual Violence*, Duke Backfile (Durham, NC: Duke University Press, 2008).

Bunyard, Tom, *Debord, Time and Spectacle: Hegelian Marxism and Situationist Theory* (Boston; Leiden: Brill, 2018).

Burdekin, Katharine, *Swastika Night* (London: Lawrence & Wishart, 1937).

Burgess, Anthony, *A Clockwork Orange* [1962] (London: Penguin, 1972).

Carr, Matt, 'You Are Now Entering Eurabia', *Race and Class*, 48:1 (2006), 1–22.

Claeys, Gregory, *Dystopia: A Natural History* (Oxford: Oxford University Press, 2017).

Coetzee, J.M., *Waiting for the Barbarians* (London: Secker & Warburg, 1980).

Collini, Stefan, *Absent Minds: Intellectuals in Britain* (Oxford: Oxford University Press, 2006).

Collins, Suzanne, *The Hunger Games*, [*Hunger Games trilogy*] bk 1 (New York: Scholastic Press, 2008).

Crick, Bernard, *George Orwell: A Life* (London: Secker & Warburg, 1980).

Crowley, Martin, 'Houellebecq – the Wreckage of Liberation', *Romance Studies*, 20:1 (2002), 17–28.

Cuarón, Alfonso, *Children of Men*, DVD (Universal Pictures (UK) Ltd, 2007).

Dalcher, Christina, *Vox* (London: HQ/HarperCollins, 2018).

Davidson, Joe P.L., 'Retrotopian Feminism: the Feminist 1970s, the Literary Utopia and Sarah Hall's *The Carhullan Army*', *Feminist Theory*, 0:0 (2021), 1–19.

Davis, Mary Elizabeth, 'On Advertising's Terms: Influence of Spatial Logic on the Weak Critiques of Consumer Capitalism in *Player Piano*, *Fahrenheit 451*, and *The Space Merchants*' (PhD, Indiana University of Pennsylvania, May 2010).

Decker, Mark, 'Biomedical Imaginaries: the Case of "The Machine Stops"', in Donald M. Hassler and Clyde Wilcox (eds), *New Boundaries in Political Science Fiction* (Columbia; London: University of South Carolina Press, 2008).

Deleuze, Gilles, *Essays Critical and Clinical*, trans. Daniel W. Smith and Michael A. Greco (Minneapolis: University of Minnesota Press, 1997).

———, *Essays Critical and Clinical*, trans. Daniel W. Smith and Michael A. Greco (London: Verso, 1998).

———, 'Postscript on the Societies of Control', *October*, 59 (Winter 1992), 3–7.

Deleuze, Gilles and Félix Guattari, *A Thousand Plateaus* [1980], trans. Brian Massumi (Minneapolis: University of Minnesota Press, 1987).

Delphy, Christine, *Separate and Dominate: Feminism and Racism after the War on Terror* [2008], trans. David Broder (London: Verso, 2015).

Dennis, Richard, '"Babylonian Flats" in Victorian and Edwardian London', *The London Journal*, 33:3 (2008), 233–47.

Desai, Radhika, *Geopolitical Economy: After US Hegemony, Globalization and Empire*, Future of World Capitalism (London: Pluto Press, 2013).

Dillon, Sarah, 'Who Rules the World? Reimagining the Contemporary Feminist Dystopia', in Jennifer Cooke (ed.), *The New Feminist Literary Studies* (Cambridge; New York: Cambridge University Press, 2020).

Donnelly, Ignatius, *Caesar's Column: A Story of the Twentieth Century* (Chicago: F.J. Schulte & Co., 1890).

Dostoevsky, Fyodor, *Notes from Underground and The Double* [1864; 1846] (London: Penguin, 2009).

Dowd, Maureen, 'Peter Thiel Explains Himself', *The New York Times*, 11 Jan. 2017. https://nyti.ms/3JSlxpr (accessed 22 January 2022).

Dwan, David, *Liberty, Equality, and Humbug: Orwell's Political Ideals* (Oxford: Oxford University Press, 2018).

Edwards, Caroline, *Utopia and the Contemporary British Novel* (Cambridge: Cambridge University Press, 2019).

Eggers, Dave, *The Circle* (London: Hamish Hamilton, 2013).

Erdrich, Louise, *Future Home of the Living God* (London: Corsair, 2017).

Evans, Timothy H., 'Authenticity, Ethnography, and Colonialism in Philip K. Dick's *The Man in the High Castle*', *Journal of the Fantastic in the Arts*, 21:3 (Nov. 2010), 366–83.

Fekete, Liz, 'The Muslim Conspiracy Theory and the Oslo Massacre', *Race and Class*, 53:3 (2011), 30–47.

Fielding, Henry, *Tom Jones* [1749], Penguin Popular Classics (London: Penguin, 1994).

Fisher, Mark, *Capitalist Realism: Is There No Alternative?* (London: Zero Books, 2009).

Forster, E.M., *Howards End* [1910], Penguin Classics (New York: Penguin Books, 2000).

——, *'The Machine Stops'* [1909], Modern Classics (London: Penguin Books, 2011).

——, *Selected Stories*, ed. David Leavitt and Mark Mitchell, Penguin Classics (London: Penguin Books, 2001).

——, *Two Cheers for Democracy* [1951] (Harmondsworth: Penguin, 1965).

Fowler, Roger, *The Language of George Orwell*, Language of Literature (Basingstoke; London: Macmillan, 1995).

Gibson, William, *Burning Chrome and Other Stories*, new ed. (London: HarperCollins, 1995).

——, *Neuromancer* [1984] (London: HarperVoyager, 2013).

Gilbert, Sophie, '*Red Clocks* Imagines America without Abortion', *The Atlantic*, 7 Feb. 2018. www.theatlantic.com/entertainment/archive/2018/02/leni-zumas-red-clocks-review/552464/ (accessed 30 July 2021).

——, 'The Remarkable Rise of the Feminist Dystopia', *The Atlantic*, 4 Oct. 2018. www.theatlantic.com/entertainment/archive/2018/10/feminist-speculative-fiction-2018/571822/ (accessed 30 July 2021).

Gopal, Priyamvada, *Insurgent Empire: Anticolonial Resistance and British Dissent* (London; New York: Verso, 2019).

Gopnik, Adam, 'The Next Thing', *The New Yorker*, 26 Jan. 2015. www.newyorker.com/magazine/2015/01/26/next-thing (accessed 30 July 2021).

Gordon, Peter E., *Adorno and Existence* (Cambridge, MA; London: Harvard University Press, 2016).

Greenslade, William M., *Degeneration, Culture and the Novel, 1880–1940* (Cambridge; New York: Cambridge University Press, 2010).

Griffith, Richard, 'The Selling of America: the Advertising Council and American Politics, 1942–1960', *The Business History Review*, 57:3 (Autumn 1983), 388–412.

Hall, Ian, 'A "Shallow Piece of Naughtiness": George Orwell on Political Realism', *Millennium*, 36:2 (2008), 191–215.

Hassler, Donald M. and Clyde Wilcox, Clyde (eds), *New Boundaries in Political Science Fiction* (Columbia: University of South Carolina Press, 2008).

Hayek, F.A., *The Road to Serfdom* [1944], ed. Bruce Caldwell, *The Collected Works of F.A. Hayek*, vol. II (Chicago: University of Chicago Press, 2007).

Hölscher, Lucian, 'Utopia', *Utopian Studies*, 7:2 (1996), 1–65.

Houellebecq, Michel, *Atomised*, trans. Frank Wynne (London: Vintage, 2001).

———, *The Map and the Territory* [2010], trans. Gavin Bowd (London: William Heinemann Ltd, 2011).

———, *Platform* [2001], trans. Frank Wynne (London: Vintage, 2003).

———, *The Possibility of an Island*, trans. Gavin Bowd (London: Phoenix, 2006).

———, *Serotonin*, trans. Shaun Whiteside (London: William Heinemann, 2019).

———, *Submission*, trans. Lorin Stein (London: William Heinemann, 2015).

———, *Whatever: A Novel* [1994], trans. Paul Hammond (London: Serpent's Tail, 1998).

Huston, Nancy, 'Michel Houellebecq: the Ecstasy of Disgust', *Salmagundi*, 152 (Fall 2006), 20–37.

Huxley, Aldous, *Brave New World* [1932] (Harmondsworth: Penguin, 1955).

———, *Ends and Means* [1937] (London: Chatto & Windus, 1946).

———, 'The Farcical History of Richard Greenow', in *Limbo* (London: Chatto & Windus, 1920).

———, *Music at Night, and Other Essays* (London: Chatto & Windus, 1931).

Huysmans, J.K., *Against Nature* [1884], trans. Robert Baldick (Baltimore: Penguin Books, 1959).

———, *En Route* [1895], trans. W. Fleming (Sawtry: Dedalus, 2002).

Ishiguro, Kazuo, *Never Let Me Go* (London: Faber, 2005).

James, P.D., *The Children of Men* (London: Faber and Faber, 1992).

Jameson, Fredric, *An American Utopia: Dual Power and the Universal Army*, ed. Slavoj Žižek (London; New York: Verso, 2016).

———, *Archaeologies of the Future: The Desire Called Utopia and Other Science Fictions* (London; New York: Verso, 2005).

———, *Brecht and Method* (London: Verso, 1998).

———, 'A Global Neuromancer', in Jameson, *The Ancients and the Postmoderns: On the Historicity of Forms* (London; New York: Verso, 2015), pp. 221–38.

———, *Late Marxism: Adorno or the Persistence of the Dialectic* [1990], Radical Thinkers 18 (London; New York: Verso, 2007).

———, *Marxism and Form: Twentieth-Century Dialectical Theories of Literature* (Princeton: Princeton University Press, 1974).

———, *The Political Unconscious: Narrative as a Socially Symbolic Act*, Routledge Classics (London: Routledge, 2002).

———, *Postmodernism, or the Cultural Logic of Late Capitalism* (London: Verso, 1991).

Kahle, Trish, 'Combustible Fictions: The Literary Novel in the Anthropocene', *Red Wedge*, 15 Aug. 2018. www.redwedgemagazine.com/online-issue/combustible-fictions-the-literary-novel-in-the-anthropocene (accessed 30 July 2021).

King, Stephen, *The Bachman Books* (London: Hodder and Stoughton, 2012).

Kornbluth, C.M., 'The Failure of the Science Fiction Novel as Social Criticism', in Basil Davenport (ed.), *The Science Fiction Novel: Imagination and Social Criticism*, 3rd ed. (Chicago: Advent, 1969).

Koselleck, Reinhart, *Sediments of Time: On Possible Histories*, trans. Sean Franzel and Stefan-Ludwig Hoffmann (Stanford: Stanford University Press, 2018).

Kumar, Krishan and Stephen Bann (eds), *Utopias and the Millennium* (London: Reaktion Books, 1993).

Kurtz, Malisa, 'After the War, 1945–65', in Roger Luckhurst (ed.), *Science Fiction: A Literary History* (London: British Library, 2017).

Landa, Ishay, *Fascism and the Masses: The Revolt against the Last Humans, 1848–1945* (London: Routledge, 2018).

Lang, Fritz, *Metropolis* [1927], DVD (London: Eureka Video, 2005).

Lefebvre, Henri, *Critique of Everyday Life. Vol. II: Foundations of a Sociology of Daily Life*, trans. John Moore (London: Verso, 2002).

Lewis, Sophie, *Full Surrogacy Now: Feminism Against Family* (London; New York: Verso, 2019).

Lilla, Mark, 'Slouching Toward Mecca', *New York Review of Books*, 2 Apr. 2015. https://bit.ly/3zGNc89.

London, Jack, *The Iron Heel* [1908] (Ware: Wordsworth Editions, 1996).

Löwy, Michael, *Fire Alarm: Reading Walter Benjamin's 'On the Concept of History'* [2001], trans. Chris Turner (London; New York: Verso, 2016).

Luckhurst, Roger (ed.), *Science Fiction: A Literary History* (London: British Library, 2017).

Lynskey, Dorian, *The Ministry of Truth: The Biography of George Orwell's 1984* (London: Picador, 2019).

Lytton, Edward Bulwer, *The Coming Race* [1871] (London: Gateway, 2015).

Macaulay, Rose, *What Not: A Prophetic Comedy* [1918] (Bath: Handheld Press, 2019).

Marin, Louis, 'The Frontiers of Utopia', in Krishan Kumar and Stephen Bann (eds), *Utopias and the Millennium* (London: Reaktion Books, 1993).

Martínez-Falquina, Silvia, 'Feminist Dystopia and Reality in Louise Erdrich's *Future Home of the Living God* and Leni Zumas's *Red Clocks*', *The European Legacy*, 26:3–4 (2021), 270–86.

Marx, Karl and Friedrich Engels, *The Communist Manifesto* [1848] (Peking: Foreign Language Press, 1977).

McLaughlin, Neil, 'Orwell, the Academy and the Intellectuals', in John Rodden (ed.), *The Cambridge Companion to George Orwell* (Cambridge: Cambridge University Press, 2007).

McManus, Patricia, 'Happy Dystopians', *New Left Review*, 105 (May/June 2017), 81–105.

Meiners, Erica R., 'Trouble with the Child in the Carceral State', *Social Justice*, 41:3 (2015), 120–44.

Merritt, Stephanie, 'Review', *The Guardian*, 8 May 2016. www.theguardian.com/books/2016/may/08/the-mandibles-lionel-shriver-review-biting-near-future-satire (accessed 30 July 2021).

Michallat, Wendy, 'Modern Life Is Still Rubbish: Houellebecq and the Refiguring of the "Reactionary" Retro', *Journal of European Studies*, 37:3 (Sept. 2007), 313–31.

Miller, Bruce, *The Handmaid's Tale* (Los Angeles: Twentieth Century Fox Home Entertainment, 2018).

Miller, Reuben Jonathan and Amanda Alexander, 'The Price of Carceral Citizenship: Punishment, Surveillance and Social Welfare Policy in an Age of Carceral Expansion', *Michigan Journal of Race and Law*, 21:2 (2016), 291–314.

Mondon, Aurélien and Aaron Winter, 'Articulations of Islamophobia: from the Extreme to the Mainstream?,' *Ethnic and Racial Studies*, 40:13 (2017), 2151–79.

More, Thomas, *Utopia* [1516], trans. Dominic Baker-Smith (London: Penguin, 2012).

Moretti, Franco, 'From The Waste Land to the Artificial Paradise' [1983], in *Signs Taken for Wonders: Essays in the Sociology of Literary Forms*, rev. ed. (London; New York: Verso, 1988).

Morris, William, *News from Nowhere* [1890], ed. Krishan Kumar (Cambridge: Cambridge University Press, 1995).

Moylan, Tom, 'Beyond Negation: the Critical Utopias of Ursula K. Le Guin and Samuel R. Delany', *Extrapolation*, 21:3 (Fall 1980), 236–51.

——, *Demand the Impossible: Science Fiction and the Utopian Imagination* [1986], ed. Raffaella Baccolini, Ralahine Utopian Studies Volume 14 (Oxford; Bern: Peter Lang, 2014).

——, *Scraps of the Untainted Sky: Science Fiction, Utopia, Dystopia*, Cultural Studies Series (Boulder; London: Westview Press, 2000).

Mulhern, Francis, *Figures of Catastrophe: The Condition of Culture Novel* (London; New York: Verso, 2016).

Mumford, Lewis, *Herman Melville* (London: Cape, 1929).

Narkunas, J. Paul, *Reified Life: Speculative Capital and the Ahuman Condition* (New York: Fordham University Press, 2018).

Negley, Glenn Robert and J. Max Patrick, *The Quest for Utopia* (College Park: McGrath Pub. Co., 1952).

Norris, Christopher (ed.), *Inside the Myth. Orwell: Views from the Left* (London: Lawrence and Wishart, 1984).

Orwell, George, *Burmese Days* [1934] (London: Penguin, 2014).

——, *Coming Up for Air* (London: Victor Gollancz, 1939).

——, *Keep the Aspidistra Flying* (London: V. Gollancz Ltd, 1936).

——, *Nineteen Eighty-Four* [1949] (London: Penguin, 2003).

——, 'Review', *New Adelphi*, March–May 1930.

——, *The Road to Wigan Pier* (London: Victor Gollancz, 1937).

Orwell, Sonia and Ian Angus (eds), *The Collected Essays, Journalism and Letters of George Orwell, Vol. I: An Age Like This, 1920–1940* (London: Secker and Warburg, 1968).

—— (eds), *The Collected Essays, Journalism and Letters of George Orwell, Vol. IV: In Front of Your Nose, 1945–1950* (London: Secker & Warburg, 1968).

Parrinder, Patrick (ed.), *Learning from Other Worlds: Estrangement, Cognition and the Politics of Science Fiction and Utopia* (Liverpool: Liverpool University Press, 2000).

Peele, Jordan, *Us*, DVD (Universal, 2019).

Piercy, Marge, *Woman on the Edge of Time* (New York: Knopf, 1976).

Piffaretti, Nadia, 'Reshaping the International Monetary Architecture: Lessons from Keynes' Plan', World Bank Policy Research Working Paper No. 5034 (1 Aug. 2009).

Plato, *The Republic*, trans. Christopher Rowe (London: Penguin, 2012).

Pohl, Frederik, *The Merchants' War* (New York: St Martin's Press, 1984).

Pohl, Frederik and C.M. Kornbluth, *The Space Merchants* [1952] (London: Orion, 2003).

Ramos, Joanne, *The Farm* (London: Bloomsbury, 2019).

Rickards, James, *Currency Wars: The Making of the Next Global Crisis* (New York: Portfolio/Penguin, 2011).

Riley, Boots, *Sorry to Bother You*, DVD (Universal Studios, 2018).

Roberts, John Michael, 'Reading Orwell through Deleuze', *Deleuze Studies*, 4:3 (2010), 356–80.

Robinson, Josh, *Adorno's Poetics of Form*, SUNY Series in Contemporary Continental Philosophy (Albany: State University of New York Press, 2018).

Robinson, Kim Stanley, 'Dystopias Now: the End of the World is Over, now the Real Work Begins', *Commune Magazine*, 2 Nov. 2018. https://communemag.com/dystopias-now/ (accessed 30 July 2021).

Rosenfeld, Aaron S., *Character and Dystopia: The Last Men* (London: Routledge, 2020).

Roubini, Nouriel, 'Europe's Poliitcs of Dystopia', *The Guardian*, 29 Oct. 2015. www.theguardian.com/business/2015/oct/29/europes-politics-of-dystopia (accessed: July 30th. 2021).

Rugoff, Ralph, 'Interview with J. G. Ballard', Frieze, 6 May 1997. www.frieze.com/article/dangerous-driving (accessed 22 January 2002).

Sargent, Lyman Tower, 'In Defense of Utopia', *Diogenes*, 53:1 (2006), 11–17.

Sartre, Jean-Paul, *What Is Literature?* [1948], trans. Bernard Frechtman (London: Methuen, 1950).

Schwartz, Alexandra, 'Lionel Shriver Imagines America's Collapse', *The New Yorker*, 30 June 2016. www.newyorker.com/books/page-turner/lionel-shrivers-american-collapse (accessed 30 July 2021).

Schweitzer, Mary M., 'State-Issued Currency and the Ratification of the US Constitution', *The Journal of Economic History*, 49:2 (June 1989), 311–22.

Scott, Ridley, *Blade Runner* (Warner Bros, 1982).

Sedgwick, Mark (ed.), *Key Thinkers of the Radical Right: Behind the New Threat to Liberal Democracy* (New York: Oxford University Press, 2019).

Seed, David, 'Take-Over Bids: the Power Fantasies of Frederik Pohl and Cyril Kornbluth', *Foundation*, 0:42 (Fall 1993), 42–58.

Sellars, Simon and Daniel F.J. O'Hara (eds), *Extreme Metaphors: Selected Interviews with J.G. Ballard, 1967–2008* (London: Fourth Estate, 2012).

Sethna, Christabelle, '"Not an Instruction Manual": Environmental Degradation, Racial Erasure and the Politics of Abortion in *The Handmaid's Tale*', *Women's Studies International Forum*, 80 (May/June 2020), 1–9.

Shatz, Adam, 'Colombey-les-deux-Mosquées', *London Review of Books*, 37:7 (9 Apr. 2015). www.lrb.co.uk/the-paper/v37/n07/adam-shatz/colombey-les-deux-mosquees (accessed 22 January 2022).

Shriver, Lionel, 'Dystopia in the Next Room', *TLS*, 3 Feb. 2017. https://bit.ly/3qaqZw6 (accessed 22 January 2022).

——, *The Mandibles: A Family, 2029–2047* (New York: HarperCollins, 2016).

——, *We Need to Talk about Kevin* [2003] (London: Serpent's Tail, 2016).

Shteyngart, Gary, *Super Sad True Love Story* (London: Granta, 2010).

Spindler, William, '2015: The Year of Europe's Refugee Crisis', 8 Dec. 2015. www.unhcr.org/uk/news/stories/2015/12/56ec1ebde/2015-year-europes-refugee-crisis.html (accessed 30 July 2021).

Spring, Dawn, *Advertising in the Age of Persuasion: Building Brand America, 1941–1961* (New York: Palgrave Macmillan, 2011).

Stock, Adam, *Modern Dystopian Fiction and Political Thought: Narratives of World Politics* (London: Routledge, 2018).

Sumner, W.G., 'Folkways: a Study of the Sociological Importance of Usages, Manners, Customs, Mores and Morals' [1907], in Philip D. Manning (ed.), *On Folkways and Mores: William Graham Sumner Then and Now* (Abingdon; New York: Routledge, 2015).

Suvin, Darko, *Metamorphoses of Science Fiction: On the Poetics and History of a Literary Genre* [1979], ed. Gerry Canavan, Ralahine Classics (Bern: Peter Lang, 2016).

———, *Positions and Presuppositions in Science Fiction* (London: Palgrave Macmillian, 1988).

Sweeney, Carole, *Michel Houellebecq and the Literature of Despair* (London; New York: Bloomsbury, 2013).

Thompson, Peter and Slavoj Žižek, *The Privatization of Hope: Ernst Bloch and the Future of Utopia* (Durham, NC; London: Duke University Press, 2013).

Titley, Gavan, Des Freedman, Gholam Khiabany and Aurélien Mondon, *After Charlie Hebdo: Terror, Racism and Free Speech* (London: Zed Books, 2017).

Urwin, Rosamund, 'Review', *The Evening Standard*, 5 May 2016. www.standard. co.uk/culture/books/the-mandibles-a-family-by-lionel-shriver-review-a3240756. html (accessed 30 July 2021).

Varsam, Maria, 'Concrete Dystopia: Slavery and Its Others', in Tom Moylan and Raffaella Baccolini (eds), *Dark Horizons: Science Fiction and the Dystopian Imagination* (New York: Routledge, 2003).

Venturi, Robert, Denise Scott Brown and Steven Izenour, *Learning from Las Vegas: The Forgotten Symbolism of Architectural Form*, rev. ed. (Cambridge, MA; London: MIT Press, 1977).

Vonnegut, Kurt, *Player Piano* [1952] (New York: Dial Press, 2006).

Walsh, Chad, *From Utopia to Nightmare* (London: Bles, 1962).

Wegner, Phillip E., *Imaginary Communities: Utopia, the Nation, and the Spatial Histories of Modernity* (Berkeley; Los Angles; London: University of California Press, 2002).

Wells, H.G., *The First Men in the Moon, and A Modern Utopia* [1901; 1905], Wordsworth Classics (Ware: Wordsworth Editions Limited, 2017).

———, *The Time Machine* [1895] (London: Everyman, 1995).

Williams, Raymond, *Orwell* [1971] (London: Fontana, 1984).

———, *Problems in Materialism and Culture* (London: Verso, 1980).

———, 'Science Fiction', *The Highway, Journal of the Workers' Educational Association*, 48 (Dec. 1956), 41–5.

Willmetts, Simon, 'Digital Dystopia: Surveillance, Autonomy and Social Justice in Gary Shteyngart's *Super Sad True Love Story*', *American Quarterly*, 70:2 (June 2018), 267–89.

Woloch, Alex, *Or Orwell: Writing and Democratic Socialism* (Cambridge, MA: Harvard University Press, 2016).

Woodcock, George, 'Utopias in Negative', *Sewanee Review*, 64:1 (Jan.–Mar. 1956), 81–97.

Ye'or, Bat, *Eurabia: The Euro-Arab Axis* (Madison: Fairleigh Dickinson University Press, 2005).

Younge, Lewis Henry, *Utopia: Or, Apollo's Golden Days* (Dublin: George Faulkner, 1747).

Zamyatin, Yevgeny Ivanovich, *We* [1924], trans. Gregory Zilboorg (London: Penguin, 1993).

Zumas, Leni, *Red Clocks: A Novel* (London: The Borough Press/HarperCollins, 2019).

Index